PUNISHMENT AND THE MORAL EMOTIONS

PUNISHMENT AND THE MORAL EMOTIONS

Essays in Law, Morality, and Religion

Jeffrie G. Murphy

UNIVERSITY PRESS

Oxford University Press is a department of the University of Oxford.
It furthers the University's objective of excellence in research, scholarship,
and education by publishing worldwide.

Oxford   New York
Auckland   Cape Town   Dar es Salaam   Hong Kong   Karachi
Kuala Lumpur   Madrid   Melbourne   Mexico City   Nairobi
New Delhi   Shanghai   Taipei   Toronto

With offices in
Argentina   Austria   Brazil   Chile   Czech Republic   France   Greece
Guatemala   Hungary   Italy   Japan   Poland   Portugal   Singapore
South Korea   Switzerland   Thailand   Turkey   Ukraine   Vietnam

Oxford is a registered trade mark of Oxford University Press
in the UK and certain other countries.

Published in the United States of America by
Oxford University Press
198 Madison Avenue, New York, NY 10016

© Oxford University Press 2012

First issued as an Oxford University Press paperback, 2014.

All rights reserved. No part of this publication may be reproduced, stored in a retrieval system,
or transmitted, in any form or by any means, without the prior permission in writing of Oxford University
Press, or as expressly permitted by law, by license, or under terms agreed with the appropriate reproduction
rights organization. Inquiries concerning reproduction outside the scope of the above should be sent to
the Rights Department, Oxford University Press, at the address above.

You must not circulate this work in any other form
and you must impose this same condition on any acquirer.

Library of Congress Cataloging-in-Publication Data
Murphy, Jeffrie G.
Punishment and the moral emotions/Jeffrie G. Murphy.
p. cm.
ISBN 978-0-19-976439-6 (hbk. : alk. paper); 978-0-19-935745-1 (paperback)
1. Punishment—Philosophy.   2. Punishment—Moral and ethical aspects.   I. Title.
K5103.M85 2011
170—dc22   2011002535

1 3 5 7 9 8 6 4 2

Printed in the United States of America
on acid-free paper

For Ellen

CONTENTS

Introduction ix
Sources and Acknowledgments xix

1. Forgiveness, Reconciliation, and Responding to Evil: A Philosophical Overview 3

2. Moral Epistemology, the Retributive Emotions, and the "Clumsy Moral Philosophy" of Jesus Christ 21

3. Christian Love and Criminal Punishment 43

4. Legal Moralism and Retribution Revisited 66

5. Shame Creeps Through Guilt and Feels Like Retribution 94

CONTENTS

6. Repentance, Mercy, and Communicative Punishment — 114

7. Remorse, Apology, and Mercy — 129

8. The Case of Dostoevsky's General: Some Ruminations on Forgiving the Unforgivable — 181

9. Response to Neu, Zipursky, and Steiker — 215

10. Jealousy, Shame, and the Rival — 234

11. Moral Reasons and the Limitations of Liberty — 244

12. The Elusive Nature of Human Dignity — 257

13. Kant on the "Right of Necessity" and other Defenses in the Law of Homicide — 274

Index — 307

Introduction

This is the fourth and, given my age, surely the last essay collection that I will publish. The essays reveal a shift in focus from much of my previous work and also some change in my views on the topics I have previously explored. The shift in focus involves an increasing interest in the *moral emotions* that can legitimately drive or can also corrupt our responses to criminals and other wrongdoers and the contribution that a religious perspective can make to our understanding of some of these emotions. By the "moral emotions" I mean emotions essentially tied to (not always correct) moral judgments–emotions such as love (in some of its forms), guilt, shame, remorse, resentment, and jealousy.

The change in perspective, a function to a large degree of my focus on the moral emotions, mainly involves a softening of my overly confident belief that punishment and other responses of strong condemnation are justified on retributive grounds, justified by what wrongdoers deserve rather than projected future good that will–it is hoped–be the consequence of condemning or punishing them. I now try to make a place for the future good of character reformation and even the common good in what is still, in its essence, a softened version of retribution. Related to this is a more generous view of when mercy and forgiveness of wrongdoers may be appropriate.

I first became interested in the role of emotions in punishment and condemnation when, in the mid-eighties, I was invited by the journal *Midwest Studies in Philosophy* to contribute an essay on punishment or a related topic. Having written so much in defense of punishment (the hard response to wrongdoing) I decided to write an essay on forgiveness (a softer response)—a topic to which I had never before given any thought at all. So I accepted the invitation in the hope that it would generate within me both ideas and enthusiasm—a hope that was indeed realized.

Following a colleague's suggestion that I work my way into the topic of forgiveness by reading Bishop Joseph Butler's sermons on resentment and forgiveness, I found myself fascinated by the topic of the emotion of resentment (what Peter Strawson called a reactive attitude) and even more fascinated by Butler's claim that this negative and potentially destructive emotion can be a legitimate part of a moral view dominated by the Christian love commandment that one should love one's neighbor as oneself.

My first views on forgiveness may be found in my chapters of the 1988 book *Forgiveness and Mercy*—a book that I joint authored with the late Jean Hampton. I contributed three of the book's five chapters (the first in essence the essay noted above), and Jean contributed two. I expressed some positive views about forgiveness, but what readers mainly noticed were the strong negative views that I expressed—suggesting that forgiveness could easily be seen, not as a virtue, but as the vice of servility, a failure to show proper self-respect. (I quoted with some glee S. J. Perelman's quip "to err is human, to forgive supine" and even defended a form of hatred that I called "retributive hatred.") What was also noticed by many readers was my totally secular—even rather antireligious—take on the topic. This was in sharp contrast to Jean's explicitly Christian commitments.

Over the years I have never abandoned my view that there is too much uncritical boosterism of forgiveness in much of the literature on the topic—a literature that does not sufficiently notice the dangers to self-respect, respect for victims, and respect for the moral order itself when forgiveness is bestowed in a hasty and uncritical way.

INTRODUCTION

I began to think, however, that my previous understanding of forgiveness had been too narrow (too limited by Butler's idea that its essence is overcoming the emotion of resentment–which cannot, for example, account for self-forgiveness) and too stingy about the conditions required before it may legitimately be bestowed. Although I still believe that repentance by the wrongdoer is the best way to open a door to forgiveness by the wronged, I tended to overestimate its role and gave rather short shrift to other possible doors. I have more recently considered with sympathy other possibly legitimate acts of forgiveness–in at least some meaningful senses of the concept of forgiveness–that do not demand repentance as a precondition.

Some of my change in view on these matters may be found in my 2003 book, *Getting Even–Forgiveness and Its Limits*–a book that revealed an increased sympathy on my part with a religious framework, particularly with Christianity and its gospel of love. Some of the essays in the present collection–particularly "The Case of Dostoevsky's General: Some Ruminations on Forgiving the Unforgivable"–expand on this sympathy and produce a view of forgiveness that is, I hope, more nuanced and complex (and even openly conflicted) than that present in my earlier work. I have stopped trying to offer a general theory of forgiveness, since I have come to believe that such theories only achieve, to use Herbert Hart's fine phrase, "uniformity at the price of distortion." Instead I seek, now stealing a phrase from Richard Rorty, simply to "advance the conversation" by sharing my current thinking, including the conflicts and uncertainties in that thinking, in the hope that this will engage in productive ways others interested in the topic. I try to defend this looser methodology (or lack of methodology if one prefers) in "Response to Neu, Zipursky, and Steiker"–drawn from an American Philosophical Association symposium, "The Work of Jeffrie G. Murphy," in which Professors Jerome Neu, Benjamin Zipursky, and Carol Steiker presented critiques of various aspects of my philosophical work. Zipursky in particular expressed his wish that I would state and defend a settled view in a more rigorous way than he had found in my writings.

As a general introduction to my transitional thinking about forgiveness, I have opened this collection with my essay "Forgiveness, Reconciliation, and Responding to Evil." This is the transcript of a keynote address I gave at a conference on "Forgiveness in the Law" at Fordham Law School in 1999. As a general introduction to my increased interest in the moral emotions and Christianity, I have included my essay "Moral Epistemology, the Retributive Emotions, and the 'Clumsy Moral Philosophy' of Jesus Christ"–which is in part a critique of Michael Moore's important essay "The Moral Worth of Retribution"–and the essay "Christian Love and Criminal Punishment."

In 2006 I was selected to be president of the American Philosophical Association, Pacific Division, and I decided that for my presidential address–"Legal Moralism and Retribution Revisited"–I would do a kind of survey of my philosophical career, particularly my career in legal philosophy that has emphasized the philosophy of punishment. In drafting this survey, I found that I was no longer comfortable with the strong versions of the retributive theory of punishment that I had earlier defended. Under the influence of such diverse people as Jesus, Freud, and particularly Nietzsche, I began some self-analysis and started to ask myself what had really drawn me to such a theory. Could it have been possible that, instead of all my high-sounding philosophical talk about justice and desert, I had been drawn in part by what Nietzsche claimed was the actual emotional basis for punishment: the passion he called *ressentiment*, an evil brew of malice, spite, envy, and cruelty? I regretfully concluded that the answer was in part *yes* and that the "reflective equilibrium" that I had attained from retributivism as a theory of punishment was probably to be explained, at least in part, not by purely intellectual considerations but by the fact that the view engaged some of my baser passions. I thus drew back from the uncritical enthusiasm of my earlier defenses and decided that considerable modification of my own defense of retribution was needed. I still thought that a version of the theory was defensible (certainly preferable to classic utilitarian theories of punishment), but this version had to be purged of any emotion of hatred (including the "retributive hatred" I had earlier defended) and had to be compatible, as I argue in "Christian Love and Criminal Punishment," with a doctrine of Christian love properly understood. What I articulate about such love, by the way, is not a happy-clappy "let us all be very nice" version of love, but one that is to some degree stern and demanding–something much more complex than simply trying to make everybody happy through preference satisfaction

At this point I had reached an awareness that emotions are deeply important in our understanding of moral judgment and legal punishment. Butler was right: legitimate emotions, such as a properly constrained resentment, can serve the interests of both morality and law. But Nietzsche was also right: just resentment can easily slide into evil *ressentiment* and corrupt morality and law at their very foundation–making them instruments of self-deceptive cruelty. So extreme caution is in order–a caution that should make us resist the temptation to see too wide a gap between us (the good and law abiding) and them (the evil and criminal) and the related temptation to think that, in punishing, we are doing God's work in the service of a righteous crusade. We simply are not good enough and do not know enough legitimately to assume such a posture of arrogance.

Once one has decided, even if a bit regretfully, that some system of punishment is required, one must start to think about the proper design of the system. One crucial component is sentencing. Following conviction, what should be relevant to the sentence actually imposed in those cases where judges or juries have some discretion? Given my increasing interest in the emotions, it was natural that I began to think about the emotions of shame, guilt, and remorse–their nature, their moral legitimacy, and the role (if any) that they might legitimately play in criminal sentencing. I explore these issues in the essays "Shame Creeps through Guilt and Feels Like Retribution," "Remorse, Apology, and Mercy," and "Repentance, Mercy, and Communicative Punishment" (a critique of an essay by Antony Duff). After arguing for the moral and spiritual importance of these emotions, I suggest that their use in criminal sentencing–although clearly relevant *in principle*–should be met with great skepticism *in practice*. Why? Because these emotions are so easy to fake; and permitting reduced sentences for people who express repentance and apology simply gives them incentives to fake and thereby cheapens the currency of the real thing. (As some Hollywood mogul once said, "Sincerity is the most precious thing in the world. When you have learned to fake that, you've got it made.") I also suggest that such expressions may have a more legitimate relevance at clemency hearings, when, typically, sufficient time has gone by to lessen the risk that the relevant authorities will be fooled by insincere claims of remorse, repentance, and moral and spiritual rebirth.

"Remorse, Apology, and Mercy" was selected as one of the core texts for the book *Criminal Law Conversations*, and I was asked to prepare an abridged version of the essay for inclusion in that volume. Critiques of the essay were presented by several insightful legal scholars: Professors Sherry F. Colb, Stephanos Bibas, Susan A. Bandes, Lisa Kern Griffin, and Janet Ainsworth. I have included my all too brief response to those critiques as an appendix to the full version of the essay reprinted in the present collection. I have also added to the appendix my brief reply in the same volume to Susan Bandes' core text "The Heart Has Its Reasons" since it pursues some of the same themes present in her critique of my own core text.

INTRODUCTION

Another situation in criminal law in which emotions play a role is, of course, in the generation of crime itself. Many crimes are generated by strong emotions (greed and anger, for example), and serious crimes–particularly crimes against women–are often generated by the emotion of *jealousy* ("If I can't have her, nobody can!"). In my essay "Jealousy, Shame, and the Rival"–a response to Jerome Neu's influential essay "Jealous Thoughts"–I try to gain an understanding of this sometimes legitimate but often dangerous emotion.

Just as punishment is rendered suspect if it is motivated by the base passion of *ressentiment*, so is criminalization rendered suspect if it is motivated by hatred. The history of constitutional challenges to the criminalization of homosexual sodomy from *Bowers v. Hardwick* (1986)–discussed in my "Moral Reasons and the Limitations of Liberty"–through *Lawrence v. Texas* (2003) illustrates the gradual realization by the US Supreme Court that mere brute hatred and disgust, no matter how widely shared by citizens, cannot justify the kind of intrusion into liberty represented by criminalization and punishment. (The Court left less severe intrusions on liberty–bans on gay marriage, for example–for another day.)

Writing for the majority in *Lawrence v. Texas*, Justice Anthony Kennedy argued that the earlier Supreme Court decision in the case of *Bowers v. Hardwick* was mistaken and thus had to be overturned. In that case, the Court had held (Justice White writing for the majority) that there is no fundamental constitutional liberty to engage in homosexual sodomy and thus that strict judicial scrutiny (requiring that the government demonstrate a compelling interest before encumbering the liberty) would not be applied. What was applied instead was what is called minimal scrutiny–a "rational basis test" that requires only that the government has a legitimate, even if not compelling, interest in encumbering the liberty in question. The state of Georgia argued that its interest was in maintaining a "decent society" by using the criminal law to enforce the strong moral convictions of the citizens of Georgia that homosexuality is morally evil. Justice White agreed that this interest was legitimate and thus upheld the constitutionality of a Georgia statute that made it a felony, punishable by up to twenty years in prison, to engage in an act of homosexual sodomy.

In *Lawrence*, Justice Kennedy did not argue that there is a fundamental liberty to engage in homosexual sodomy and thus did not apply strict scrutiny. He did, however, argue that–when the encumbrance to liberty is something as intrusive as criminal imprisonment–a proper application of the rational basis test requires strong if not compelling government interest. Certainly more is required than the mere animus of the citizenry.

I would be willing to bet the farm that my essay "Moral Reasons and the Limitations of Liberty" was never read by Justice Kennedy and certainly never influenced him in any way. I take a certain amount of pleasure, however, in knowing that his line of reasoning about the rational basis test–with which I generally agree–overlaps substantially with an essay I wrote some time before the *Lawrence* decision. And this essay, like many of the others in the present collection, ties in with the topic of emotions. In it, I argue that a decent society cannot count as a good reason for incarcerating people the mere fact that citizens–even a majority–have an emotion of hatred (Justice Kennedy's word is "animus") or disgust toward certain kinds of people and the liberties they would like to enjoy.

The background moral vision that sets the framework for all the essays in the present collection remains my commitment to a quasi-Kantian idea of human dignity, but this increasingly strikes me (contra Kant) as needing a religious foundation–the idea that human beings have a special moral preciousness because they are created in the image of God and are his beloved children. This is a foundation about which, alas, I run hot and cold, sometimes embracing it and at other times dominated by skepticism. The essay,

INTRODUCTION

"The Elusive Nature of Human Dignity," explores the various ways in which the concept of human dignity might be understood and defended.

The final essay in the collection, "Kant on the 'Right of Necessity' and other Defenses in the Law of Homicide," has not been previously published. In it, I return to the subject of most of my first writings in philosophy: Kant's moral, political, and legal theory. Here I explore the three criminal defenses that Kant discusses in his writings on punishment: the kind of necessity often claimed for killing to save one's life in cases of shipwreck, a woman killing at birth her illegitimate baby, and a soldier killing another soldier in a duel. Although much of Kant's discussion is surprisingly unsatisfactory, he does explore some issues relevant to the theme of the present collection—the role, for example, that shame might play as an excusing condition that might at least mitigate homicide in such a way as to remove it from the class of homicides for which the death penalty is appropriate. Kant's commitment to human dignity is also addressed in order to expand and sometimes to critique Kant's discussion of these possible defenses.

One final word: All of the essays in this collection were written by invitation–written to be given as public lectures, presented at symposia, or for volumes on specific topics. Because of the different venues and audiences, I could never assume that my listeners or readers would be familiar with the general framework I bring to bear on the topics in question. As a result, there is some overlap in material in the essays I have here included. Also, since written at different times, there are some inconsistencies or at least tensions among some of them. In spite of these overlaps and tensions, however, I have tried to make sure that each essay selected for inclusion contains substantial material that is not duplicated in discussions in any of the other essays.

SOURCES AND ACKNOWLEDGMENTS

1. "Forgiveness, Reconciliation, and Responding to Evil: A Philosophical Overview." This article was originally published in the *Fordham Urban Law Journal* as "Forgiveness, Reconciliation and Responding to Evil: A Philosophical Overview," 27 FORDHAM URB. L.J. 1353 (2000). Reprinted with permission.
2. "Moral Epistemology, the Retributive Emotions and the 'Clumsy Moral Philosophy' of Jesus Christ." This essay is reprinted with permission from *The Passions of Law*, edited by Susan A. Bandes, copyright © 1999 New York University Press.
3. "Christian Love and Criminal Punishment." This essay is reprinted with permission from *Christianity and Law: An Introduction*, edited by John Witte Jr. and Frank S. Alexander, copyright © 2008 Cambridge University Press.
4. "Legal Moralism and Retribution Revisited." This article originally appeared in *Criminal Law and Philosophy*, Volume 1, Number 1 (January 2007), copyright © 2007 Springer Netherlands. Reprinted with permission.

5. "Shame Creeps through Guilt and Feels Like Retribution." This essay originally appeared in *Law and Philosophy*, Volume 18, Number 4 (July 1999), copyright © 1999 Springer Netherlands. Reprinted with permission.
6. "Repentance, Mercy, and Communicative Punishment" originally appeared in *Crime, Punishment, and Responsibility: The Jurisprudence of Antony Duff*, edited by Rowan Cruft and Matthew H. Kramer, copyright © 2011 Oxford University Press. Reprinted with permission.
7. "Remorse, Apology, and Mercy" originally appeared in *Ohio State Journal of Criminal Law*, Volume 4, Number 2 (Spring 2007), and is reprinted with permission. The appendix to this essay is drawn from pp. 203–205 and 647–649 of *Criminal Law Conversations*, edited by Paul H. Robinson, Stephen Garvey, and Kimberly Kessler Ferzan (copyright © 2009 Oxford University Press) and is reprinted with permission.
8. "The Case of Dostoevsky's General: Some Ruminations on Forgiving the Unforgivable" originally appeared in *The Monist*, Volume 92, Number 4 (October 2009), copyright © 2009 The Monist: An International Quarterly Journal of General Philosophical Inquiry, Open Court Publishing Company, Chicago, Illinois. Reprinted with permission.
9. "Response to Neu, Zipursky, and Steiker" originally appeared as a portion of a symposium "The Work of Jeffrie G. Murphy" held at the meetings of The American Philosophical Association (APA), Pacific Division, 2008, and sponsored by the Committee on Law and Philosophy, American Philosophical Association. The symposium was originally published in the Newsletter of the Committee on Law and Philosophy (copyright © 2008 American Philosophical Association) and was reprinted, with APA permission, in *Criminal Justice Ethics*, Volume 27, Number 2 (Summer/Fall

SOURCES AND ACKNOWLEDGMENTS

2008). It is here reprinted with permission of The American Philosophical Association.

10. "Jealousy, Shame, and the Rival." This essay was originally published in *Philosophical Studies*, Volume 108, Number 2 (March 2002), copyright © 2002 Springer Netherlands. Reprinted with permission.
11. "Moral Reasons and the Limitations of Liberty" originally appeared in *William and Mary Law Review*, 40 Wm. & Mary L. Rev. 947 (1999). Reprinted with permission.
12. "The Elusive Nature of Human Dignity" originally appeared in *The Hedgehog Review*, Volume 9, Number 3 (Fall 2007), copyright © 2007 Institute for Advanced Studies in Culture. Reprinted with permission.
13. "Kant on the 'Right of Necessity' and other Defenses in the Law of Homicide" has not previously been published.

I want here to thank the Divinity Faculty of Cambridge University for their invitation to deliver the 2010 Stanton Lectures. Health problems prevented my giving the lectures in person—just as well since volcanic ash from Iceland closed Heathrow Airport the day I was scheduled to arrive—and Cambridge kindly arranged for me to give the lectures with the assistance of video conference technology. These lectures drew heavily on some of the essays contained in this collection, and preparing them helped me to form the judgment (which I hope is correct) that the essays do hang together around common themes and thus make the present collection a genuine book and not just a random assortment.

Since I have become an old man, and since this will surely be among the last things that I will publish, I want to express here my gratitude for the many undeserved blessings that I have received in the course of my life and career. I had loving and supportive parents who lived lives of integrity and dedication—my father making a career in the United States Navy during periods of war and my mother often left to manage things on her own during these difficult times. They always made me feel safe in the world—even when (as I later came to realize) their own safety was threatened by war, separation, and (after my father's retirement) financial distress. They made considerable sacrifices so that I could have a chance for success and happiness in life, and one of my greatest regrets is that I never expressed to them the full nature of my love, gratitude, and admiration for them—something that I did not bring to my full consciousness until I outgrew being consumed by the claims of my "dear self" (to use Kant's phrase).

I have also been blessed with two fine sons who are good and honorable men whom I love and of whom I am very proud. They have had their share of problems and disappointments in life, but these have never deflected them from their core values. As Gandhi said, "all else is dross." Their mother, my first wife, is a good person who has been kind to them and has assisted their development into the men that they are.

I have had the good fortune to have had a few exceptional teachers, colleagues, and students who have stimulated and supported my intellectual life and improved my work through their discussion, criticism, and example. Many of these people have been noted and thanked in my earlier publications, but I would here like to add the names of Svetlana Beggs, Richard Dagger, and Mary Sigler.

Finally, I want to thank, as I always do, my wife Ellen Canacakos for the valuable discussions we have on my intellectual work. She draws on her experience as a lawyer and a psychotherapist in illuminating ways and, even more important, brings to bear on our discussions—and our entire life together—her remarkable moral decency and goodness. These are qualities that I envy and admire. I know that she is the primary cause of the happiness in my life, and

SOURCES AND ACKNOWLEDGMENTS

I think and hope that she also influences me toward being a better person. Just being in the same room with her and our beloved dogs gives me a kind of peace and contentment that I find nowhere else in my life and without which I could not work up enthusiasm for my intellectual work or, indeed, for anything else. I dedicate this book to her with love.

Jeffrie G. Murphy
Tempe, Arizona
August 5, 2011

PUNISHMENT AND THE MORAL EMOTIONS

Chapter 1

Forgiveness, Reconciliation, and Responding To Evil
A Philosophical Overview

INTRODUCTION

I am honored to be a part of what promises to be a rich and varied symposium on forgiveness. What I have been asked to do is to present a philosophical overview on the topic of forgiveness in order to provide a framework for the day's later discussions. I have also been asked to limit my remarks to thirty minutes. This time limit will, of course, entail that most of what I say will be quite general, since I shall not be able to make the kinds of qualifications and refinements that would be possible if I had more time. Being general is not the same as being shallow, however, and I will do my best to avoid this latter pitfall.

Before getting into the details of my discussion, I would like to make three preliminary points.

First, I should note that most of my thinking and writing on forgiveness and reconciliation has concerned what might be called interpersonal forgiveness and reconciliation—e.g., forgiveness of an unfaithful spouse, a betraying friend, a malicious colleague, a government agent by whom one has been tortured, or a criminal by whom one has been victimized. With respect to law, my focus has been more on criminal than private law.

I have only recently started to think and write about what might be called group forgiveness and reconciliation as possible responses to such mass violence as genocide and apartheid. My views on this topic are still in a very early stage, and thus I feel very fortunate that I shall be able to join you all this afternoon in listening to the talk by Professor Martha Minow. She is the author of the truly splendid book, *Between Vengeance and Forgiveness: Facing History After Genocide and Mass Violence*.[1]

The second preliminary point I want to make concerns my own qualifications to speak on the topic in question. I have been thinking and writing about this topic for many years, and over the years I have developed increasingly positive views about the value of forgiveness. (Indeed, my early views on the topic were perceived as so negative that a colleague once suggested that my chapters in the book *Forgiveness and Mercy* should be subtitled "An Outsider's View.") However, I want to make it clear that my current views are essentially intellectual and theoretical rather than autobiographical in nature. Although I have over the years suffered my share of petty slights and insults, I have led an astoundingly fortunate life in the realm of victimization. I have experienced some small scale immorality, but nothing that I would indentify as evil. I have never to my knowledge been betrayed by a loved one or friend; I have never been tortured; I have never been raped: I have never been violently assaulted or been the victim of any crime more serious than auto theft—nor has anyone close to me. Thus, when I speak of forgiveness as a virtue, I know that I may be open to the charge "easy for you to say." When those who have been seriously victimized can emerge from their victimization without hate, there is nobility and moral grandeur to be found in their capacity to forgive. Nelson Mandela seems to be such a person.

---

1. Martha Minow, Between Vengeance and Forgiveness: Facing History After Genocide and Mass Violence (1998).

I have no idea, however, if I could rise to this in similar circumstances; and thus I will express my admiration for such people without ever meaning to suggest that I know that I could act in a comparable way.

The third and final preliminary point I want to make concerns the level of precision that one can expect on the topic of forgiveness. With Aristotle, I tend to think that it is generally a mistake in ethics to aim for a level of precision not really allowed by what is in fact a quite messy and conflicted subject matter. Neat theories in ethics generally produce not illumination but rather (in Herbert Hart's fine phrase) "uniformity at the price of distortion."[2] (I am convinced, indeed, that a really insightful book in ethics would not have as a title "The Theory of…." but rather something like "Muddling Through" or "Stumbling Along."[3]) Thus all one can hope to do is to enrich the discussion a bit by exposing some of the value choices at the heart of forgiveness—a point well made by Professor Minow in her book when she says that she will resist "tidiness" and "temptations of closure" in her own thinking and writing about forgiveness.[4]

Preliminaries out of the way, I shall now move to my "philosophical overview." But what exactly is it that philosophers do? Well, first they draw a lot of distinctions. (Indeed, I think it was J. L. Austin who once suggested that the drawing of distinctions might be the occupation and not just the occupational disease of philosophers.) Thus I shall begin by attempting to explain what forgiveness is and, in the process, distinguish it from various other things it is not but with which is has often been confused. After that, I will explore what can be said against forgiveness and then close with a discussion of what can be said in its favor.

---

2. H.L.A. Hart, The Concept of Law 38 (2d ed. 1994).
3. The second title was suggested to me in conversation by D.Z. Phillips.
4. *See* Minow, *supra* note 1, at 4, 24.

THE NATURE OF FORGIVENESS

I think that one of the most insightful discussions of forgiveness ever penned is to be found in Bishop Joseph Butler's 1726 sermon "Upon Forgiveness of Injuries."[5] In that sermon, Bishop Butler offers a definition of forgiveness that I have adapted in my own work on the topic.[6] According to Butler, forgiveness is a moral virtue (a virtue of character) that is essentially a matter of the heart, the inner self, and involves a change in inner feeling more than a change in external action. The change in feeling is this: the overcoming, on moral grounds, of the intense negative reactive attitudes—the vindictive passions of resentment, anger, hatred, and the desire for revenge—that are quite naturally occasioned when one has been wronged by another responsible agent. A person who has forgiven has overcome those vindictive attitudes and has overcome them for a morally creditable motive—e.g., being moved by repentance on the part of the person by whom one has been wronged. Of course, such a change in feeling often leads to a change of behavior—reconciliation, for example; but, as our ability to forgive the dead illustrates, it does not always do so.

On this analysis of forgiveness, it is useful initially to distinguish forgiveness from other responses to wrongdoing with which forgiveness is often confused: justification, excuse, mercy, and reconciliation. Although these concepts are to some degree open textured and can bleed into each other, clarity is—I think—served if one at least starts by attempting to separate them. I will discuss each of them briefly.

1. *Justification*: To regard conduct as justified (as in lawful self-defense, for example) is to claim that the conduct, though normally

---

5. See sermon IX, in SERMONS OF JOSEPH BUTLER 127–141 (W. E. Gladstone ed., 1897).
6. My adaptation of Butler is free, and I make no pretense that what follows is a solid piece of Butler scholarship. I have been inspired by Butler's discussion; and thus, even when I have modified or added to that discussion, I hope that I have always been loyal to its essential spirit.

wrongful, was—in the given circumstances and all things considered—the right thing to do. If I have suffered because of conduct that was right—e.g., had my nose bloodied by someone defending himself against my wrongful attack—I have not been wronged, have nothing legitimately to resent, and thus have nothing to forgive.

2. *Excuse*: To regard conduct as excused (as in the insanity defense, for example) is to admit that the conduct was wrong but to claim that the person who engaged in the conduct lacked substantial capacity to conform his conduct to the relevant norms and thus was not a fully responsible agent. Responsible agency is, of course, a matter of degree; but to the degree that the person who injures me is not a responsible agent, resentment of that person would make no more sense than resenting a sudden storm that soaks me. Again, there is nothing here to forgive.

3. *Mercy*: To accord a wrongdoer mercy is to inflict a less harsh consequence on that person than allowed by institutional (usually legal) rules. Mercy is less personal than forgiveness, since the one granting mercy (a sentencing judge, say) typically will not be a victim of wrongdoing and thus will not have any feelings of resentment to overcome. (There is a sense in which only victims of wrongdoing have what might be called standing to forgive.) Mercy also has a public behavioral dimension not necessarily present in forgiveness. I can forgive a person simply in my heart of hearts, but I cannot show mercy simply in my heart of hearts. I can forgive the dead, but I cannot show mercy to the dead. I can forgive myself, but I cannot show mercy to myself.

This distinction between mercy and forgiveness allows us to see why there is no inconsistency in fully forgiving a person for wrongdoing (that is, stop resenting or hating the person for it) but still advocate that the person suffer the legal consequence of criminal punishment. To the degree that criminal punishment is justified in order to secure victim satisfaction, then—of course—the fact that the victim has forgiven will be a relevant argument for reducing the criminal's sentence, and the fact that a victim still resents and hates will be a relevant argument for increasing that sentence. It is highly controversial, of course, that criminal punishment should to any degree be harnessed to victim desires.[7] Even if it is, however, it must surely be admitted that the practice serves other values as well—particularly crime control and justice; and, with respect to these goals, victim forgiveness could hardly be dispositive. In short: It would indeed be inconsistent for a person to claim that he has forgiven the wrongdoer and still advocate punishment for the wrongdoer in order to satisfy his personal vindictive feelings. (If he still has those feelings, he has not forgiven.) It would not be inconsistent, however, to advocate punishment for other legitimate reasons. Of course, the possibilities for self-deception are enormous here.

4. *Reconciliation*. The vindictive passions (those overcome in forgiveness) are often a major barrier to reconciliation; and thus, since forgiveness often leads to reconciliation, it is easy to confuse the two concepts. I think, however, that it is important also to see how they may differ—how there can be forgiveness without reconciliation and reconciliation without forgiveness.

First let me give an example of forgiveness without reconciliation. Imagine a battered woman who has been repeatedly beaten and raped by her husband or boyfriend. This woman—after a religious conversion, perhaps—might well come to forgive her batterer (i.e., stop hating him) without a willingness to resume her relationship with him. "I forgive you and wish you well" can, in my view, sit quite consistently with "I never want you in this house again." In short, the fact that one has forgiven does not mean that one must also trust or live again with a person.

---

7. For a survey of the arguments, pro and con, on allowing victim desires to influence criminal sentencing, see the majority and dissenting opinions in *Booth v. Maryland*, 482 U.S. 496 (1987), overruled by *Payne v. Tennessee*, 501 U.S. 808, 825 (1991).

As an example of reconciliation without forgiveness, consider the example of the South African Truth and Reconciliation Commission.[8] In order to negotiate a viable transition from apartheid to democratic government with full black participation, all parties had to agree that there would in most cases be no punishment for evil acts that occurred under the previous government. Wrongdoers, by making a full confession and accepting responsibility, would typically be granted amnesty. In this process the wrongdoers would not be required to repent, show remorse, or even apologize.

I can clearly see this process as one of reconciliation—a process that will allow all to work toward a democratic and just future. I do not so easily see this process as one of forgiveness, however. No change of heart was required or even sought from the victims—no overcoming of such vindictive feelings as resentment and hatred. All that was required of them was a willingness to accept this process as a necessary means to the future good of their society.

In my view, this counts as forgiveness only if one embraces what is (to me) a less morally rich definition of forgiveness: forgiveness merely as the waiving of a right. Examples of this are found in the private law idea of forgiving a debt or in Bishop Desmond Tutu's definition of forgiveness as "waiving one's right to revenge."[9] But surely one can waive one's right for purely instrumental reasons; reasons having nothing to do with the change of heart that constitutes forgiveness as a moral virtue. One can even waive one's rights for selfish reasons—e.g., the belief that one's future employment prospects will be better if one simply lets bygones be bygones. I am not saying that it is wrong to act for instrumental reasons—indeed, for South Africa, it may have been the only justified course. Neither am I saying that instrumental justifications can never be moral justifications. To

---

8. For a survey of the operation of the Commission, see MINOW, *supra*, note 1, at 52–90.
9. Interview by Bill Moyers with Bishop Desmond Tutu, PBS (April 27, 1999).

attempt reconciliation for the future good of one's society, for example, is surely both instrumental and moral. I am simply saying that, however justified acting instrumentally may sometimes be, it is—absent the extinction of resentment and other vindictive passions—something other than what I understand as the moral virtue of forgiveness. In short: if all we know is that two parties have decided to reconcile, we do not know enough to make a reliable judgment about whether the moral virtue of forgiveness has been realized in the reconciliation.

Another point worth making about the relation between reconciliation and forgiveness is this: if one always delayed reconciliation until forgiveness had taken place, then some vitally important kinds of reconciliation might not be possible. Thus the realization that forgiveness is often a helpful step toward reconciliation should not lead us into the mistaken belief that forgiveness is a necessary condition for reconciliation. Indeed, it is surely sometimes the case that reconciliation, coming first and adopted for instrumental reasons, opens the door to future forgiveness. After learning that one can work with one's victimizer toward a common goal, a sense of common humanity might emerge and one's vindictive passions toward that person might over time begin to soften.

Let me now discuss the evaluation of forgiveness as I—following Bishop Butler—have defined it.

THE DANGERS OF HASTY FORGIVENESS

In addition to his powerful sermon on forgiveness, Bishop Butler authored an equally powerful sermon with the title "Upon Resentment."[10] In that sermon, Butler started to make a case for the

---

10. See *Sermon VIII*, in SERMONS OF JOSEPH BUTLER, *supra* note 5, at 115–126.

legitimacy of resentment and other vindictive passions—arguing that a just and loving God would not have universally implanted these passions within his creatures unless the passions served some valuable purpose. The danger of resentment, he argued, lies not in having it, but rather in being dominated and consumed by it to such a degree that one can never overcome it and acts irresponsibly on the basis of it. As the initial response to being wronged, however, the passion stands in defense of important values—values that might be compromised by immediate and uncritical forgiveness of wrongs.

What are the values defended by resentment and threatened by hasty and uncritical forgiveness? I would suggest two: respect for self and respect for the moral order. A person who never resented any injuries done to himself might be a saint. It is equally likely, however, that his lack of resentment reveals a servile personality—a personality lacking in respect for himself and respect for his rights and status as a free and equal moral agent. (This is the point behind the famous quip: "To err is human; to forgive, supine."[11]) Just as indignation or guilt over the mistreatment of others stands as emotional testimony that we care about them and their rights, so does resentment stand as emotional testimony that we care about ourselves and our rights.

Related to this is an instrumental point: Those who have vindictive dispositions toward those who wrong them give potential wrongdoers an incentive not to wrong them. If I were going to set out to oppress other people, I would surely prefer to select for my victims persons whose first response is forgiveness rather than persons whose first response is revenge. As Kant noted in his *Doctrine of Virtue*, "One who makes himself into a worm cannot complain if people step on him."[12]

---

11. I have heard this quip attributed to the comic writer S. J. Perelman (who often wrote for the Marx Brothers), but I am not certain if the attribution is accurate.
12. IMMANUEL KANT, THE DOCTRINE OF VIRTUE, PART II OF THE METAPHYSICS OF MORALS 103, (Mary J. Gregor trans., 1964).

Resentment does not simply stand as emotional testimony of self-respect, however. This passion—and the reluctance to hastily transcend it in forgiveness—also stands as testimony to our allegiance to the moral order itself. This is a point made forcefully by Aurel Kolnai in his important essay on forgiveness.[13] According to Kolnai, we all have a duty to support—both intellectually and emotionally—the moral order, an order represented by clear understandings of what constitutes unacceptable treatment of one human being by another. If we do not show some resentment to those who, in victimizing us, flout those understandings, then we run the risk of being "complicitous in evil."

If I had more time, I could say many more things in defense of the vindictive passions. (Indeed, I am soon to publish an essay with the title "Two Cheers for Vindictiveness."[14]) I hope I have said enough, however, to support Butler's claim that these passions have some positive value. Having such value, these passions are unlike, say, malice—pure delight in the misfortunes and sufferings of others. Malice is by no means universal but is, where present, intrinsically evil or diseased or both. Butler essentially wants to apply Aristotle's idea of the mean to the passion of resentment—developing an account of the circumstances that justify it and the degree to which it is legitimate to feel and be guided by it.[15] But the doctrine of the mean does not apply to malice; for the proper amount of this passion is always zero.

Uncritical boosters for quick forgiveness have a tendency to treat resentment and the other vindictive passions as though, like malice, they are intrinsically evil—passions that no decent person would

---

13. See AUREL KOLNAI, *Forgiveness*, in PROCEEDINGS OF THE ARISTOTELIAN SOCIETY 91, 95–98 (1973–74).
14. *See* Jeffrie G. Murphy, *Two Cheers for Vindictiveness*, in PUNISHMENT AND SOCIETY (forthcoming).
15. *See* ARISTOTLE, NICHOMACHEAN ETHICS 1107a, reprinted in NICHOMACHEAN ETHICS 44–46 (Terence Irwin trans., 1985).

acknowledge.[16] In this, I think that they are quite mistaken. In the *Oresteia*, Athena rightly made an honorable home for the Furies (representatives of the vindictive passions)—so constraining their excess by due process and the rule of law that they become the Eumenides (the Kindly Ones), protectors of law and social stability.[17] There is no honorable home for malice, however.

Let me summarize what I have argued to this point: the problem with resentment and other vindictive passions is not (as with malice) their very existence. In their proper place, they have an important role to play in the defense of self and of the moral and legal order. The problem with these passions is rather their tendency to get out of control—to so dominate the life of a victimized person that the person's own life is soured and, in his revenge seeking, he starts to pose a danger to the very moral and legal order that rightly identifies him as a victim of immorality. It is here—as a limiting and overcoming virtue—that forgiveness has its important role to play.

FORGIVENESS AS A VIRTUE

It is, of course, possible to take one's revenge against others in measured and proportional and peaceful ways—ways as simple as a cutting remark before colleagues or a failure to continue issuing lunch invitations.

Very often, however, a victimized person will allow vindictiveness to take over his very self—turning him into a self-righteous fanatic so involved—even joyous—in his outrage that he will be satisfied only with the utter annihilation of the person who has wronged him. Such

---

16. I sometimes think I find such uncritical boosterism among certain voices within what might be called the "forgiveness movement" in clinical psychology. *See* JEFFRIE G. MURPHY, *Forgiveness in Counseling: A Philosophical Perspective*, in CHARACTER, LIBERTY AND LAW: KANTIAN ESSAYS IN THEORY AND PRACTICE 223–238 (1998).
17. *See* AESCHYLUS, ORESTEIA (Robert Fagles trans., 1979).

a person is sometimes even willing to destroy, as symbolic stand-ins, persons who have done him no wrong or who may even be totally innocent.[18] Such a person is a danger to himself—very like, as I think Nietzsche once said, a scorpion stinging itself with its own tail—and poses a threat to the morality and decency of the social order. A person under the power of such vindictiveness can, often unconsciously, even use the language of justice and crime control as a rationalization for what is really sadism and cruelty. I cannot help thinking, for example, that many of the unspeakably brutish conditions that we tolerate in our prisons flow not from the stated legitimate desires for justice and crime control, but rather from a vindictiveness so out of control that it actually becomes a kind of malice.

Against such a background, forgiveness can be seen as a healing virtue that brings with it great blessings—chief among them being its capacity to free us from being consumed by our angers, its capacity to check our tendencies toward cruelty, and its capacity to open the door to the restoration of those relationships in our lives that are worthy of restoration. This last blessing can be seen in the fact that, since each one of us will sometimes wrong the people that mean the most to us, there will be times when we will want to be forgiven by those whom we have wronged. Seeing this, no rational person would desire to live in a world where forgiveness was not seen as a healing virtue. This is, I take it, the secular meaning of the parable of the unforgiving servant.[19]

We are faced, then, with a complex dilemma: How are we to reap the blessings of forgiveness without sacrificing our self-respect or our respect for the moral order in the process?

---

18. The von Kleist story *Michael Kohlhaas*—retold by E. L. Doctorow in his novel, *Ragtime* (1974)—is a famous illustration of this. A good English translation of Heinrich von Kleist's 1808 novella *Michael Kohlhass* may be found in HEINRICH VON KLEIST, THE MARQUISE OF O AND OTHER STORIES 114–213 (David Luke & Nigel Reevs trans., 1978).
19. See Matthew 18:21–35.

One great help here—and make no claim that it is the only help or even a necessary condition for forgiveness—is sincere repentance on the part of the wrongdoer. When I am wronged by another, a great part of the injury—over and above any physical harm I may suffer—is the insulting or degrading message that has been given to me by the wrongdoer; the message is that I am less worthy than he is, so unworthy that he may use me merely as a means or object in service to his desires and projects. Thus failing to resent (or hastily forgiving) the wrongdoer runs the risk that I am endorsing that very immoral message for which the wrongdoer stands. If the wrongdoer sincerely repents, however, he now joins me in repudiating the degrading and insulting message—allowing me to relate to him (his new self) as an equal without fear that a failure to resent him will be read as a failure to resent what he has done. In short: It is much easier to follow St. Augustine's counsel that we should "hate the sin but not the sinner" when the sinner (the wrongdoer) repudiates his own wrongdoing through an act of repentance.[20]

My point here is that sincere repentance on the part of the wrongdoer opens the door to forgiveness and often to reconciliation. This is not to suggest, however, that we should always demand repentance as a condition for forgiveness and reconciliation. When a person comes to repentance as a result of his own spiritual growth, we are witness to an inspiring transformation of character. Any repentance that is simply a response to a demand or external incentive, however, is very likely to be fake. In what could be read as a commentary both on certain aspects of the Federal Sentencing Guidelines[21] and on remarks

---

20. St. Augustine's remark, so often rendered as it is here, more literally reads "with love of mankind and hatred of sins." THE OXFORD DICTIONARY OF QUOTATIONS 37 (Angela Partington ed., rev. 4th ed. 1996) (citing *Letter 211*, reprinted in 33 PATROLOGIAE LATINAE (J. P. Minge ed., 1845)).
21. *See* U.S. SENTENCING COMMISSION GUIDELINES MANUAL § 3E1.1 (1998) ("If the defendant clearly demonstrates acceptance of responsibility for his offense, decrease the offense level by 2 levels.").

made by some of our current crop of elected officials, Montaigne wrote: "These men make us believe that they feel great regret and remorse within, but of atonement and correction or interruption they show us no sign... I know of no quality so easy to counterfeit as piety."[22] Montaigne's observation also suggests that the South Africans were perhaps wise in not making repentance a condition for amnesty under their Truth and Reconciliation Commission.

So let us welcome repentance when we find it, and let us do what we can to create a climate where it can flourish and open the door to the moral rebirth of the wrongdoer and to forgiveness by the wronged. But, out of respect for the genuine article, let us not demand or otherwise coerce it. Demanding tends to produce only lying and may even be degrading to the wrongdoer—inviting his further corruption rather than his moral rebirth. David Lurie, the central character in J. M. Coetzee's novel *Disgrace*, could save his job if he simply expressed the kind of repentance demanded of him by the university disciplinary board that has authority over him. I find myself sympathizing with the reasons he gives for not giving them what they want when he says:

> We went through the repentance business yesterday. I told you what I thought. I won't do it. I appeared before an officially constituted tribunal, before a branch of the law. Before that secular tribunal I pleaded guilty, a secular plea. That plea should suffice. Repentance is neither here nor there. Repentance belongs to another world, to another universe of discourse.... [What you are asking] reminds me too much of Mao's China. Recantation, self-criticism, public apology. I'm old fashioned, I would prefer simply to be put against a wall and shot.[23]

---

22. Michel de Montaigne On Repentance (1588), in The Complete Essays of Montaigne 617 (Donald Frame trans., 1958).
23. J. M Coetzee, Disgrace 58, 66 (1999).

There has in recent times been much cheap and shallow chatter about forgiveness and repentance—some of it coming from high political officials and some coming from the kind of psychobabble often found in self-help and recovery books. As a result of this, many people are, I fear, starting to become cynical about both. For reasons I have developed here, repentance may pave the way for forgiveness. It is less likely to do so, however, in a world where we come to believe that too many claims of repentance are insincere and expedient—talking the talk without (so far as we can tell) walking the walk.

I have reached a point where I fear that I have both used up my time and worn out my welcome. So I will now move to bring my remarks to a close by touching briefly on one additional issue.

FORGIVENESS AND CHRISTIANITY

At a symposium on forgiveness sponsored by a distinguished Catholic university, it would be fitting for me to close my talk with a few general remarks about the relationship between religion—particularly Christianity—and forgiveness. As someone who is neither devout nor trained in theology, I am hardly the best person to do this—either spiritually or intellectually. However, I will take a brief stab at it nonetheless.

There are, I think, at least three ways in which a Christian perspective on the world might make the struggle toward forgiveness— not easy, surely—but at least slightly less difficult than it otherwise might be. (Similar perspectives might also be present, of course, in other religions and world views.)[24]

First, I think that Christianity tends to introduce a humbling perspective on one's self and one's personal concerns—attempting to

---

24. *See, e.g.,* the discussion of the background world view that underlies the Judaic conception of forgiveness in Louis E. Newman's *The Quality of Mercy: On the Duty to Forgive in the Judaic Tradition*, 15 JOURNAL OF RELIGIOUS ETHICS 155 (1987). For the context provided

counter our natural tendencies of pride and narcissistic self-importance. According to this perspective, we are all fallible and flawed and all stand in deep need of forgiveness. This perspective does not seek to trivialize the wrongs that we suffer, but it does seek to blunt our very human tendency to magnify those wrongs out of all reasonable sense of proportion—the tendency to see ourselves as morally pure while seeing those who wrong us as evil incarnate. By breaking down a sharp us-them dichotomy, such a view should make it easier to follow Auden's counsel to "love your crooked neighbor with your crooked heart."[25] This should make us more open to the possibility of forgiving those who have wronged us and should also help us to keep our justified resentments from turning into malicious hatreds and our demands for just punishment from serving as rationalizations for sadistic cruelty.

Related to this is a second Christian teaching that might help open the door to forgiveness—a teaching that concerns not the status of the victim, but the status of the wrongdoer. According to Christianity, we are supposed to see the wrongdoer, as we are supposed to see each person, as a child of God, created in His image, and thus as ultimately precious. This vision is beautifully expressed by the writer William Trevor in his novel *Felicia's Journey*. He speaks with compassion and forgiveness even of the serial killer who is a central character of that novel and writes of him: "Lost within a man who murdered, there was a soul like any other soul, purity itself it surely once had been."[26] Viewing the wrongdoer in this way—seeing in him the innocent child he once was—should make it difficult to hate him with the kind of abandon that would make forgiveness of him utterly impossible.

---

by Stoicism, see Seneca, *On Anger* and *On Mercy*, in 1 MORAL ESSAYS 106–449 (John W. Basore trans., 1994). For a discussion of forgiveness in capital murder cases from an Islamic perspective, see Azizah al-Hibri, *The Muslim Perspective on the Clergy-Penitent Privilege*, 29 LOY. L.A. L. REV. 1723, 1728–29 (1996).

25. W.H. AUDEN, *As I walked Out One Evening*, in COLLECTED POEMS 135 (1991).
26. WILLIAM TREVOR, FELICIA'S JOURNEY 212 (1994).

Third and finally, Christianity teaches that the universe is—for all its evil and hardship—ultimately benign, created and sustained by a loving God, and to be met with hope rather than despair. On this view, the world may be falling, but—as Rilke wrote—"there is One who holds this falling/with infinite softness in his hands."[27]

If I could embrace such a view of the universe and our place in it—a view for which there is surely no proof, requiring a faith that is properly called religious—then perhaps I would not so easily think that the struggle against evil—even evil done to me—is my task alone, all up to me.[28] If I think that I alone can and must make things right—including making sure that the people I have branded as evil get exactly what is coming to them—then I take on a kind of self-importance that makes me not only unforgiving but dangerous—becoming the kind of person Nietzsche probably had in mind when he warned that we should "mistrust those in whom the urge to punish is very strong."[29] If I were capable of a certain kind of faith, then perhaps I could relax a bit the clenched fist with which I try to protect myself, sustain my self-respect, avenge myself, and hold my world together all alone.

This brings to a close my brief ruminations on forgiveness—ruminations that have, I hope, helped a bit to provide a framework for the discussion to follow today. As much as I love my own discipline of philosophy, however, I believe that it is the poets and other literary

---

27. RAINER MARIA RILKE, *Autumn*, in THE BOOK OF IMAGES (Edward Snow trans., 1991).
28. I came to see the value of this perspective when it was used by philosopher-theologian Marilyn Adams in her critique of some of my earlier writing on forgiveness. *See* Marilyn Adams, *Forgiveness: A Christian Model*, 8 FAITH AND PHILOSOPHY 277–304 (1991). I have also recently come to see the wisdom in Herbert Morris's use of the thought of Simone Weil on these matters. *See* Herbert Morris & Jeffrie G. Murphy, *Exchange on Forgiveness*, 7 CRIMINAL JUSTICE ETHICS 3, 22 (Summer/Fall 1988).
29. FRIEDRICH NIETZSCHE, *Thus Spoke Zarathustra, Second Part, On the Tarantulas*, in THE PORTABLE NIETZSCHE 212 (Walter Kaufmann trans., 1970). I pursue Nietzsche's thoughts on punishment in somewhat greater detail in my *Moral Epistemology, the Retributive Emotions, and the "Clumsy Moral Philosophy" of Jesus Christ*, in THE PASSIONS OF LAW 149 (Susan Bandes ed., 1999).

artists who do the best job of providing a vision around which not just our thinking but our sensibilities can be organized. And thus I shall give my last word to the poet Seamus Heaney and simply read to you a brief excerpt from his play, *The Cure at Troy*:

> Human beings suffer.
> They torture one another.
> They get hurt and get hard.
> No poem or play or song
> Can fully right a wrong
> Inflicted and endured.
>
> The innocent in gaols
> Beat on their bars together.
> A hunger-striker's father
> Stands in the graveyard dumb.
> The police widow in veils
> Faints at the funeral home.
>
> History says, Don't hope
> On this side of the grave.
> But then, once in a lifetime
> The longed-for tidal wave
> Of justice can rise up.
> And hope and history rhyme.
>
> So hope for a great sea-change
> On the far side of revenge.
> Believe that a further shore
> Is reachable from here...[30]

---

30. SEAMUS HEANEY, THE CURE AT TROY 77 (1991). This play is Heaney's performing version of Sophocles's *Philoctetes*.

Chapter 2

Moral Epistemology, the Retributive Emotions, and the "Clumsy Moral Philosophy" of Jesus Christ

In her opinion the troubles in life were started by people who never looked into their own souls.

Oscar Hijuelos, *Mr. Ives' Christmas*

INTRODUCTION

Nietzsche's writings have a remarkable capacity to trouble the soul, and I have recently found my own soul troubled by reflection on his remarks on retribution as a theory of punishment, a theory that I have long endorsed and defended.[1]

---

1. Nietzsche's reflections on punishment are spread throughout most of his major works. The best place to begin reading him on this and related issues is probably the Second Essay ("'Guilt,' 'Bad Conscience,' and the Like") of the 1887 *On the Genealogy of Morals*. (Friedrich Nietzsche, *On the Genealogy of Morals*, translated by Walter Kaufmann, New York: Vintage, 1989.) Nietzsche's remarks are about punishment in general, with no specific references to retributivism. I think it is obvious, however, that what he has in mind is punishment with a retributive justification—the idea that, in punishing, we are giving people what they in justice deserve. As will be noted later, he sometimes speaks favorably of punishment when the practice is defended with a nonretributive justification. My own defenses of the retributive theory of punishment may be found in my collection of essays *Retribution, Justice and Therapy* (Dordrecht: Reidel, 1979); my chapters in the book *Forgiveness and Mercy* by Jeffrie G. Murphy (Chapters 1, 3, and 5) and Jean Hampton (Chapters 2 and 4) (Cambridge:

Nietzsche does not, of course, give intellectual arguments against the claims of retributivism—arguments that could perhaps be met by counter-arguments. Rather, he offers a diagnosis of those who favor punishment on such grounds—speculating that, for all their high talk about justice and desert, they are actually driven by a variety of base and irrational passions—malice, spite, envy—passions for which Nietzsche uses the French noun *ressentiment*. At their best, retributivists—with their scorekeeping and their tit for tat—have the sensibilities of accountants: "their souls squint."[2] At their worst, retributivists are simply cruel.[3] Small wonder, then, that Nietzsche offers the following counsel: "Mistrust all in whom the impulse to punish is powerful."[4]

I see in myself, alas, a person whose impulse to punish has been—at least in some cases—very powerful, and Nietzsche has caused me to mistrust myself and the abstract theories I have been inclined to use to rationalize that impulse. In this essay I share with you the nature of my mistrust.[5]

Cambridge University Press, 1988), and in my essay "Getting Even: The Role of the Victim," reprinted in my essay collection *Retribution Reconsidered* (Dordrecht: Kluwer, 1992).

2. "While the noble man lives in trust and openness with himself…, the man of *ressentiment* is neither upright nor naive nor honest and straightforward with himself. His soul squints." (Nietzsche, *Genealogy, supra* note 1, p. 38.)
3. "Almost everything we call 'higher culture' is based on the spiritualization of cruelty." (Friedrich Nietzsche, *Beyond Good and Evil*, translated by Walter Kaufmann, New York: Vintage, 1989, p. 158.) More cautiously expressed versions of similar thoughts may, of course, be found in other writers. See, for example, Chapter III of Thomas Hobbes' *De Cive*, and Karen Horney's marvelous essay "The Value of Vindictiveness" in *American Journal of Psychoanalysis* (Volume 8, 1948, pp. 3–12).
4. *Thus Spoke Zarathustra*, Second Part, "On the Tarantulas," in *The Portable Nietzsche*, translated by Walter Kaufmann (New York: Viking, 1970), p. 212.
5. I have been assisted in reaching this not totally welcome self-perception not simply by Nietzsche but also by some essays by Marilyn Adams and Herbert Morris that are critical of my work on resentment, punishment, and forgiveness—essays that suggest, ever so politely and ever so indirectly, that views such as mine may grow out of excessive self-involvement, mistrust, and a lack of generosity of spirit. See Marilyn Adams's "Forgiveness: A Christian Model," in *Faith and Philosophy* (Volume 8, Number 3, 1991, pp. 277–304) and Herbert Morris' and Jeffrie G. Murphy's "Exchange on Forgiveness" in *Criminal Justice Ethics* (Volume 7, Number 2, 1988, pp. 3–22).

In the main, I shall be focusing on Michael Moore's widely anthologized and justly admired essay "The Moral Worth of Retribution."[6] In that essay, Moore takes seriously the Nietzschean challenge to retributivism and argues that this challenge can be successfully defused if only we draw the proper distinctions.

In the course of his essay, Moore seeks to explore the use of emotions in moral epistemology, arguing that some emotions are epistemically reliable—pointing us in what is morally the correct direction—whereas other emotions are epistemically unreliable—pointing us toward moral error. He grants that if the retributive urge must be grounded in the family of base passions that Nietzsche labels *ressentiment*, then retribution is indeed undermined. He then argues that retribution does not have to be so basely grounded but should be seen as grounded instead in the rational and good emotion of guilt.

In what follows I shall argue that Moore's attempt to defuse the Nietzschean challenge fails. I think that many of his general points about emotions and moral epistemology are mistaken and shall argue that guilt fares just as badly as *ressentiment* as an honorable emotional basis for retribution.

As I reflect on my own personal and philosophical struggles with retribution and related concepts over the years, I find myself increasingly making autobiographical references in the recent writings that reflect these struggles. I do this not (I hope!) merely as narcissistic self-indulgence but rather in the spirit of another insight by Nietzsche: "Gradually it has become clear to me what every philosophy so far has been: namely, the personal confession of its author and a kind of involuntary and unconscious memoir." (Nietzsche, *Beyond Good and Evil, supra* note 3, p. 13.) A similar thought has been expressed by Thomas Nagel: "Philosophical ideas are acutely sensitive to individual temperament, and to wishes." (Thomas Nagel, *The View from Nowhere,* New York: Oxford University Press, 1986, p. 10.) To the degree that Nietzsche and Nagel are correct about this, then, it might be useful if philosophers in general would "fess up" concerning the internal struggles that motivate some of their abstract speculations.

6. Michael Moore, "The Moral Worth of Retribution," in *Responsibility, Character, and the Emotions,* edited by Ferdinand Schoeman (Cambridge: Cambridge University Press, 1987), pp. 179–219. Although I am here selecting certain aspects of Moore's essay with which I want to quarrel, I want to make it clear to the reader how very much I admire the essay and how much I have learned from it.

I shall also argue that the main value of Nietzsche's challenge emerges if his claims are interpreted as what might be called lessons in moral humility—lessons that (ironically enough) are similar to those found in the famous New Testament report of Jesus stopping the stoning of an adulteress by saying, "He that is without sin among you, let him first cast a stone at her" (John 8:7).[7] Moore ridicules this remark and characterizes its use by Jesus, in the context of punishment, as "pretty clumsy moral philosophy."[8] Against Moore, I shall argue that the remark is not clumsy at all but is, rather, deeply insightful and deeply cautionary. I will also suggest (another irony) that a version of this same insight may be found in the ethical writings of that arch-retributivist Immanuel Kant.

MORAL EPISTEMOLOGY AND THE EMOTIONS

In introductory logic we warn our students against committing the genetic fallacy—the fallacy of thinking that the falsity of a proposition can be demonstrated by a causal claim concerning the origins of the belief in that proposition. It might be tempting to dismiss Nietzsche's challenge to retributivism as an instance of that fallacy, and Moore is correct in seeing that this move would be too hasty.

It is, of course, logically possible for a proposition to be true even if the person believes that proposition for a variety of suspect reasons—e.g., retribution could be the correct theory of punishment,

---

7. I am well aware that I am using some of Nietzsche's insights for my own purposes and taking them in directions he would not welcome. Here, for example, is what he has to say about humility: "When stepped on, a worm doubles up. That is clever. In that way he lessens the probability of being stepped on again. In the language of morality: humility." (Friedrich Nietzsche, *Twilight of the Idols*, in *The Portable Nietzsche*, translated by Walter Kaufmann, New York: Viking, 1970, p. 471.)
8. Moore, *supra* note 6, p. 188. Moore is willing to concede (p. 193) that the passage may "charitably" be read as a counsel against falling victim to mob psychology, but he sees no deeper message in it.

people could really in justice deserve the punishment they receive, even if those advocating their punishment on retributive grounds were motivated not by justice but by a variety of hateful passions.

However, as Moore rightly notes, this logical point should not blind us from realizing that the causation of a belief can be epistemically relevant to the degree of confidence we place in that belief. Are we not properly skeptical, for example, of the testimony we receive from those who made their observations while drunk? It is logically possible, of course, that the beliefs that they formed in this state are true. However, given the high correlation between beliefs formed in this state and false beliefs, we are surely reasonable in our skepticism.

Moore claims that emotions, while not able logically to undermine truth or establish falsity, might still be used as what he calls *heuristic guides* to moral truth. By this, I interpret him to mean something like the following: We know that certain emotions are highly correlated with correct moral judgments, and other emotions are highly correlated with moral error—e.g., we know that *ressentiment*-based moral judgments are likely to be erroneous, whereas guilt-based moral judgments are likely to be correct. Thus he writes:

> [W]e should ask ourselves what [the criminal] deserves by asking what we would deserve had we done such an act. In answering this question we should listen to our guilt feelings, feelings whose epistemic import is not in question in the same way as are those of *ressentiment*. Such guilt feelings should tell us that to do an act like [that of a vicious murderer] is to forfeit forever any light-hearted idea of going on as before. One should feel so awful that the idea of again leading a life unchanged from before, with the same goals and hopes and happiness, should appear revoltingly incomprehensible.[9]

9. Ibid., p. 216.

Thus, according to Moore, is Nietzsche answered. Insofar as we are guided by *ressentiment* in forming our punitive judgments, then—as Nietzsche rightly points out—our judgments are likely to be erroneous. When guided by guilt, however—a possibility Nietzsche did not consider—our retributive judgments are likely to be correct. Thus the way to avoid Nietzsche's problem is to make sure that our retributive judgments are grounded in guilt rather than in *ressentiment*.

Alas, all this simply will not work. It both concedes too much to Nietzsche and concedes too much to guilt. First of all, the concession to Nietzsche. Of course, *ressentiment* is going to be highly correlated with error since *ressentiment* is, by definition, an irrational and base passion. It means, roughly, "spiteful and malicious envy." It thus makes no sense to speak of rational or justified or honorable *ressentiment*— just as it makes no sense to speak of rational or justified or honorable malice.

But suppose instead we employ the English noun "resentment." It seems that we can speak of rational or justified resentment (just as we can speak of rational or justified indignation), and thus it would take more than a few Nietzschean sermons against *ressentiment* in order to make us reasonably doubt the epistemic reliability of resentment as a foundation for retributive judgments. I will below express some skepticism about regarding any emotion as the legitimate foundation of retributive judgments, but, if we are going to seek for such a foundation, I see no reason for thinking that resentment will be any less reliable than guilt.[10]

10. In my chapters in *Forgiveness and Mercy* (*supra* note 1), I argue that some degree of resentment may be justified as an assertion of self-respect and may thus form part of a virtuous life. This is the good side of resentment, but perhaps (if Nietzsche is correct) it has a tendency to slide into *ressentiment* without our being aware of this. Guilt also, of course, has a good side insofar as it is a testament to the fact that we care for others and our moral duties to them. But perhaps (as I shall suggest below) it has a tendency to slide into neurosis— everything from moral silliness to pathological self-loathing.

But is guilt epistemically reliable? Does it merit the celebration that Moore conducts for it? I think not. Although guilt may not have its epistemic import challenged "in the same way" as *ressentiment*, it still faces some deep challenges. We all know (even without reading Freud) that our guilts are often neurotic—misplaced and irrational and destructive. Thus it is hard to see how any useful or fair idea of what others deserve can be generated merely by projecting from our own imagined feelings of guilt. Given a certain sort of upbringing and consequent neurotic or simply narrow personality, for example, a person might use his own imagined guilt feelings to demand very serious punishment for conduct that is (in my view) objectively trivial or entirely unobjectionable—e.g., masturbation or homosexuality or romance outside a particular religious or ethnic or racial group.

Should we then project only from guilt feelings that are rational? But what will these be—those that are based on a proper idea of wrongdoing and desert? If so, then the whole enterprise begins to look hopelessly circular: we are using prior concepts of evil and desert to decide which guilt feelings may be projected to yield an idea of what others deserve. But if we already know what level of suffering is deserved for certain evils, why not just give other people (and ourselves) that level of suffering and forget all this talk about guilt and projections from it?[11]

---

11. Moore (*supra* note 6, p. 183) suggests two ways in which one, using coherence to assess the adequacy of a moral theory, might attempt to defend a retributive theory of punishment. One strategy is to show that retributivism follows from some more general principle of justice that we think is true. The other strategy, favored by Moore, is to show that retributivism "best accounts for those of our more particular moral judgments that we also believe to be true." This strategy, called by John Rawls the methodology of "reflective equilibrium," selects as the best theory the theory that accounts for the largest set of our pretheoretical convictions. (John Rawls, *A Theory of Justice*, Cambridge: Harvard University Press, 1971, pp. 20ff.) But what if Nietzsche is correct about the origin and nature of our pretheoretical convictions concerning desert and punishment—that, whatever we may consciously think, these pretheoretical convictions are self-deceptive covers for *ressentiment*? Or what if we can tell a plausible story to plant comparable skepticism about pretheoretical convictions generated by guilt? What does this do to the use of reflective equilibrium methodology?

A DIGRESSION ON RETRIBUTION

I would now like to explore the ways in which our personal shortcomings—including our emotional shortcomings—may legitimately serve to undermine our confidence in some of our retributive judgments. Prior to this exploration, however, I think it will be useful to distinguish several different senses of retribution, for only one of them is clearly vulnerable to the challenges I shall raise.

Retribution is, of course, punishment that involves giving wrongdoers what they deserve. There are at least five senses of desert, however, and thus at least five senses of retribution. The five are these: desert as legal guilt; desert as involving *mens rea* (e.g., intention, knowledge); desert as involving responsibility (capacity to conform one's conduct to the rules); desert as a debt owed to annual wrongful gains from unfair free-riding (the Herbert Morris theory)[12]; and, finally, desert as involving ultimate character—evil or wickedness in some deep sense.

I shall call this fifth kind of retributivism "character retributivism."[13] Although Kant defends different accounts of punishment at

---

12. See Herbert Morris' "Persons and Punishment" in his *On Guilt and Innocence* (Berkeley: University of California Press, 1976), pp. 31–63.
13. I explore in greater detail the distinction between character retributivism (the view I am attributing to Moore) and grievance retributivism (the Morris view) in my "Repentance, Punishment and Mercy" in *Repentance: A Comparative Perspective*, edited by Amitai Etzioni and David Carney (Lanham, Md.: Rowman & Littlefield, 1997), pp. 143–170. In another essay, Moore rejects character (and favors choice) as a basis for criminal liability and excuse. ("Choice, Character, and Excuse," *Social Philosophy and Policy*, Volume 7, Issue 2, Spring 1990, pp. 29–58.) In "The Moral Worth of Retribution," *supra* note 6, however, his concern seems to be with punishment as deserved suffering as this value might be reflected not in judgments of liability but in sentencing; here issues of character move to center stage. Consider, for example, the weight that Moore gives (pp. 213ff.) to the murderer Richard Herrin's "shallowness"—his lack of guilt and remorse—in thinking about the punishment that Herrin deserves. For an instructive discussion of the very different roles that character might play in conviction and sentencing, see James Landon's "Character Evidence: Getting to the Root of the Problem Through Comparison," in *American Journal of Criminal Law* (Volume 24, Number 3, Summer 1997, pp. 581–615).

various places in his *The Metaphysics of Morals,* character retributivism is clearly his position in the famous passage where he argues that murderers must be punished, even if civil society disbands, so that these wrongdoers will receive what is properly proportional to their "inner wickedness" (*inneren Bösartigkeit*).[14] I have also on occasion defended this view—e.g., in *Forgiveness and Mercy,* where I reject Augustine's "hate the sin but not the sinner" counsel and advocate what I call retributive hatred toward certain unrepentant wrongdoers.[15]

Michael Moore, as I interpret him, embraces a particularly ambitious and robust version of character retributivism: state punishment as pursuing the same objective that older traditions assigned to God. Character retribution, the idea that evil people are to be punished in proper proportion to their inner wickedness, had its first and best home in the context of divine punishment—something that God might properly administer, on that final Day of Judgment, when he consults the ledger book of a whole human life and character. Whatever one might think of this as a theology, most writers on punishment—even most retributivists—would probably reject it as a legitimate objective of state punishment. But not Moore. Indeed, Moore claims that if he believed in God he probably would not favor this account of secular, state punishment. However, as an atheist, he claims that the state must take on the punitive task that older traditions reserved for God. Otherwise the task of apportioning punishment to evil would be left undone, and that would be morally intolerable.[16]

I have, in several earlier essays, expressed skepticism that an account of state punishment based on this robust version of character retributivism is consistent with the idea of a liberal, secular state, and I do not propose to

---

14. Immanuel Kant, *The Metaphysics of Morals,* translated by Mary Gregor (Cambridge: Cambridge University Press, 1991), p. 142.
15. *Supra* note 1, Chapter 3.
16. Moore, *supra* note 6, p. 217.

rehearse my arguments here.[17] In those same essays, however, I accepted (even celebrated) the moral legitimacy of character retributivism and expressed some regret that I might be forced to choose between it and liberalism. In the present essay I will explain why I have come to doubt even the moral legitimacy of character retributivism and will argue not simply that the liberal state should not pursue this goal but that virtuous individuals should not embrace or welcome it either—even as something to hope for from God. Here (ironically enough) I have an ally in Kant—at least when he is thinking not about state punishment but about punishment and personal virtue. In *The Metaphysics of Morals*, he writes:

> It is a duty of virtue not only to refrain from repaying another's enmity with hatred out of mere revenge but also *not even to call upon the judge of the world* for vengeance, partly because a man has enough guilt of his own to be greatly in need of pardon and partly, and indeed especially, because no punishment, no matter from whom it comes, may be inflicted out of hatred. It is therefore a duty of men to be *forgiving*.[18]

In some sense, the remainder of the present essay may be seen as simply an expansion—with the help of Jesus and Nietzsche—of this Kantian insight.

---

17. Jeffrie G. Murphy, "Retributivism, Moral Education, and the Liberal State" (in *Retribution Reconsidered*, supra note 1, pp. 15–30), and "Legal Moralism and Liberalism," in *Arizona Law Review* (Volume 37, Number 1, Spring 1995, pp. 73–94).
18. *Supra* note 14, p. 253 (first italics mine). Kant does not always follow his own counsel on this matter. In his famous "moral proof" for the existence of God, for example, he argues that it is so vital (the *summum bonum*) that wrongdoers receive their just deserts (and good people their proper rewards) that—given that we cannot attain this goal in this world—we must postulate the existence of God as an agent who can bring this about in the next world. Of course we know that God will not be motivated by hate. How can we be so sure, however, that we are not so motivated when we believe in God in the hope that he will punish wrongdoers as they truly deserve? Are those who are charmed by Kant's moral proof subject to a Nietzschean diagnosis?

A FRESH START: RETRIBUTION AND MORAL HUMILITY

It is not a logical truth, of course, that character retributivists will be motivated by hatred, and indeed most (and surely Moore and my previous self) would claim that they are not so motivated. If Nietzsche is right, however, the possibilities for self-deception here are enormous.[19] Once we think we are in a position to make judgments about a person's deep character—about that person's ultimate worth or value as a human being—then it is almost certain that we shall be tempted, once we have labeled some people as evil or "rotten to the core," to come to think of them as so much scum and to respond to them contemptuously. And the road from contempt to cruelty strikes me as a short one. The transition from "you have a bad character" to "you are evil" to "you are scum" to "you deserve to be treated with contempt" to "you deserve whatever cruel indignity I choose to inflict on you" is not a logical transition. It is, however—and this is the insight I draw from Nietzsche—a rather compelling psychological transition, one that should make us very cautious about basing our justification of punishment on assessments of ultimate character.[20]

Those of us who are sophisticated philosophers may, of course, think that we can detach our intellectual retributivist views from the kind of self-deceptive cruelty against which Nietzsche warned. But

---

19. Moore, *supra* note 6, admits this (p. 216), but the admission strikes me as possibly perfunctory, for it seems in no degree to undermine Moore's own willingness to make supremely confident judgments about what suffering others—e.g., Richard Herrin—deserve. His response to Herrin and the other criminals he discusses could be read as superior and contemptuous. I think, alas, that such a response is also obviously present in some of my own previous work. It is possible, of course, that I misinterpret Moore here because I want company—desiring to draw another prominent retributivist into my tent so that I will not have to feel alone in my fear that I have perhaps fallen victim to some bad passions.
20. Recall again (*supra* note 13) that my concern here is mainly with criminal sentencing, not with criminal liability.

self-deceiving people always think that they can do this; this is part of what it means to say that they are in a state of self-deception. Even if we could do it, however, do we want to put forth views that—given the psychological connections noted by Nietzsche—might well be used by others to feed the fires of social cruelty, fires that currently rage nearly out of control in the American public's current viciousness toward criminals? I hope not, and I think that Judge Richard Posner—hardly my idea of a soft-on-crime, bleeding-heart sentimentalist—agrees with me. In a recent opinion, in language that is persuasive and eloquent, he warned against the irrationality and cruelty toward criminals that is increasingly driving our system of criminal justice in America:

> There are different ways to look upon the inmates of prisons and jails in the United States in 1995. One way is to look upon them as members of a different species, indeed as a type of vermin, devoid of human dignity and entitled to no respect.
>
> I do not myself consider the 1.5 million inmates of American prisons and jails in that light. We should have a realistic conception of the composition of the prison and jail population before deciding that they are scum entitled to nothing better than what a vengeful populace and a resource-starved penal system chooses to give them. We must not exaggerate the distance between "us," the lawful ones, the respectable ones, and the prison and jail population; for such exaggeration will make it too easy for us to deny that population the rudiments of humane consideration.[21]

I do not know if Judge Posner would welcome being located in the Nietzschean camp, but it is Nietzsche, I think, who provides the

---

21. Johnson v. Phelan, No. 93-3753, United States Court of Appeals, Seventh Circuit, 1995 WL 621777 (7th Cir.[Ill.]).

most plausible explanation of the psychological and social forces that Judge Posner rightly wishes to oppose.

In short: realizing that we might be motivated not by justice but by cruelty should make us pause before we confidently march forward under the banner of character retributivism. This is Nietzsche's lesson in moral humility.

Nietzsche's lesson in moral humility is not the only such lesson relevant to an assessment of character retributivism, however. Two additional ones are provided by Kant as he seeks to mine his Christian background for moral nuggets of secular value. Let me quote at some length passages from his *Critique of Pure Reason* and his *Religion Within the Limits of Reason Alone*, the final passage rivaling Nietzsche in its passion and in the profundity of its psychological insight:

> The real morality of actions, their merit or guilt, even that of our own conduct, remains entirely hidden form us. Our imputations can refer only to the empirical character. How much of this character is ascribable to the pure effect of freedom, how much to mere nature, that is, to faults of temperament for which there is no responsibility, or to its happy constitution (*merito fortunae*), can never be determined; and upon it therefore no perfectly just judgments can be passed.[22]

> We call a man evil, however, not because he performs actions that are evil (contrary to law) but because these actions are of such a nature that we may infer from them the presence in him of evil maxims. In and through experience we can observe actions contrary to law, and we can observe (at least in ourselves) that they are preformed in the consciousness that they

---

22. Immanuel Kant, *Critique of Pure Reason*, translated by Norman Kemp Smith (London: Macmillan, 1933), p. 475.

are unlawful; but a man's maxims, sometimes even his own, are not thus observable; consequently the judgment that the agent is an evil man cannot be made with certainty if grounded on experience.[23]

[People] may picture themselves as meritorious, feeling themselves guilty of no such offenses as they see others burdened with; nor do they ever inquire whether good luck should not have the credit, or whether by reason of the cast of mind which they could discover, if they only would, in their own in-most nature, they would not have practiced similar vices, had not inability, temperament, training, and circumstances of time and place which serve to tempt one (matters which are not imputable), kept them out of the way of these vices. This dishonesty, by which we humbug ourselves and which thwarts the establishing of a true moral disposition in us, extends itself outwardly also to falsehood and deception of others. If this is not to be termed wickedness, it at least deserves the name of worthlessness, and is an element in the radical evil of human nature, which (inasmuch as it puts out of tune the moral capacity to judge what a man is to be taken for, and renders wholly uncertain both internal and external attribution of responsibility) constitutes the foul taint of our race.[24]

In these passages Kant seems to be raising both cognitive and moral obstacles to the legitimacy of imputing deep character responsibility to others (and perhaps even to ourselves)—calling into question our capacity to judge such matters. The passages raise the question "Who are we to judge?" Do we know enough to occupy this

---

23. Immanuel Kant, *Religion Within the Limits of Reason Alone*, translated by T. M. Greene and Hoyt H. Hudson (New York: Harper, 1960), p. 16.
24. *Ibid.*, pp. 33–34.

role without gross negligence and error? Are we virtuous enough to occupy this role without hypocrisy?

COGNITIVE OBSTACLES TO CHARACTER RETRIBUTIVISM

The deeper we probe in our retributive judgment, the more prone to error we are, and character retributivism requires the deepest probing of all.[25] For the inquiry here is not simply into wrongful acts (harm or free riding), or into voluntary control, or into such fairly surface parts of the mind as intention or knowledge (*mens rea*), or even into episodic motive. It is, rather, a search into deep character—into such matters as whether the defendant possesses (to use the language of some capital sentencing guidelines) a "hardened, abandoned and malignant heart."[26] But are we in a position to know such deep character or to know the degree to which, if at all, people are responsible for the possession of such character? Kant suggests, in the first two of the three passages quoted, that the answer to these questions is no.

We face here the formidable epistemological problem that philosophers call "the problem of other minds" and perhaps even deep metaphysical worries about free will and determinism. It is hard

---

25. The cognitive and moral obstacles to character retribution that I present here were first developed with respect to the imputation of responsibility in my essay "Cognitive and Moral Obstacles to Imputation" (*Jahrbuch für Recht und Ethik*, Band 2, 1994, pp. 67–79).
26. In many American states, capital murder's *mens rea* requirement of "malice aforethought" may be inferred from recklessness if a killer is said to have the mental state or character defect variously characterized as "an abandoned and wicked heart," "a depraved heart," "a malignant heart," "a depraved mind," "wickedness of disposition, hardness of heart, cruelty, recklessness of consequences and a mind regardless of social duty," "wickedness of heart or cruelty," or (in the *Model Penal Code*) "extreme indifference to the value of human life." See generally Joshua Dressler's *Understanding Criminal Law* (New York: Matthew Bender, 1987), p. 461. Even when a concern with inner wickedness does not find its way into the definition of the crime, it often arises dramatically when character is considered for purposes of criminal sentencing—particularly in capital sentencing. See generally London, *supra* note 13.

enough—given human capacity for self-deception—to be very certain of one's own motives and fundamental desires, and there are staggering obstacles in the way of our making such judgments about others.[27]

Kant's own theory of imputation and desert, placing so much weight upon the radically free noumenal self that is unknowable through any empirical means (the only ones we have, alas), faces this problem in a particularly dramatic way.[28] Any theory that places weight on the inner life in determining desert, however, will face the problem to some degree. Even the attribution of such familiar (from the American *Model Penal Code*) *mens rea* conditions as purpose or recklessness faces nontrivial cognititve problems. And, of course, when we seek to target even deeper aspects of ultimate character and responsibility—to target "inner wickedness" or a "hardened, abandoned and malignant heart"—the cognitive problems become even more awesome.

It seems to me that these epistemological problems cannot, in justice, simply be ignored. If we really do not have the knowledge required to impute deep character depravity to others with any degree

---

27. E. M. Cioran: "How to imagine other people's lives when our own seems scarcely conceivable?" (I copied this down years ago from one of Cioran's works, but I can no longer find the source.) For a careful and insightful exploration of the issues of this section of my paper—an exploration from which I learned a great deal—see Rebecca Dresser's "Culpability and Other Minds" in *Law & Southern California Interdisciplinary Law Journal* (Volume 2, Number 1, Spring 1993, pp. 41–88).

28. If we claim that responsibility is a property of the noumenal self, we preserve a strong sense of desert because the noumenal self is (according to Kant) metaphysically free. The noumenal self, however, cannot be known through empirical means—e.g., observation of behavior. We can get around this cognitive problem by claiming that responsibility is a property of the empirical self. But the empirical self is (according to Kant) subject to causal determination, and this would seem to spell the end of any strong sense of desert. Any attempt to link up the two selves in a common theory would, of course, face the classic problem of interactionism familiar from the debates over Cartesian dualism. These problems might be overcome, but we are currently in no position to justify cheerful optimism that we really know what we are doing here.

Although I cannot pursue the matter here, it is possible (as my colleague Michael White has suggested) that attribution of desert in a deep sense might involve conceptual as well as cognitive obstacles. The concept of responsible inner wickedness might involve a notion of the self (or true self) that is incoherent.

of reliability, then we act recklessly in inflicting misery on people as the suffering they deserve for their inner wickedness.[29]

What, then, are we to do? We could attempt a Thomas Nagel strategy and return to our strong retributive practices with a certain sense of irony and detachment.[30] This probably would not work, however, since the emotions required for strong retributivism are probably not consistent with irony and detachment. We could also adopt an essentially consequentialist theory of punishment, perhaps with some deontological side constraints—e.g., the negative retributive side constraint that we not punish anyone to a degree greater than he deserves. This will only work, of course, if we can analyze the concept of desert in such a way that it does not raise all the same problems noted above—e.g., "punish him no more than he deserves" had better not mean "punish him no more than demanded by his inner wickedness."

Perhaps the most promising prospect is to seek a weaker or more modest version of retributivism, one whose epistemological and metaphysical commitments are less deep. We could, for example, employ Herbert Morris' justification of criminal punishment: the claim that the criminal, as a free rider on a mutually beneficial scheme of social cooperation, must be punished in order to annul the unfair advantage

---

29. In my view, there are two probably unanswerable questions that would need answers before we could confidently claim to be punishing people in proper proportion to their inner wickedness: (1) Have we in fact accurately determined the ultimate character of the individual? (2) Was the individual freely responsible for the development of that character? Not everyone, of course, thinks that the second question is relevant. John Kekes, for example, in his book *Facing Evil* (Princeton: Princeton University Press, 1990), thinks that the issues of free choice and responsibility are irrelevant to assessing a character as evil or wicked, and thus our failure to know about such matters must be irrelevant also. For Kekes, a person has an evil character if that person possesses (for whatever cause or reason) traits that tend to inflict harm on innocent people. I can see this as one possible analysis of evil and can also see it as a basis for a utilitarian response to evil—e.g., respond to people who are evil in this way by taking steps to neutralize the harm that they might cause. What I cannot see, however, is how any interesting concept of deserved suffering can be applied to persons who are evil only in this way.
30. See Thomas Nagel's "The Absurd" in his collection *Mortal Questions* (Oxford: Oxford University Press, 1979), pp. 11–23.

his wrongful failure to exercise self-restraint has given him over those citizens who have been law-abiding.[31] Although this theory does not involve deep notions of inner wickedness, it may still properly be called retributive because it is a non-consequentialist theory of punishment that bases the justification of punishment on considerations of justice or fairness. (Free riders violate a duty of fair play to those who have given the law their voluntary compliance.) Some notion of desert is also captured—e.g., according to Morris, the criminal has a right to punishment and owes it as a debt to his fellow citizens. This theory would also require some consideration of states of mind and character (e.g. free riding is an intentional act), but ones that, given the less deeply retributive purpose of the practice in which the consideration will arise, will probably stretch our cognitive powers to a much less worrisome degree. Such a "moral balance" theory is, of course, not without its problems—and may even be open to the Nietzschean charge that some with the score-keeping souls of accountants will be drawn to it.[32] It does not, however, seem to flirt with cruelty.

31. *Supra* note 12.
32. In *The Dawn*, Nietzsche speaks of "our abominable penal codes, with their shopkeeper's scales." (*The Portable Nietzsche, supra* note 4, p. 86.) Some of the problems faced by Morris' theory (a theory I once embraced wholeheartedly) are these: How are we to use this version of retributivism to grade criminal offenses on a scale of seriousness? It does not seem that murder (clearly a more serious crime than theft) is more unfair than theft. And if the criminal owes us a debt solely because we have exercised self-restraint and the criminal has not, then the criminal's punishment would have to be a function of how difficult it was for us to obey the law (i.e., how great a burden we found our own self-restraint). But this might produce a highly unpredictable and bizarre ranking of criminal offenses. Most of us who are normal and well brought up are probably not very tempted to murder or rape and are thus not aware of taking on much of a burden in refraining from these activities. The burden of self-restraint exercised here is, for most of us, far less than the burden we feel when paying our taxes. Do we then want to punish tax evasion as a more serious offense than murder or rape? Additional problems for Morris' view are generated by Robert Nozick's critique of the principle of fairness itself in *Anarchy, State and Utopia* (New York: Basic Books, 1974, pp. 90ff) and perhaps by my argument that given the radical inequality of benefits in actual societies, the principal of fairness will not impose upon all citizens equal obligations of obedience to law. On this issue, see my essay "Marxism and Retribution" in my collection *Retribution, Justice and Therapy, supra* note 1, pp. 93–115.

To summarize: Even though the necessities of maintaining civilized life and schemes of just cooperation require that we sometimes make and act on our best judgments of wrongdoing and criminal responsibility (that we have trials and jails, in short), we should be very cautions about overdramatizing and overmoralizing what we must (regretfully) do here by portraying it as some righteous cosmic drama—as a holy war against ultimate sin and evil. Such a view would, among other things, tempt us to dangerous excesses—excesses that would harm others through our unjust treatment of them and harm us through our own corruption—as one is always corrupted when one would presume to occupy a role best reserved for the gods. As mere humans, with radically finite knowledge, it is perhaps better for us to admit that we are not totally clear about what we are up to here.

MORAL OBSTACLES TO CHARACTER RETRIBUTIVISM

There are at least two ways in which retributive judgments might seem inappropriate (unvirtuous and likely—but not necessarily—mistaken) because of moral failings in the person who makes them. First, they could involve the vice of hypocrisy: our demanding that others receive their just deserts when we ourselves are no better. (I take it that Jesus' "He that is without sin..." remark is an attempt to identify the hypocrisy in at least some acts of punishment.) Second—as noted by Nietzsche—retributive judgments could be seen as running a nontrivial risk of being motivated by such base passions as envy, malicious hatred, and spite, passions included by Nietzsche under the term *ressentiment*. I have already discussed the Nietzschean challenge, and I will close this essay by a discussion of the hypocrisy challenge.

Michael Moore, you will recall, attempts to make short work of Jesus' "He that is without sin..." remark, calling it "pretty clumsy moral philosophy." He writes:

> It is true that all of us are guilty of some immoralities, probably on a daily basis. Yet for most people reading this essay, the immoralities in questions are things like manipulating others unfairly; not caring deeply enough about another's suffering; not being charitable for the limitations of others; convenient lies; and so forth. Few of us have raped and murdered a woman, drowned her three small children, and felt no remorse about it.[33]

Moore's point seems to be this: In the relevant sense most of us *are* without sin, and so we might as well feel free to pick up some stones and cast away.

Is this an adequate answer to Jesus and to the passage quoted earlier from Kant's *Religion*? I think not. The response is too shallow, for it fails to reflect the kind of serious moral introspection that Jesus and Kant are attempting to provoke. The point is not to deny that many people lead lives that are both legally and morally correct. The point is, rather, to force such people to face honestly the question of why they have lived in such a way. Is it (as they would no doubt like to think) because their inner characters manifest true integrity and are thus morally superior to those people whose behavior has been less exemplary? Or is it, at least in part, a matter of what John Rawls has called "luck on the natural and social lottery"?[34] Perhaps, as Kant suggests, their favored upbringing and social circumstances, or the fact that they have never been placed in situations where they have been similarly tempted, or their fear of being found out, has had considerably more to do with their compliance with the rules of

---

33. *Supra* note 6, p. 188. In the film "Dead Man Walking," Sister Helen Prejean cautions that no person should be judged solely on the basis of the worst thing that the person has done. Moore seems not to exercise such caution.

    If one visualizes even this worst of criminals as the small child he once was, one might reach the moral wisdom expressed toward a serial killer by Felicia in William Trevor's novel *Felicia's Journey*: "Lost within the man who murdered, there was a soul like any other soul, purity itself it surely once had been" (London: Viking, 1994, p. 212).
34. John Rawls, A *Theory of Justice, supra* note 11, Chapter 2.

law and morality than they would like to admit. Perhaps if they imagined themselves possessed of Gyges' ring (a ring that, in Plato's myth in Book 2 of *Republic*, makes its wearer invisible), they might—if honest with themselves—have to admit that they would probably use the ring not to perform anonymous acts of charity, but to perform some acts of considerable evil—acts comparable, perhaps, to the acts for which they often seek the punishment of others.[35] If they follow through honestly on this process of self-examination, they (like Angelo in *Measure for Measure*) will have discovered the potential for evil within themselves and will have learned an important lesson in moral humility.[36]

CONCLUSION

This brings to a close my little sermonette on moral humility. I have suggested the following: (1) From Nietzsche we learn that our retributive judgments may be based not on justice but on cruelty and that we may be in a state of self-deception about this. (2) From Kant we learn that we may not be in a position to know that persons possess the responsible and evil character that we seek to target in the desert judgments of character retributivism. (3) From Jesus and Kant we learn that our own evil or our own potential for evil is such that, rather than seeking to give others the suffering they deserve for their evil, we should leave that task to God (or leave it undone) and seek to put our own personal moral house in order.

---

35. The Gyes' ring thought experiment could perhaps be used to help Morris' theory overcome one of the objections raised above in note 32—the objection that most of us are not aware of repressing impulses to murder and rape and thus do not demand that murderers and rapists be punished because they have failed to restrain impulses that we have restrained. But perhaps we are not aware of repressing impulses to murder and rape because these impulses have been so successfully repressed that they are generally unconscious, If we imagine ourselves possessed of Gyges's ring, however, we perhaps open a door that allows these impulses to become conscious.
36. See Walt Whitman's poem "You Felons on Trail in Courts." Saying of himself "beneath this face that appears so impassive hell's tides continually run," he concludes the poem thus: "And henceforth I will not deny them—for how can I deny myself?"

Does this mean that we should abandon institutions of punishment in some sentimental orgy of love and self-doubt? Of course not. What it does mean is that, in punishing, we should act with caution, regret, humility, and with a vivid realization that we are involved in a fallible and finite human institution—one that is necessary but regrettable. The danger arises when we forget—as some of us who are retributivists sometimes, I fear, do forget—that nothing but iniquity and madness awaits us if we let ourselves think that, in punishing, we are involved in some cosmic drama of good and evil—that, like the Blues Brothers, we are on a mission from God.

Let me then close, appropriately, with a final word from Nietzsche: "Whoever fights with monsters should take care that in the process he does not become a monster."[37]

---

37. Nietzsche, *Beyond Good and Evil, supra* note 3, Epigram 146, p. 89. Nietzsche concludes the epigram with this observation: "When you look long into an abyss, the abyss also looks into you."

Nietzsche is best known, of course, for his suggestion that the idea of just or deserved punishment may be a mask for cruelty, may turn us into the very kind of monsters we seek to punish. He is also well aware, however, that sloppy sentimentality, an uncritical ethic of pity, and hasty tendencies to forgive can also infect punitive practices. In *Beyond Good and Evil* (*supra* note 3, p. 114) he writes: "There is a point in the history of society when it becomes so pathologically soft and tender that among other things it sides with even those who harm it, criminals, and does this quite seriously and honestly. Punishing somehow seems unfair to it, and it is certain that imagining 'punishment' and 'being obligated to punish' hurts it, arouses fear in it. 'It it not enough to render him undangerous? Why still punish? Punishing itself it terrible.' With this question, herd morality, the morality of timidity, draws its ultimate consequence."

This is a very puzzling passage. In part, the passage seems to make the point that society must take steps to protect itself against criminals and that worries about *ressentiment* should not impede those steps. But the passage also seems to suggest that protection is not enough—that, in addition to neutralizing the criminal, we should also feel free to strike out against the criminal in some more robust way, that only timidity stands in our way of such a response. However, Nietzsche's own warnings about punishment's link to *ressentiment* seem to give powerful support to the very timidity and reluctance he here condemns. Perhaps there is some unescapable tension at the heart of punishment—a tension that will always generate anxiety in those who are aware of it—and perhaps this anxiety is a good thing. Perhaps it is good that, when we recommend punishment, we should always feel conflicted and slightly unclean about what we are doing. This might at least blunt our tendencies toward cruelty.

Chapter 3

Christian Love and Criminal Punishment

What would law be like if we organized it around the value of Christian love, and if we thought about and criticized law in terms of that value? Christian love as a divine command is, of course, not identical with either *philia* (friendship love) or *eros* (erotic love), although it may incorporate elements of both. Christian love is rather that kind of universal (that is non-particular) love called *agape* or love of neighbor. American philosopher John Rawls claimed that justice is the first virtue of social institutions. But what if we considered *agape* to be the first virtue? What would social institutions – law in particular – be like?

My primary focus in this chapter will be to explore criminal law and the practice of criminal punishment from a perspective of Christian love. Why should anyone really care about such an exploration? Almost everyone would acknowledge that Christianity's emphasis on the moral and spiritual significance of the inner life exercised great influence on the development of a comparable emphasis on this in Western criminal law – for example, the idea that *mens rea* (intention, for instance) is generally required for conviction of any serious crime. But this general rejection of strict liability, one might think, has more to do with justice than with love, and this may still leave one with the question of why one should care about the value of love in thinking about criminal law.

One might begin to answer this question by noting that one does not have to choose between love and justice and that, indeed, justice (properly understood) may be entailed by love (properly understood). Former Archbishop of Canterbury William Temple put it this way: "It is axiomatic that love should be the predominant Christian impulse and that justice is the primary form of love in social organization."[1] To say that one is acting in a loving way while subjecting a person to unjust oppression can only be seen as a sick joke.

In addition to welcoming Archbishop Temple's invitation to think of justice as a part of love, I also have some personal reasons for caring about the issue of love and punishment. Because of my upbringing, I have always been someone whose moral sensibilities are grounded – even when in the past I called myself an atheist – in the Christian tradition, a religious tradition that makes love of neighbor central. When a person brought up a Christian becomes an atheist, he tends to become a Christian atheist. The questions he chooses to make central and many of the answers that tempt him are often framed, even if he does not realize it, by the very set of beliefs he claims to reject. I suspect that this is true for other religions as well. I suspect, for example, that my Protestant upbringing had a great deal to do with the fact that I was early in my studies so drawn to the moral philosophy of German philosopher Immanuel Kant, a philosopher who has been interpreted, with some justice, as seeking a secular and rational defense for what is essentially a Protestant moral vision. The child is father of the man, as Wordsworth reminded us.

Of course, even those outside the Christian tradition generally celebrate some version of the value of love. We know from popular culture and music that "love makes the world go round," that "love conquers all," and that "all we need is love." One might thus find it

---

1. Quoted in Lord Denning, *The Influence of Religion on Law* (Alberta, Canada: Canadian Institute for Law, Theology, and Public Policy, 1997), 3.

both interesting and puzzling to consider how, if at all, that value can consistently sit with law – particularly criminal law, which often seems a very harsh and unloving institution.

Finally, there is a great deal of public sermonizing from politicians these days – far too much for my taste – that purports to draw the basic tenets of Christianity into political decision-making. It might be useful to examine what the actual legal consequences of Christianity properly interpreted would be, consequences that could turn out to be quite different from those represented in much current political posturing. As the bloody record of historical Christianity clearly reveals, those in power who speak the language of love do not always act in loving ways but can instead be vessels of intolerance, persecution, hatred, and cruelty.

I realize that I cannot speak for all Christians or survey Christian scholarship in a brief chapter, but I can, at most, give my own "take" on what Christianity has to offer on the topics of crime and punishment. Neither can I explore every aspect of the relationship between criminal law and love. So I shall focus on only one aspect: the nature of *forgiveness* – often seen as a paradigm Christian virtue – and its relation to criminal law and criminal justice. I focus on this aspect because many people seem to think that forgiveness is at odds with criminal punishment, that to the degree we are forgiving then to that degree we will oppose punishment. Indeed, in a provocative essay, Notre Dame law professor Thomas Shaffer goes even farther than this. In developing what he calls a "jurisprudence of forgiveness," Shaffer argues that forgiveness is not simply incompatible with criminal punishment but with the very idea of law itself. Speaking of those prisoners securely imprisoned on death row, he writes:

> There is no rational argument any longer to kill them – much less the common good argument Caiaphas had for killing Jesus. Legal power, it seems, has to kill them anyway, if only because it

would not be legal power if it didn't. Law here cannot take the risk of forgiveness. Forgiveness would remove the fear, the accountability, and the responsibility that law provides – and this, as law sees it, would invite chaos [because]...forgiveness disrupts legal order.[2]

Shaffer's claim strikes me as deeply wrong – confused all the way down, if I may say so. I think that he misunderstands both forgiveness and love and thus misunderstands the relationship that forgiveness and love bear to law and punishment. I realize that this is a strong claim made against a distinguished academic who has produced much admirable work, and I will have an uphill fight making a case for it. Since many people share some version of this confusion, however, unmasking it is worth a shot.

THE LOVE COMMANDMENT

Before getting into the details of a law-versus-loving forgiveness debate, however, let me begin with a bit of background, and remind you of the Christian love commandment itself. It occurs most famously in Luke 10:25–37 when a lawyer – yes, a lawyer – interrogates Jesus and asks him how one might gain eternal life. Jesus answers that the lawyer knows the answer to this question already, for it is found in Jewish law: "You shall love the Lord your God with all your heart, and with all your soul, and with all your strength, and with all your mind; and your neighbor as yourself." Continuing his cross-examination, the lawyer then asks: "And who is my

---

2. Thomas L. Shaffer, "The Radical Reformation and the Jurisprudence of Forgiveness," in *Christian Perspectives on Legal Thought*, ed. Michael W. McConnell, Robert E. Cochran, Jr. and Angela C. Carmella (New Haven, CT: Yale University Press, 2001), 325–26.

neighbor?" Jesus replies not with a definition of "neighbor" but with the parable of the Good Samaritan.

Two things relevant to the present chapter are worth noting about this scriptural passage. First, it must be emphasized that, for the Christian, what happens to the human soul – in this life and the next – is of primary concern. Note that the love commandment is endorsed by Jesus as the correct answer to the question, "What must I do to inherit eternal life?" Thus a central question for the Christian with respect to punishment must be, not simply what will happen to the body, but what will happen to the soul. (Those who prefer a less metaphysically rich term might provisionally – but only provisionally – here substitute "character" for "soul.") One who is impatient with this concern must necessarily be impatient with Christianity at its core and thus with much of what Christianity will have to say about punishment.

Second, and intimately related to the first point, is the importance of not mistakenly interpreting the role played by the parable of the Good Samaritan in this scriptural passage. If one mistakenly sees this parable as primarily an answer to the question, "What is love?" one might be led to see *agape* as nothing more than what could be called liberal compassion – helping the sick, the despised, and the poor. The love commandment surely involves that, as it involves justice, but I think that it also involves much more. The actual question answered through the parable, however, is not "What is love?" but is rather "Who is my neighbor?" The answer that seems to emerge from the parable is that *all human beings* are to be seen as neighbors. As Danish theologian and philosopher Søren Kierkegaard puts it: "when you open the door that you shut in order to pray to God and go out the very first person you meet is the neighbor whom you *shall* love"[3] – regardless of whether that person is your enemy, a member of some

---

3. Søren Kierkegaard, *Works of Love*, ed. and trans. Howard V. Hong and Edna H. Hong (Princeton, NJ: Princeton University Press, 1995), 51.

despised group, your king, a criminal, or someone who strikes you as intrinsically and grotesquely unlovable.[4] This is a doctrine of universalism, in contrast to tribalism, with respect to loving concern. Some Christians like to claim that it is unique to the moral outlook of Christianity, but in fact a similar kind of moral universalism can be found in some aspects of Stoicism and Judaism, and I suspect elsewhere as well.

There are, of course, many fascinating questions that could be raised about the love commandment. Does it command love as an emotion or simply that we act in a certain way? Kant, convinced that we can be morally bound only to that which is in our control and believing (hastily in my view) that emotions are not in our control, called emotional love *pathological love* and claimed that it could not be our duty to feel it. What is actually commanded he called *practical love*, which is simply acting morally as Kant conceived it. In the century after Kant, Kierkegaard, in his *Works of Love*, famously raised a variety of additional puzzles about Christian love of neighbor. He assumed that we would all agree that most human beings seem to be anything but lovable. (If you think it is possible to love everyone, just look around in a supermarket as Ayn Rand once suggested.) Given the apparent unlovability of those Kierkegaard called "your very unpoetic neighbors," would it be possible to love them absent a divine command to do so? Kierkegaard thought not.[5] And to what degree, if at all, is the command of love of neighbor compatible with those particular loves of lovers, spouses, children, parents, friends, and one's own country that Kierkegaard calls "preferential"? This was a question of great concern to Kierkegaard. Such loves seem to many of us among the

---

4. Ibid., 17–90.
5. Ibid.

crowning glories of human life and thus most of us will not look with favor upon Jesus' teaching that "any one [who] comes to me and does not hate his own father and mother and wife and children and brothers and sisters, yes, and even his own life...cannot be my disciple" (Luke 14:26). Even most devout Christians will seek some way of interpreting this remark to keep it from having the unhappy consequence it seems to have upon first reading.

Given my limited purpose to explore the place of agapic forgiveness in the context of law, particularly criminal punishment, I think that all I will need to say about love here is the following, what I hope most interpreters of Christianity would find noncontroversial: *agape* is not simply a matter of being nice and cuddly – of giving everyone a warm hug, saying "have a nice day," and sending them on their way. In spite of what the secular mind and even some religious believers might wish, the full doctrine of *agape* is to be found not simply in the social gospel films of Frank Capra but also in the grim stories of Flannery O'Connor and in the hard and demanding theologies of Augustine and Kierkegaard. "God loves you whether you like it or not," as the bumper sticker says.

One of the things that is manifestly not cuddly about *agape*, at least as I understand it, perhaps shows the influence of ancient Greek thought on love and friendship (*philia*). It is this: such love is concerned not simply with satisfying preferences, alleviating distress, providing for people's material well-being, and thereby making their lives more pleasant – what I earlier called liberal compassion. It is also centrally concerned with promoting their moral and spiritual good – helping their souls or characters to grow in *virtue*. (Recall Aristotle's discussion of what he calls "the perfect form of friendship."[6]) In this way, a legal order dominated by *agape* would almost certainly be more paternalistic than would be

---

6. Aristotle, *Nichomachean Ethics*, 1156b.2f, and generally bks. 8–9.

acceptable to the more value-neutral and libertarian versions of political liberalism of, say, John Rawls or Ronald Dworkin. Those motivated by *agape*, as a basic principle, will (subject no doubt to some major side-constraints of a prudential nature) seek to design legal practices and institutions with a view to the moral and spiritual improvement in virtue of affected citizens.

In the area of free expression, just to give one example, such persons will probably seek greatly to restrain the corrupt and corrosive availability of pornography – refusing to see its production, distribution, and consumption as an important human liberty. They might very reluctantly allow pornography for practical or instrumental reasons – if they think that it is impossible to design a legal prohibition that would not constrain legitimate expression. But they would never seek to protect it in principle under the general heading of a fundamental right of personal autonomy. Rather than seeing basic rights as rights to exercise unrestrained "do your own thing" autonomy, they would tend to see such rights (as some perfectionist liberals see them) as rights to choose only among options that could all be part of a good life. Thus they would see conversation about the good life as being central to law and politics, not as in principle a "private" matter that should be left out of the political and legal domains. This suggests that there may be some interesting tensions between some forms of political liberalism and *agapic* love as I have conceptualized it – tensions that might force some choices that many would find hard and unattractive.

For the law of crime and punishment, those motivated by *agape* will seek punitive practices that contribute to, or at least do not retard, the moral and spiritual rebirth of criminals. It is perhaps regrettable but true that there may be little that the state can do actively to promote virtuous character. This might be because the state is sometimes nothing but a collection of inept apparatchiks who cannot even deliver the mail. Or it could be because, even as its best, the state must be very cautious about using state power to encourage a particular vision of the good life, in an environment of religious pluralism and free exercise of religion. For such a vision may capture the moral view from only one segment of those with deep and serious commitments to seeking what they deem to be the good life. I, for one, am less concerned about those who are indifferent to the good life and want only to revel under an uncritical "do your own thing" conception of liberty.

But surely, even under these constraints, it ought to be possible to do *something* for prisoners that is potentially character-building. If Aristotle is right, then virtue is often acquired through a process of *habituation* – becoming by doing – and encouraging certain habits might promote, for example, a virtuous kind of empathetic kindness often absent or greatly limited in criminal wrongdoers. A small start in this direction might involve something as simple as the Prison Dog Project, a program in which prisoners care for dogs and thereby perhaps develop some of the virtues that come from the receiving and giving of love they have been missing in their prior lives. This program is only one small thing, but great things often consist of many small things.

Even those who remain skeptical of all positive programs of character reform, however, should still at the very least seek to create a prison environment where opportunities for positive character development are not radically minimized or even extinguished by unspeakable conditions. For example, those who claim to champion agapic love should be on the forefront of any movement to eliminate those current aspects of criminal punishment and prison life such as gang rape, that – to put it mildly – are hardly likely to encourage the reflection, repentance, and spiritual rebirth that should be hoped for from those culpable of serious wrongdoing. In this case, religious believers and traditional secular liberals should find, and have found, themselves united. The Prison Rape

Elimination Act, for example, enacted by Congress in 2003, was supported by such diverse agencies and individuals as Amnesty International, Human Rights Watch, Senator Ted Kennedy, the Southern Baptist Ethics and Religious Liberty Commission, and Charles Colson's Prison Fellowship Ministries.

Of course, none of this is even worth thinking about if Shaffer is correct that (1) the duty to forgive is mandated by the love commandment and (2) forgiveness is incompatible with criminal punishment. I think he is right about (1) but dead wrong about (2), and so I will now move to a discussion of forgiveness, its nature, value, and relation to punishment.

FORGIVENESS AND PUNISHMENT

What is forgiveness? I think that one of the most insightful discussions of forgiveness ever penned is to be found in Bishop Joseph Butler's 1726 sermon "Upon Forgiveness of Injuries" and its companion sermon "Upon Resentment."[7] These sermons are long and carefully reasoned philosophical essays on the character of forgiveness, and they must have greatly tried the patience of his congregation. According to Butler, forgiveness is a moral virtue (a virtue of character) that is essentially a matter of the heart, the inner self, and involves a change in inner feeling more than a change in external action. The change in feeling is the overcoming, on moral grounds, of the intensely negative and reactive attitudes that are quite naturally occasioned when one has been wronged by another – the passions of resentment, anger, even hatred, and the desire for revenge. We may call these the vindictive passions. A person who has forgiven has overcome those vindictive passions

---

7. Both sermons are collected in *Works of Joseph Butler*, vol. ii, *Sermons*, ed. W. E. Gladstone (Oxford: Clarendon Press, 1896), 136–167.

and has overcome them for a morally creditable motive – for example, being moved by repentance on the part of the person by whom one has been wronged. Of course, such a change in feeling often leads to a change of behavior – reconciliation, for example. But, as our forgiving of the dead illustrates, change in feeling does not always change behavior. Forgiveness, so understood, is often a good thing because it may allow us to reconcile and restore relationships of value, free us from the inner turmoil that may come from harboring grudges, and free us from an overly narcissistic involvement with our own unjust victimizations, for it seems that the common human tendency is often to magnify such victimizations out of all reasonable proportion.

None of this shows, however, that forgiveness – particularly hasty and uncritical forgiveness – is *always* a good thing. Sometimes forgiveness mistakenly tempts us into restoring relationships that would be better left permanently ruptured. Also, hasty overcoming of anger and resentment through forgiveness may sometimes show insufficient self-respect, since feeling such reactive emotions when wronged is a characteristic sign of self-respect. This is no doubt the point of S. J. Perelman's famous quip: "to err is human; to forgive, supine." The popular self-help literature on forgiveness tends to stress only its benefits, but I think it is important to note at least some of its potential costs.[8]

On my Butler-inspired analysis of forgiveness as a victim's change of heart toward culpable wrongdoing, it is useful initially to distinguish forgiveness from four other responses to wrongdoing with which forgiveness is often confused: justification, excuse, mercy, and reconciliation. Although these concepts are to some degree

---

8. Butler believed the benefit of forgiveness is a God-given check on the valuable passions of resentment and anger, which are necessary to defend one's own rights, the rights of others, and the moral order itself. For uncannily similar observations, see Reinhold Niebuhr, "Anger and Forgiveness," in *Discerning the Signs of the Times – Sermons for Today and Tomorrow* (London: SCM Press, 1946), 26–39.

open-textured and can bleed into each other, clarity is served if one at least starts by attempting to separate them. I discuss each of them briefly.

Justification

To regard conduct as justified (as in lawful self-defense, for example) is to claim that the conduct, though normally wrongful, was the right thing to do in the given circumstances and all things considered. In such cases, there is nothing legitimately to resent and thus nothing to forgive.

Excuse

To regard conduct as excused (as in the insanity defense, for example) is to admit that the conduct was wrong but to claim that the person who engaged in the conduct was not a fully responsible agent. Responsible agency is, of course, a matter of degree. But to the degree that the person who injures me is not a responsible agent, resentment of that person would make no more sense than resenting the wasp that stings me. Again, there is nothing here to forgive.

Mercy

To accord a wrongdoer mercy is to inflict a less harsh consequence on that person than allowed by institutional (usually legal) rules. Mercy is less personal than forgiveness, since the one granting mercy (a sentencing judge, say) typically will not be a victim of wrongdoing and thus will not have any feelings of resentment to overcome. (There is a sense in which only victims of wrongdoing have what might be called *standing* to forgive.) Mercy also has a public behavioral dimension not necessarily present in forgiveness. I can forgive a person simply in my heart of hearts, but I cannot show mercy simply in my heart of hearts. I can forgive the dead, but I cannot show mercy to the dead.

This distinction between mercy and forgiveness allows us to see why there is no inconsistency in fully forgiving a person for wrongdoing but still advocating that the person suffer the legal consequence of criminal punishment. Here you see one of my primary disagreements with Professor Shaffer. To the degree that criminal punishment is justified in order to secure victim satisfaction, then of course the fact that the victim has forgiven will be a relevant argument for reducing the criminal's sentence and the fact that a victim still resents will be a relevant argument for increasing that sentence. It is highly controversial, of course, that criminal punishment should to *any* degree be harnessed to a victim's desires. Such considerations are generally considered only in assessing damages in a private suit in tort. Even if the criminal punishment is partly calibrated by the victim's desires, however, it must surely be admitted that the practice of punishment serves other values as well, such as crime control and justice. With respect to these values, a victim's forgiveness could hardly be dispositive. In short, it would indeed be inconsistent for a person to claim that he has forgiven the wrongdoer and still advocate punishment for the wrongdoer in order to satisfy his personal vindictive feelings. If he still has those feelings, he has not forgiven the wrong or the wrongdoer. It would not be inconsistent, however, to advocate punishment for other legitimate reasons – for example, crime control and just deserts. Of course, the possibilities for self-deception are enormous here. As Friedrich Nietzsche reminded us, our high-sounding talk about justice and public order is often simply a rationalization for envy, spite, malice, and outright cruelty – the cluster of emotions for which Nietzsche used the loaded French term *ressentiment*.[9]

But what about mercy itself as a virtue independent of forgiveness? Is it not also required, as an aspect of Christian love, to exhibit mercy in dealing with wrongdoers? And would this not involve mercy to criminals? I think that the answer to this question is *yes*. Yet it is important to see that the requirement to exhibit mercy is best understood not as a requirement never to punish but rather as a requirement to develop a character that is not hardened and rigidly formalistic – a requirement that leaves room for considering relevant features of a criminal (remorse, repentance, or apology, for example) that might legitimately incline one to favor a reduced sentence for that criminal. This is most appropriately done in an executive clemency decision rather than at the time of sentencing.

Reconciliation

The vindictive passions (those overcome in forgiveness) are often a major barrier to reconciliation. Since forgiveness often leads to reconciliation, it is thus easy to confuse the two concepts. I think, however, that it is important also to see how they may differ – how there can be forgiveness without reconciliation, and how there can be reconciliation without forgiveness.

---

9. As I have argued in my "Legal Moralism and Retribution Revisited," *Proceedings of the American Philosophical Association* 80:2 (2006): 45–62, one must be careful about how one understands the idea of criminal just desert. This idea legitimately focuses our attention on the criminal's act, the intentionality of that act, and the degree of responsibility for that act. However, if one employs the concept of just desert to target deep character, ultimate evil, or what Kant called "inner viciousness," then one is presuming to judge what no human being should presume to judge. For "thou, [God] thou only, knowest the hearts of all the children of men" (I Kings 8:39). It is hard enough for us to discern the shallows of intentions to surmise the utter futility of probing the depths of character – for whether, to use some language from American homicide law, the criminal has "a hardened, abandoned, and malignant heart" or a character that is "cruel, heinous and depraved."

For an example of forgiveness without reconciliation, imagine a battered woman who has been repeatedly beaten and raped by her thuggish husband or boyfriend. This woman – after a religious conversion, perhaps – might well come to forgive her batterer (for example, stop being angry with him) without a willingness to resume her relationship with him. "I forgive you and wish you well" can, in my view, sit quite consistently with "I will never allow you in this house again." In short, the fact that one has forgiven does not mean that one must also trust or live again with a person.

For an example of reconciliation without forgiveness, consider the example of the South African Truth and Reconciliation Commission. In order to negotiate a viable transition from apartheid to democratic government with full black participation, all parties had to agree that there would in most cases be no punishment for evil acts that occurred under the previous government. Politically motivated wrongdoers, by making a full confession and accepting responsibility, would typically be granted amnesty. In this process the wrongdoers would not be required to repent, show remorse, or even apologize. I can clearly see this process as one of reconciliation (although I might prefer the term cooperation) – a process that will allow all to work toward a democratic and just future. I do not so easily see this process as one of forgiveness, however. No change of heart was required or even sought from the victims – no overcoming of such vindictive feelings as anger or resentment or hatred. All that was hoped of them was a willingness to accept this process as a necessary means to the future good of their society.

It should now be obvious why I reject Shaffer's claim that agapic forgiveness is incompatible with legal punishment. On my view, following Bishop Butler, forgiveness is mainly a matter of a change of heart, not of external practice.

So can forgiveness of a person, so understood, still be compatible with the continued demand that the person be punished – perhaps even executed? In my view the answer to this question is yes. It all depends on the *motive* or *reason* for the demand. If the motive or reason is to satisfy one's vindictive passions, then of course there is immediate inconsistency. If one still retains those passions, one has not forgiven. Thus an appeal to agapic forgiveness does constitute a powerful attack on legal punishment to the degree that such punishment is driven by vindictive passions, particularly by hatred.

Of course, if one is doing something truly horrendous to another human being, the chance that hatred and cruelty are behind it should not be too quickly dismissed. In fact, many present penal practices in America are, alas, hard to understand on any other terms. To return to my earlier example of prison conditions, Mary Sigler has recently written on such terrible conditions as subjecting inmates to repeated acts of forced sodomy that are generally tolerated by prison officials and the public. She notes that the popular media freely makes jokes about this. For example, there was a soft drink commercial in which someone is handing out cans to prison inmates, drops one on the floor, and notes that in this environment it probably would not be a good idea to bend over and pick it up. The commercial closes with a scene in which the soft drink huckster is shown sitting at a table with a large inmate who has an arm around him. The voice-over says that this drink makes friends, the inmate tightens his arm, and the huckster says in dismay "not that kind of friend." What kind of a society is it that knows about forced sodomy in prison and feels comfortable making jokes about it? In trying to answer this question, the words "hatred" and "cruelty" certainly come to my mind.[10]

I think that callous indifference also deserves a place next to hatred as something that is ruled out by *agape* – something that should be guarded against in the realm of punishment. Recall the New Testament

---

10. See Mary Sigler, "By the Light of Virtue: Prison Rape and the Corruption of Character," *Iowa Law Review* 91(2006): 561–607.

parable in which a servant, forgiven his debt out of compassion from his master, is blind to the suffering of one of his own servants and shows no compassion when that servant cannot pay a debt to him (Matthew 18:23–35). The sin of the forgiven servant inflicting harsh treatment on his own servant was not based on any hatred he felt toward his servant. It was, rather, a radical failure of compassion, a total indifference to the adverse life circumstances that caused the servant to become indebted and to fear harsh punishment for failing to pay the debt – the very kind of life circumstances that the master, out of compassion, had taken account of in showing mercy to the unforgiving servant for the nonpayment of his own debt. As Raimond Gaita, drawing on Simone Weil, argued in his book, *A Common Humanity*, our indifference to the suffering of those whom we regard as outsiders – an indifference that makes them, as Weil said of the poor, invisible to us – often flows from an incapacity to see anything that could *go deep* in their inner lives, a failure to find it even intelligible that someone could love them. This is, I think, at least part of what Weil meant when she said that "love sees what is invisible."[11]

Suppose, however, that the motive or reason for punishment is not grounded in any vindictive passion or in callous indifference of the kind just noted. Suppose, rather, that it is grounded in the sincere belief that punishment of the kind prescribed is necessary to control crime and thereby promote the common good. Or suppose that it is required by justice (what the criminal deserves for his wrongdoing), or that it will be instrumental in the moral and spiritual transformations of the criminal. Then, even if one has doubts about one or more of these justifications, those doubts cannot legitimately be grounded in the claim that they are inconsistent with the demands of Christian love.

---

11. Quoted in Raimond Gaita, *A Common Humainty: Thinking About Love and Truth and Justice* (London: Routlege, 2000), 84.

The main point, then, is this: *agape* does not forbid punishment. What it forbids is *punishment out of hatred or other vindictive passions.* What Jesus counseled, it will be recalled, is that we visit and comfort those in prison; he did not counsel the abolition of prisons (Matthew 25:36). To visit and comfort those in prison – even those justly there – is a way of saying that they are still loved and not hated, that their essential humanity is still being acknowledged, and that we have not presumed to banish them from the domain of loving concern. Such loving concern is quite consistent, however, with thinking that it is proper that they be in prison – because they deserve it or for the common good, for example.

As stated above, the possibilities of self-deception here are enormous – particularly the possibility that, as Nietzsche warned, we use the rhetoric of justice and the common good in order to hide from ourselves the fact that our actual motives are instances of *ressentiment* – spite, malice, envy, and cruelty. Thus, although I think that Shaffer overreaches when he uses the virtue of forgiveness to condemn all law and punishment, he has offered an important corrective to much of what we are *actually* doing in contrast to what we say and think we are doing, a contrast dramatically illustrated when we consider the actual conditions present in many of our jails and prisons. For this he deserves our gratitude.

LOVE AND THE DEATH PENALTY

In closing, let me briefly say something about *agape* and capital punishment. The death penalty is so extreme that many might think that, even if much punishment is consistent with *agape*, this punishment cannot be. This was certainly the view of Catholic theologian Bernard Häring. He acknowledged that the Old Testament is filled with what appear to be robust defenses of capital punishment, but then claimed that "it would not be in harmony with the unique fullness of salvation and its loving kindness to apply drastic [Old Testament] directives without any qualification as obligatory in the present order of salvation and grace."[12]

Not all Christians would agree with Häring, of course, and the fact that so many prominent Christian philosophers and theologians have through the ages been supporters of capital punishment should make us pause before hastily assuming that the practice is inconsistent with *agape*. However, the enthusiasm expressed by these thinkers for capital punishment has often been radically overstated by supporters of the death penalty. The radio show host and newspaper columnist Dennis Prager, for example, has cited Augustine as a Christian authority to support his belief in the legitimacy of capital punishment. He quoted this passage from *The City of God:* "It is in no way contrary to the commandment 'thou shalt not kill' to put criminals to death according to law or the rule of natural justice."[13]

Augustine did indeed make this claim, but it takes a great deal of creative free association to turn this into a statement of support for the death penalty. And getting Augustine right is a matter of some importance, since, after Jesus and Paul, he has probably done more than anyone else to set what might be called "the moral tone" of Christianity, at least among educated people. I read Augustine – and here I impose on him a modern distinction – as asserting the *right* of the state to execute but also arguing that *it is almost always wrong for the state to exercise that right*. The state may not be denied to have, in the abstract, the right to execute if this promotes the common good or gives the criminal the punishment that he in justice deserves or promotes the personal repentance and rebirth of the wrongdoer – the only three objectives that could justify it. (And, before you laugh

---

12. Bernard Häring *The Law of Christ*, 3 vols. (Westminster, MD: The Newman Press, 1966), III:124.
13. Quoted in Dennis Prager, Editorial, "There's A Moral Reason That McVeigh Must Die," *Los Angeles Times* (June 8, 2001): B-17.

dismissively at the idea of capital punishment as personal reform, recall Samuel Johnson: "Depend upon it, Sir, when a man knows he is to be hanged in a fortnight, it concentrates his mind wonderfully."[14]) One can hold this view of capital punishment's three possible justifications, however – common good, just deserts, and personal rebirth – and also consistently hold that in every particular case that one knows of or can imagine, that execution either does not promote these goals or does not promote them any better than less drastic means. Augustine sometimes argues in this way and indeed, for all his reputation to the contrary, offers some of the most eloquent objections to capital punishment ever given in our culture. For example, in a letter to Marcellinus, the special delegate of the Emperor Honorius to settle the dispute between Catholics and Donatists, Augustine is concerned with the punishment to be administered for what must have, to him, seemed the most vicious of crimes: the murder of one Catholic priest and the mutilation of another by members of a radical Donatist faction. He wrote:

> I have been prey to the deepest anxiety for fear your Highness might perhaps decree that they be sentenced [to death]. Therefore, in this letter, I beg you by the faith which you have in Christ and by the mercy of the same Lord Christ, not to do this, not to let it be done under any circumstances... We do not wish that the martyrdom of the servants of God should be avenged by similar suffering, as if by way of retaliation... We do not object to wicked men being deprived of their freedom to do wrong, but we wish it to go just that far, so that, without losing their life or

---

14. Quoted in *Boswell's Life of Johnson*, 2nd edn, 6 vols., ed. George Birkbeck Hill, revised by L. F. Powell (1934; Oxford: Clarendon Press, 1964), III:167 Or, as Flannery O'Connor's Misfit said of his victim: "She would of been a good woman if it had been someone there to shoot her every minute of her life." Flannery O'Connor, "A Good Man Is Hard to Find," in *Collected Works* (New York: Library of America, 1998 8), 153.

being maimed in any part of their body, they may be restrained by the law from their mad frenzy, guided into the way of peace and sanity, and assigned some useful work to replace their criminal activities. It is true, this is called a penalty, but who can fail to see that it should be called a blessing rather than a chastisement when violence end cruelty are held in check, but the remedy of repentance is not withheld?[15]

Of course capital punishment is far too complex an issue and too dependent on a variety of contested empirical claims to be settled here. And philosophy, an *a priori* discipline, is certainly in no position simply to pronounce finally on whether the fear of death as a punishment could ever promote the common good or could ever provoke spiritual rebirth on the part of the criminal. So let me close by making a claim that I can in conscience endorse: to the degree that our willingness to support the death penalty is based on the thoughtless, cruel hatred or indifference to the humanity of criminals (and I suspect that much of it is), then it manifestly is not consistent with *agape*, a love that teaches that all human beings, even the worst among us, are precious because created in the image of God. And thus Christians, Jews, and those from many other religions should, I think, be willing to join in endorsing these words of Ezekiel 33:11: "I have no pleasure in the death of the wicked; but that the wicked should turn from his way and live."

RECOMMENDED READING

Brugger, E. Christian. *Capital Punishment and Roman Catholic Moral Tradition*. Notre Dame, IN: University of Notre Dame Press, 2003.

---

15. Quoted in Donald X Burt *Friendship and Society: An Introduction to Augustine's Practical Philosophy* (Grand Rapids, MI: Wm. B. Eerdmans Publishing, 1999), 195–96.

Burtt, Donald X. *Friendship and Society: An Introduction to Augustine's Practical Philosophy*. Grand Rapids, MI: Wm. B. Eerdmans Publishing, 1999.

Butler, Joseph. "Sermons VIII and IX," in *Works of Joseph Butler*. Vol. II, *Sermons*. Edited by W. E. Gladstone. Oxford: Clarendon Press, 1896, 136–167.

Denning, Lord. *The Influence of Religion on Law*. Alberta, Canada: Canadian Institute for Law, Theology, and Public Policy, 1997.

Gaita, Raimond. *A Common Humanity: Thinking about Love and Truth and Justice*. London: Routledge, 2000.

Gorringe, Timothy. *God's Just Vengeance*. Cambridge: Cambridge University Press, 1996.

Griswold, Charles L. *Forgiveness: A Philosophical Exploration*. Cambridge University Press, 2007.

Häring, Bernard. *The Law of Christ*. 3 vols. Westminster, MD: The Newman Press, 1966.

House, H. Wayne and John Howard Yoder. *The Death Penalty Debate*. Dallas, TX: Word Publishing Company, 1991.

Kant, Immanuel. *Practical Philosophy*. Translated by Mary Gregor. Cambridge: Cambridge University Press, 1996.

Kierkegaard, Søren. *Works of Love*. Edited and translated by Howard V. Hong and Edna H. Hong. Princeton, NJ: Princeton University Press, 1995.

Murphy, Jeffrie G. "Repentance," In *Repentance*. Edited by Amitai Etzioni. Totowa, NJ: Rowman and Littlefield, 1997, 143–170.

"Moral Epistemology, the Retributive Emotions, and the 'Clumsy Moral Philosophy' of Jesus Christ," in *The Passions of Law*. Edited by Susan Bandes. New York: New York University Press, 1999, 49–167.

Getting Even: Forgiveness and Its Limits. Oxford: Oxford University Press, 2003.

"Legal Moralism and Retribution Revisited." *Proceedings of the American Philosophical Association* 80:2 (2006): 45–62. This essay has also appeared in *Criminal Law and Philosophy* 1 (January 2007): 5–20.

"Remorse, Apology, and Mercy." *Ohio State Journal of Criminal Law* 4 (2007): 423–453.

Murphy, Jeffrie G. and Jean Hampton, *Forgiveness and Mercy*. Cambridge: Cambridge University Press, 1988.

Murphy, Jeffrie G., Stephen P. Garvey, R. A. Duff, Joseph Vining, John Witte Jr., and Patrick McKinley Brennan. "Religion and the Criminal Law: Legal and Philosophical Perspectives." Special issue, *Punishment and Society* 5:3 (2003).

Niebuhr, Reinhold. "Anger and Forgiveness," in *Discerning the Signs of the Times – Sermons for Today and Tomorrow*. London: SCM Press, 1946, 26–39.

O'Connor, Flannery. "A Good Man Is Hard to Find," in *Collected Works*. New York: Library of America, 1988, 136–167.

Owens, Eric C., John D. Carlson, and Eric P. Elshtain, eds. *Religion and the Death Penalty: A Call for Reckoning*. Grand Rapids, MI: Wm. B. Eerdmans Publishing, 2004.

Sigler, Mary. "By the Light of Virtue: Prison Rape and the Corruption of Character." *Iowa Law Review* 91 (2006): 561–607.

Shaffer, Thomas L. "The Radical Reformation and the Jurisprudence of Forgiveness," in *Christian Perspectives on Legal Thought*. Edited by Michael W. McConnell, Robert E. Cochran Jr. and Angela C. Carmella. New Haven, CT: Yale University Press, 2001, 321–39.

Chapter 4

Legal Moralism and Retribution Revisited

INTRODUCTION

I never expected to be a president of the American Philosophical Association, and I still do not know how to process this recognition. There is, of course, very little money or real power in the academic world, and so those of us in this world sometimes have a tendency to be motivated to a large degree by vanity. Because of this, it is easy for us to overestimate the importance of academic titles, awards, and honors and to become puffed up with an unseemly self-importance when they come our way.

Sometimes, however, the universe—through fate, the grace of God, or pure chance—arranges it so that we are usefully brought down from the lofty heights of self-adoration. The *very day* after I received notification of my selection as president, my wife and I went to see the François Ozan film *The Swimming Pool*. Early in that film, the Charlotte Rampling character—commenting on literary and academic awards—makes this remark: "Awards are like hemorrhoids—eventually every asshole gets one." I turned to my wife and whispered, "I do not like the timing of that remark one bit."

One acceptable practice for the presidential address, I hope, is to summarize and comment upon some of the ideas for which one has become known. This, at any rate, is the practice that I will follow in my address this afternoon—presenting a kind of intellectual autobiography or career retrospective. Because of time limitations, my discussion today will of necessity be compressed and oversimplified.

So what have I been up to, as a philosopher, for the past forty years? I have worked on Kant's moral and legal philosophy, worked on theories of punishment and responsibility, and have most recently worked on forgiveness, mercy, and the moral emotions of resentment, guilt, remorse, and shame. In this afternoon's address, I will attempt to draw some of these past and current interests together; and I will start with the past.

When, in the mid-sixties, I first began working on the philosophy of punishment, two related issues tended to dominate the discussion: (1) legal moralism and (2) explorations of the degree to which, if at all, a retributive justification of punishment could be rendered consistent with a consequentialist justification.

The legal moralism controversy had at its core the Hart-Devlin debate. Lord Patrick Devlin, in his influential Maccabaean Lecture "The Enforcement of Morals," had challenged the liberal idea that, as a matter of *principle*, some things are simply not the legitimate business of the criminal law. In particular, Devlin challenged the famous harm principle that John Stuart Mill had introduced in his *On Liberty*. According to this principle, the only purpose that justifies society in coercing any one of its members is to prevent harm to others, where harm is understood as posing what Justice Holmes would later call a clear and present danger to the rights or interests of others. Coercion for a person's own good or coercion for the perceived general long-range moral good of society is in most cases to be ruled out. Devlin's own view came to be called "legal moralism" because of his belief that one legitimate use of the criminal law is to enforce the moral values of the community, even if these values have little or nothing to do with the kinds of harm that Mill had in mind. (Devlin was as concerned with harm as was Mill, but the two men had very different understandings of what constitutes relevant harm.) Devlin argued that the appeal to Mill's harm principle—or, indeed, to any other totally general and abstract principle—obscures rather than clarifies the values that are at stake in criminal punishment, and he suggested that the limits on the scope of the criminal law should be thought of primarily in pragmatic terms. In his book *Law, Liberty and Morality*, Herbert Hart mounted a sustained attack on almost every aspect of Devlin's account. My first publication in legal philosophy was an uncritical endorsement of Hart's critique and a muddled expansion of that critique—a publication so truly dreadful that I no longer even list it on my CV.

With respect to the second issue—the issue of consequentialism versus retributivism—the dominant characterization generally given of retributivism in the sixties, though appearing quite insightful at the time, now seems rather inane. Retributivism was seen, for example by John Rawls and Herbert Hart, as an answer to the question, "How should punishment be distributed?" and consequentialism was seen as an answer to the quite different question, "What is the general justifying aim of punishment?" The classic retributivist concept of desert was reduced to the concept of legal guilt, and the distributive principle that defined retributivism was simply this: that punishment should fall only on the legally guilty, never the legally innocent. Given this simple characterization of retributivism as the injunction that the state should never intentionally punish the legally innocent, it was thought fairly easy to show that consequentialism and retributivism are compatible—indeed, that consequentialism provides the best support for the respectable core of retributivism. The general justifying aim of punishment is consequentialist—to control dangerous antisocial conduct (this is the good consequence)—but we should employ this coercive mechanism only on the legally guilty, never on the legally innocent. And if one asks why, then the typical answer given—by both Rawls and sometimes Hart—was consequentialist, a version of rule-utilitarianism. Simply put, the argument was this: a social rule or practice that would allow the intentional punishment of the legally innocent would, in the long run, have many more bad than good consequences—e.g., it would prevent citizens from using the criminal law as a guide to their susceptibility to state coercion and would thus make citizens insecure with respect to that coercion.

In the remainder of my address, I want to contrast how I think about these two issues of legal moralism and retributivism today with the way in which I thought about them when I first started out. Obviously, I believe that my present way of thinking about these issues is an improvement over my old way, but that is ultimately for you to judge. Even if my change in views is a big mistake, however, my address may still have value as a cautionary tale—an illustration of how one's mind can deteriorate as one ages.

I will begin with a discussion of my evolving views of legal moralism and the Hart-Devlin debate.

LEGAL MORALISM AND THE HART-DEVLIN DEBATE

While I still think that there is much that is quite wrong in Lord Devlin's view, I have now come to think that it is not simply to be dismissed as dangerous and silly. I think that it contains some positive insights and also, when sympathetically interpreted, exposes some contradictions—or at least tensions—in traditional liberal theories of criminal law—the theories that start with Mill, run through Hart and Herbert Morris, and perhaps culminate in the extensive four-volume work of Joel Feinberg.

Unless one applies the principle of charity in interpretation, Devlin's view is indeed easy to ridicule and dismiss because of the excessive way in which he puts points that, if expressed more cautiously, might have some merit. Believing that society is bound together in part by shared moral values, Devlin argued that those who violate the most fundamental of these values—e.g., through private sexual conduct such as homosexual sodomy that society regards as a vice—threaten and undermine society in a way that is analogous to *treason*. Hart and others could not, of course, resist rubbing Devlin's nose in the nuttiness of this weird analogy. In an often cited remark, Hart said that Devlin's belief that private acts of consensual sodomy tend, like treason, to undermine society is evidentially on a par with the Emperor Justinian's belief that homosexuality causes earthquakes.

It does seem to me, however, that one could develop a more cautious version of the Devlin view that would at least be worth discussing. One might, for example, argue that open toleration of the flouting of sexual norms threatens the honorific position historically accorded the traditional nuclear family and that such a threat risks undermining the social stability generated by such family units. I have no idea of the degree to which conservative claims of this nature are true; and, indeed, I tend to be quite skeptical about many of them—particularly skeptical when they are directed solely against homosexuality, but less skeptical when they are directed against routine divorce, adultery, and general promiscuity—"hooking up," I think it is now called. It does not strike me as absurd, for example, to suggest that the sexual revolution of the sixties, and the resulting freedom many men felt to abandon their marriages and family responsibilities for sexual and other forms of so-called self-fulfillment, generated considerable social harm—particularly for women and children.

These claims may well be false, but they are not in my view—like Devlin's treason analogy—just plain *silly*. They merit a rational response based on a fair weighing of all available evidence and not merely rejection with a variety of liberal platitudes and slogans. If it should turn out that evidence renders plausible the claim that significant social decay is likely to result from a particular form of sexual excess, then I tend to agree with Devlin that the solemn invocation of Mill's Harm Principle does not by itself constitute a conclusive reason why dealing with such a concern could never be part of the criminal law's legitimate business. I think that it probably would be a very great mistake to use the criminal law for such ends, but many of my reasons would now be pragmatic—one being that the criminal law is a blunt and dangerous instrument and, as such, is generally maladapted as a tool for social engineering.

My increasing skepticism about Mill's Harm Principle does not mean, however, that I have abandoned *all* principles and would limit myself solely to pragmatic considerations when thinking about the legitimate use of the criminal law. I believe that, in trying to think rationally about legitimate state coercion, one would need to do something that Mill's Harm Principle, speaking of liberty and coercion only in grandly general terms, does not do—namely, assess the importance, both socially and to the individual, of the particular *kind* of liberty that the state is proposing to encumber. Later sections of *On Liberty* reveal that Mill really does not believe that all liberties are created equal. He clearly sees that some liberties (e.g., freedom of speech) are far more important than many others. This nuance is not present, however, in the often quoted sections of *On Liberty* in which the Harm Principle is most famously stated.

So just how important, for example, is sexual liberty when compared with other liberties? If that liberty is really important or fundamental, then I believe that this would provide a principled reason for demanding that the state show public harm before encumbering that liberty—perhaps even the kind of great harm that the United States Supreme Court has said that the state has a compelling interest in preventing. If the liberty is not all that important, however, then I see no reason why the state would necessarily have to demonstrate harm at all before encumbering it—offense, for example, might be enough. I will return to this issue a bit later.

Mill's own defense of the Harm Principle was, in general, utilitarian—the general argument being that, of all the rules that a society might adopt to regulate state coercion, the harm principle is the one that will bring about the greatest balance of good over bad social consequences. I have no idea how in the world one could tell if this claim is true—but then I have the same doubts about Mill's famous utilitarian defense of free speech principles. And Devlin's argument is itself, as I have previously noted, a kind of harm and thus utilitarian argument, since his argument is that society will be better off in the long run if it uses effective means to preserve its shared morality—even if the core of that morality does not always overlap the values that an educated elite tends to favor. But, again, how does one tell if such a claim is true?

Since many utilitarian-based principles rest on very uncertain and often merely anecdotal hunches about matters that are empirical and complex, it is not surprising that some philosophers find it attractive to attempt to find some *a priori* foundation for their favorite principles—the Harm Principle, for example.

A natural strategy, if one wishes to remain in the realm of principle, is to try to derive the Harm Principle from some more general principle that is arguably more foundational in liberal theory than the Harm Principle itself. Many liberal philosophers—and I think here mainly of Ronald Dworkin—will draw on some version of a principle of governmental *neutrality*. This principle, which Dworkin believes defines a liberal society, is that—out of respect for the right of moral independence held by each citizen—the state must never use its coercive power to pursue or to force individuals to pursue a particular vision of the good life. A liberal state must, of course, concern itself with the moral issues of public peace and order. However, moral issues of personal vice and virtue, of personal worth or goodness of character, are simply not the law's business. The liberal state must remain neutral on such matters. If the law, particularly the criminal law, concerned itself with such matters it would by definition violate the principle of neutrality and thereby fail to treat all citizens with the equal concern and respect demanded by the right of moral independence—the right to form and freely pursue (subject to certain restraints such as the Harm Principle) one's own vision of the good life, even if that vision is not shared or is even deplored by most people in one's society.

Limitations of both time and talent will prevent my subjecting this line of argument to criticism. What I propose instead is simply to grant it for purposes of discussion and then, drawing inspiration from Lord Devlin, to suggest that this liberal line of argument may ultimately be inconsistent with—or at least in tension with—two other values that many if not all liberals embrace. I call these values *fundamental rights constitutionalism* and *character retributivism in criminal sentencing*.

Since I here want to emphasize character retributivism in criminal sentencing. I will in the present context simply state in a bald and undefended way my view on fundamental rights constitutionalism—a view that I have developed and defended elsewhere. The view is this: if one were designing an ideal constitutional bill of rights, then some liberties—free exercise of religion and sexual liberty, for example—would have their best chance of earning legitimate status as fundamental constitutional liberties (liberties demanding, in American constitutional law, that the state show some compelling interest before encumbering them) through a good argument that these liberties instantiate or promote and secure some basic human good, that they assist individuals to live lives that are—as judged by some nonneutral standard—meaningful and worthwhile. This is, indeed, the very kind of argument made by Justice Kennedy in the 2003 case *Lawrence v. Texas* (539 U.S. 558). He based his decision to overturn the 1986 case *Bowers v. Hardwick* (478 US 186), an earlier case that had refused to recognize sexual liberty for homosexuals as a fundamental right, by arguing for the centrality of freedom of intimate sexual relations in a fully realized and meaningful human life. (Note that I am not here arguing a point of actual United States constitutional law. Even if a case can be made that a particular liberty would merit fundamental right status in an ideal constitutional system, it does not follow that the United States Supreme Court would act properly in claiming to find that right in our actual constitutional system.) [p. xvi more accurately describes this case.]

Of course, if the best argument for recognizing religious liberty or sexual liberty as fundamental rights depends on making a case for the central value of these liberties in meaningful human lives, it follows—I think—that the best attack on the claim that such liberties should be regarded as fundamental will be a good argument that the liberties do *not* secure any basic human good but are more like, say, mere recreational liberties—jet skis for some, religion and sexual intercourse for others. If I am right about this, then liberals may not consistently intone the principle "the state must be neutral on the good life" to defend the Harm Principle while simultaneously regarding as fundamental liberties that presuppose some nonneutral vision of the good life. (I do not mean to suggest, of course, that religious liberty and sexual liberty stand or fall together, since it is certainly possible to believe that the one is fundamental and the other is not. My point is simply that nonneutral views about a good or meaningful human life are central to the position we might reasonably take on either.)

This line of argument concerning the nonneutral nature of fundamental liberties (a line of argument that we now associate not simply with conservatives but with those thinkers often called perfectionist liberals) was only hinted at indirectly by Lord Devlin, and my ideas on that topic represent an attempted rational reconstruction and expansion of those hints. Devlin explicitly raises the issue I have called "character retributivism in criminal sentencing," however, and argues that liberals such as Mill and Hart probably want to count such virtuous states of character as remorse and repentance as relevant factors in sentence reduction. And this is certainly true of such later liberal theorists as Joel Feinberg, Herbert Morris, and the late Jean Hampton, since they have all argued that the truly repentant criminal in general deserves less punishment than the unrepentant criminal. But, asked Devlin, if such beliefs about personal virtue and vice are legally relevant here—at this point in the criminal law—how could it be in principle wrong to make all questions of personal virtue and vice relevant to deciding what to criminalize in the first place? So if a certain sexual practice is regarded as a moral vice and the liberal seeks to argue against criminalizing the practice on those grounds, he cannot in consistency give as his reason the general principle "issues of personal vice and virtue have no place in the criminal law"—not, at any rate, unless he wants to give up his belief that they are relevant in criminal sentencing.

Jean Hampton and Herbert Morris are two liberal theorists who embraced a version of Joel Feinberg's view that the criminal law should be grounded in what he called "grievance morality"—a morality solely concerned with protecting the rights and interests of others, rights that give rise to a legitimate grievance on the part of those who find them violated; and yet all three of these philosophers also claimed that remorseful and repentant criminals should receive less punishment than remorseless and unrepentant criminals. According to Jean Hampton, to quote just one of these philosophers, "what makes a state liberal…is its rejection of the idea that any enforcement of moral behavior should include punishment of immoral behavior which nonetheless has no victim other than the offender himself." But if a sentencing judge, after giving the criminal a punishment properly proportional to the injury he has inflicted, adds on a little extra because of the defendant's vicious character—his smug unrepentance, say—is that not simply to punish him for an aspect of his character that has no victim? If so, is not the liberal who approves this inconsistent when he crusades against using the criminal law against victimless immorality? What does repentance have to do with grievance or rights violation?

Now there is one way in which one might attempt to make repentance relevant to grievance—at least with respect to certain kinds of crimes—and thereby keep alive at least a part of the argument defended by Feinberg, Morris, and Hampton. I have defended such a view in other writings, and I will sketch it here although I am no longer totally convinced of its merits. It goes like this: for at least some crimes (rape is perhaps a good example) part of the injury itself (and thus the grievance) may be a function of the *symbolic message* that the criminal act conveys—the message, "I matter in a way that you do not and can use you, like a mere thing or object, for my own purposes." This is a degrading and insulting message, one that the victim would surely want to reject. If the wrongdoer manifests sincere repentance, however, then the evil message is being withdrawn—the wrongdoer now standing with the victim in condemning the act—and the victim might now, for example, forgive the wrongdoer without fearing a compromise of self-respect. Or so at least I have argued in the book on forgiveness and mercy that I did with Jean Hampton. I have come to have doubts about this view, however, in part because it does not seem to work at all for some crimes and in part because I may have overestimated the importance of symbolic messaging even in the crimes for which it does seem to work. To the degree that it does work, however, then to that same degree will victim grievance be less as a result of repentance and thus repentance could count toward sentence reduction even in a theory of criminal punishment based entirely on grievance.

Having introduced the idea of retributive punishment in the context of the legal moralism debate, I would now like to discuss it as an issue in its own right.

RETHINKING RETRIBUTIVISM

In discussing retributivism as a theory of criminal punishment, I am here simply going to sketch a few of the reasons why I no longer have the unqualified enthusiasm for the theory that I once did. I hope that the reasons will reveal—not just my own personal anxieties—but matters that really do deserve more thought from all of us.

Put in the simplest terms, a retributivist is a person who believes that the primary justification for punishing a criminal is that the criminal *deserves* it. The devil (or maybe the angel) is in the details, of course, and so what is really needed to defend retributivism is a persuasive answer to three questions: (1) What is desert? (2) Why is it morally important that punishment be based on desert? (3) Why should the *state* (which does not seek, after all, to promote all moral values) be concerned with moral desert as an aim in its system of criminal punishment? (I have written on question 3, but I will not have time to discuss it here.)

I have already mentioned the characterization of desert given by those writers, such as Rawls and Hart, who wanted to render retributivism compatible with consequentialism: desert is simply *legal guilt*. This is surely unsatisfying as a full account of retributivism, however, and hardly captures the robust view that such classic retributivists as Kant had in mind. It is the robust versions of retributivism that will concern me in the remainder of my address—versions that do not analyze desert merely as legal guilt and will not regard desert merely as a side constraint on a system that has, as its primary purpose, the utilitarian objective of crime control. To use Hart's language, the robust retributivist will see desert as central in answering the question, "What is the general justifying aim of punishment?" and the retributivist answer to this question is this: *to give criminal wrongdoers the punishment that they deserve.*

According to the retributivist, the substantive offenses of the criminal law should be designed to prohibit acts of moral evil, and the punishments mandated by such a system should be proportional to the personal evil displayed by the criminal in what he has done and by his reasons and motives for doing it. Kant defended such a version of retributivism in terms of the classic principle of *lex talionis*—a principle that is often unhelpfully rendered as "an eye for an eye." What Kant actually advocated was that punishment be proportional to the moral iniquity that the crime represents, and he saw this iniquity as a function both of the injustice of the criminal's act and of what he called the "inner viciousness" (*inneren Bösartigkeit*) of the criminal in performing that act.

There will, of course, be very welcome crime control benefits from such a system, but those benefits are—for the true retributivist—secondary to the primary purpose of imposing on criminals the suffering that they deserve.

If so much weight is going to be placed on the concept of desert, then we need a very clear understanding of exactly what we are going to mean by desert. If desert is not simply to be understood as legal guilt, then what is it? We know that for the retributivist the desert in question must be *moral* desert. But what is that?

In seeking to answer this question, I was once very charmed by a version of retributivism that analyzes desert in terms of the concept of a *debt* owed for free riding and which has sometimes been referred to as a theory of *moral balance*. Instead of taking retributive justice as a foundational primitive in one's moral and legal theory, the moral balance theory seeks to derive a justification of retributive punishment from a more general moral principle—a principle of fairness. The best defense of this view is to be found in Herbert Morris' 1968 essay "Persons and Punishment." This essay, one of the classics of twentieth-century jurisprudence, almost singlehandedly rescued robust retributivism from obscurity and rendered it philosophically respectable again.

The essence of the moral balance version of retributivism is this: every citizen benefits from living under the rule of law—a benefit that is possible only because most citizens, most of the time, give the law their voluntary obedience. This compliance involves assuming the burden of self-restraint—refraining, simply because the law requires it, from doing things we would very much like to do or that would benefit us. The criminal, on this model, violates a basic principle of fairness by being a free rider on this cooperative scheme since he derives the benefits without making the appropriate sacrifice. His punishment is thus a debt that he owes to those of us who have been law abiding, for without it the unfair advantage he has taken of us will be allowed to stand—a result that is clearly unfair. This is why the criminal deserves punishment. To this fairness-based theory Morris also adds the important Hegelian idea that criminals have a *right* to punishment, since punishing them is a way of showing that we respect them as free and responsible beings rather than viewing them as sick and nonresponsible.

As anyone familiar with my 1973 essay "Marxism and Retribution" will recall, I very early in my career expressed grave doubts about the legitimacy of *applying* this version of retributivism to a society of great inequality. In the essay I drew on some insights from Marx, but I could have made my main point just as well by drawing on John Rawls' idea of luck on the natural and social lottery or even on some wonderful lines from William Blake. (It will give you some idea of how old I am that I was actually required in school to memorize these and many other passages from plays and poems.) The lines are these:

> Every night and every Morn
> Some to Misery are Born.
> Every Morn and Every Night
> Some are Born to sweet delight.
> Some are Born to sweet delight,
> Some are Born to Endless Night.

Although I realize that this is an overly simplistic way of putting my concern, societies of radical inequality often seem to be societies in which the "sweet delight" folks are imposing punishment on the "endless night" folks and adding insult to injury by justifying this to the "endless night" folks by telling them that they owe this sacrifice to the community as a kind of debt. Unless they pay this debt, so the story goes, they will be unfair free riders on a mutually beneficial scheme of social cooperation, receiving all the benefits of the society in which they live without making the sacrifice of obedience to law required to make the system work. This might make a kind of sense for corporate criminals or other members of the "sweet delight" club, but it strikes me as rather indecent to say this sort of thing to those who might understandably have a difficult time naming all the wonderful benefits that have supposedly put them in debt to the rest of us.

Even given the worries about inequality that I expressed in that 1973 essay, I for quite some time remained committed to the debt/moral balance version of retributivism at the ideal theoretical level even if not at the level of concrete application. Eventually, however, under the influence of Richard Burgh, David Dolinko, Joshua Dressler, Antony Duff, Robert Nozick, and others, I came to doubt this and certain other versions of retributivism even at the theoretical level. With respect to moral balance retributivism, I came to find problematic the idea that one could acquire such important obligations merely from the passive receipt of benefits and thus became suspicious of any debt model of crime and punishment. Also, I came to think that the theory could not provide a plausible ranking of criminal offenses on a scale of severity. Murder and rape, for example, should surely be ranked as much more serious crimes than tax evasion, but I—like most decent, well brought up, and (let's face it) lucky people—am conscious of exercising no self-restraint in not raping or not murdering while being very conscious of great self-restraint in being honest in filling my tax returns. Others may have different priorities here, of course, but even that would illustrate the radical and unpredictable subjectivity that would be introduced into ranking offenses if one tried to do it in terms of some notion of the burden of self-restraint. Finally, it struck me that the moral balance theory at least flirts with explaining the obvious in terms of the controversial. If someone asks me why a murderer deserves to be punished, I would be far more inclined to answer this question simply by saying with emphasis "because he is a *murderer*," rather than by saying, "because he is a free rider."

So I moved away from regarding desert merely as legal guilt and moved away from regarding desert as merely owing a debt. But I still had very strong retributivist intuitions—was even prepared to defend some degree of vengeance and, in the book *Forgiveness and Mercy* that I wrote with Jean Hampton, to defend an emotion that I called "retributive hatred." Gradually I began to realize that what had always really drawn me to retributivism was some version of Kant's idea of punishing, not just wrongdoing, but human *evil*—vile deeds performed by people of "inner viciousness." I learned that such a notion had even found its way into American homicide law where such phrases as "cruel, heinous, and depraved" and "flowing from a hardened, abandoned and malignant heart" occurred in statutes and in sentencing guidelines. This appealed to me.

Such a strong notion of just deserts is, of course, in some ways a secular analogue to traditional notions of divine justice—the judgment that God will administer in the Last Assizes. Indeed, Michael Moore (the legal philosopher, not the maker of propaganda films) defends a robust version of retributivism very like the one that I am sketching here but claims that, if he believed in God, he would not be so concerned to organize secular systems of criminal law around retributive values. As an atheist, however, he sees no other way to target moral desert in punishment and regards this value as too important to leave unrealized.

This analogy with divine punishment is interesting; but it should, I now believe, alert us to some dangers of thinking of secular punishment along these lines. It is not for nothing that we often find ourselves condemning people who—as we put it—"play God," and even Scripture famously teaches, "Judge not that ye be not judged."

The Living Bible, that wonderful source of unintended theological humor, renders "judge not that ye be not judged" as "Don't criticize, and then you won't be criticized." But the true point of the passage is surely not a prohibition against making any critical moral judgments at all but is rather a caution against making final judgments of deep character—of presuming to declare any fellow human being as simply vermin or disposable garbage—evil all the way down—and a legitimate object of our hatred. And why should we be reluctant to make such judgments? There are two reasons: (1) we do not know enough ("only God can read the heart" as Scripture puts it) and (2) we are not ourselves good enough to presume such a sharp us/them distinction. This, I take it, is at least part of the point of Jesus' remark, "Let him who is without sin among you be the first to cast a stone at her."

Jesus' remark can, I think, be taken as potentially applicable to cases other than that of a woman caught in adultery. According to Michael Moore, however, Jesus' remark—when thus generalized—may be an inspiring slogan but is—as he puts it—"pretty clumsy moral philosophy." He writes as follows:

> It is true that all of us are guilty of some immoralities, probably on a daily basis. Yet for most people...the immoralities in question are things like manipulating others unfairly; not caring deeply enough about another's suffering; not being charitable for the limitations of others; convenient lies; and so forth. Few of us have raped and murdered a woman, drowned her three small children, and felt no remorse about it.

Moore's point seems to be this: in the relevant sense most of us *are* without sin, and so we might as well feel free to pick up some stones and cast away.

Is this an adequate answer to the concern raised by Jesus? I think not. The response is too shallow, for it fails to reflect the kind of serious introspection that the passage should provoke. The point is not to deny that many people lead lives that are legally and morally correct. The point is, rather, to force such people to face honestly the question of *why* they have lived in such a way. Is it (as they would like to think) because their inner characters manifest true integrity and are thus morally superior to those people whose behavior has been less exemplary? Or is it, at least in part, a matter of what John Rawls has called "luck on the natural and social lottery"? Perhaps, because of favored circumstances, they have never been adequately tempted, for example. Perhaps if they imagined themselves possessed of Gyges' ring (a ring that in Plato and Herodotus makes its wearer invisible) they might—if honest with themselves—have to admit that they might use the ring, not to perform anonymous acts of charity, but to perform some acts of considerable evil—acts, if not identical to, then still comparable in evil to those for which they seek the punishment of others. "There, but for grace of God, go I" is a thought that might well occur to them at this point.

Many persons will, of course, associate the perspective I have just been outlining with a kind of sloppy sentimentality about crime and criminals. In an attempt to lay such associations to rest, let me call your attention to passages from two writers—Immanuel Kant and Judge Richard Posner—who can hardly be regarded as bleeding-heart, soft-on-crime sentimentalists.

Those who know only Kant's rather bloodthirsty passages on retribution from his *Metaphysical Elements of Justice* may be surprised by this passage on blame and self-deception from his *Religion Within the Limits of Reason Alone*:

[People] may picture themselves as meritorious, feeling themselves as guilty of no such offenses as they see others burdened with; nor do they ever inquire whether good luck should not have the credit, or whether by reason of the cast of mind which they could discover, if they only would, in their own inmost nature, they would not have practiced similar vices, had not inability, temperament, training, and [nonimputable] circumstances of time and place which serve to tempt one, kept them out of the way of these vices. This dishonesty, by which we humbug ourselves and which thwarts the establishing of a true moral disposition in us is, if not to be termed wickedness, at least deserves the name worthlessness, and is an element of the radical evil in human nature which constitutes the foul taint of our race.

And here is Judge Richard Posner writing in dissent in *Johnson v. Phelan*, a case dealing with prison conditions:

I do not myself consider [the inmates of prisons and jails] as a type of vermin, devoid of human dignity and entitled to no respect. We should have realistic conceptions [of these people] before deciding that they are scum entitled to nothing better than what a vengeful populace and a resource-starved penal system chooses to give them. We must not exaggerate the distance between "us," the lawful ones, the respectable ones, and the prison and jail populations; for such exaggeration will make it too easy for us to deny that population the rudiments of humane consideration. (No. 93-3753, United States Court of Appeals, Seventh Circuit, 1995 WL 621777 7th Cir.[III.])

Finally, as a further step on the road to my increasing lack of enthusiasm for robust retributivism, vengeance, and retributive hatred, I was pulled up short when, in teaching my undergraduate course in Existentialism (a recent interest of mine), I had my students reflect on Nietzsche's claim that we should mistrust any person in whom the urge to punish is strong. It seemed to me that Nietzsche had a potentially profound insight here and the insight made me uncomfortable about my own long-standing defense of a retributive theory of punishment—uncomfortable because of a fear that my defense of such a theory perhaps in part grew out of my own strong and unexamined urge to punish rather than exclusively from objective moral and intellectual considerations. If Nietzsche was in part justified in his skepticism about the conscious rationales of justice, rights, and desert that we generally give for retribution, and if he was partly correct in diagnosing the retributive urge as *ressentiment* (an ugly emotional brew of malice, spite, envy, and cruelty) then one will, to put it mildly, want to rethink one's own urge to punish and any theories one builds on that urge. Surely I needed at least to consider the possibility that the retributive theory had put me and many others in what Rawls called "reflective equilibrium" in part because our pretheoretical intuitions about punishment and wrongdoing were corrupt. Those who embrace, as I do, reflective equilibrium as an important test for the adequacy of a moral theory must be willing to explore the deep psychology of their pretheoretical intuitions and not simply dismiss such explorations as examples of the genetic fallacy.

THE TWO FACES OF RETRIBUTION

I now come to the final section of this address—a section I call "The Two Faces of Retribution." I will note one face that draws us, in its stress on moral desert, toward the recognition of human dignity and responsibility and another face that tempts us to self-deceptive cruelty. It is this second face that has given me second and even third thoughts about retributivism. And where do these second and third thoughts leave me? They leave me as what I will call a "reluctant retributivist." I still hold a variety of retributivist convictions, but I hold many of them much more cautiously than was once the case for me.

To the degree that a retributive outlook on punishment involves a respect for the dignity of human beings as free and responsible agents—even if it sometimes tempts us to overstate their degree of responsibility—then retributivism surely makes an important point and is, as Herbert Morris has persuasively argued, dramatically preferable to some alternatives—e.g., advocacy of a therapeutic state in which wrongdoing is regarded as illness and criminals are subjected to involuntary chemical and other personality-destroying intrusions in order to turn them into compliant members of the social order. Some concept of desert, even if not what might be called "desert all the way down," is vital to our conception of ourselves and others as responsible beings, having the value that Kant called "dignity." This insight by itself is sufficient to keep me somewhere within the retributivist camp.

Also consider this: A retributive outlook on punishment is often identified with excessive harshness in punishment. This is a mistake, however. Such an outlook can, of course, sometimes urge us toward harsh punishments, but it can just as frequently urge us to greater concern with the humanity of criminals and thus to greater justice, goodness, and decency in our punitive practices. For example, surely one of the most powerful ways to confront the conditions of terror, assault, and rape that are common in the pest holes of many American jails and prisons is to remind ourselves that the people in those facilities are our fellow human beings, possessed of the basic human rights that attach to such a status. As such they simply do not *deserve* to be treated in such inhumane ways—no matter how much criminal deterrence society gets, and perhaps subconsciously welcomes, from such abusive treatment. Many of the people in these facilities have committed crimes for which such a level of abuse is radically disproportionate—e.g., on what theory of *lex talionis* is it just to ignore repeated gang rapes inflicted on persons who have been convicted of drug possession, or of criminal fraud? And even in cases where we may be tempted to think that the inmate has done such malicious evil that an environment of rape is properly proportional punishment for him, the Kantian retributivist will surely be guided by Kant's own injunction that all punishments, even those directed at the worst criminals, must be kept free of any maltreatment that would degrade the humanity of the criminal or of those administering the punishment. If the worst criminals are not human beings possessed of basic human rights, then the whole language of desert and just punishment would not even apply to them—as it does not apply to beasts. Thus, in spite of the deviation from strict proportionality, a decent society—according to Kant—will not torture the torturer or rape the rapist.

Given that I acknowledge some considerable virtues present within a retributive outlook on punishment—virtues that represent a very good face—why have I qualified my endorsement of retributivism and called myself a "reluctant retributivist"? To answer this question, let me briefly explore the bad face of retribution.

One of Nietzsche's great insights, I think, was his realization that our abstract theorizing—at least in moral theory—cannot fully be divorced from its social setting and from our own personal human psychology, a psychology that may affect us in ways of which we are not fully conscious. He claimed that all philosophy should be seen as the psychological autobiography of its writer, and—following in his footsteps—Iris Murdoch said that the first question that should be asked of any philosopher is, "What is he afraid of?" C. D. Broad put a similar point in his characteristically flip way simply by observing that "we all learn our morality at our mother's knee or at some other joint." All of these statements are obviously exaggerations, but they still contain important insights.

Although, like any decent philosopher, I try to get some critical distance from all these social and psychological and autobiographical factors, I am sure that to some degree I remain a prisoner—in ways of which I am often unaware—of my own resentful and vindictive Irish nature, some tendencies toward self-righteousness, a certain rigidity of character, and my lifelong back-and-forth struggle between the gospel of love stressed in my Christian upbringing and my not-always-loving personality. At the very least, these factors surely influence the framework I choose for discussion—the questions that I decide to ask first. At most and at worst, these factors may have inclined me to favor philosophical accounts for less than fully honorable reasons—reasons that may reveal that my enthusiasm for settling scores and restoring balance through retributive justice may in part have been extensions of what Nietzsche called "a soul that squints"—the soul of a shopkeeper or an accountant. If I had been a kinder person, a less angry person, a person of more generous spirit and greatness of soul, would robust retributivism have charmed me to the degree that it at one time did? I suspect not.

Let me emphasize, by the way, that this observation about my character is not a narcissistic confession of some unique and perhaps even perversely heroic depravity on my part. I do not think that I am at all unique in the way in which some of my principled intellectual views may at least to some degree be an extension of less than admirable aspects of character. If what is now usually called virtue ethics teaches us to worry about such matters, then I think that virtue ethics teaches a good lesson and should be welcomed by those of us who might have mistakenly thought that our Kantianism could proceed without such introspective reflection.

Let me take the slippery slope of retributive thinking as an example to illustrate the concerns that I have expressed above. The transition from "because your act and your mental state at the time of your act were blameworthy, you deserve punishment" to "you have a vicious character" to "you have a hardened, abandoned, and malignant heart" to "you are evil and rotten to the core" to "you are scum" to "you deserve whatever cruel indignity I choose to inflict on you" is, of course, not a logical transition. Not a single step logically follows from its predecessor. I fear, however, that the transition is *psychologically* a rather common and in some ways compelling one, one that ultimately may tempt us to endorse cruelty and inhumanity. I fear that I have myself sometimes succumbed to this temptation while talking the grand abstract language of just deserts, and I know that others have—and always will—succumb to this temptation as well. As recent reports of torture and humiliation of prisoners—both by "our side" and by "their side"—have reminded us, there are enormous subterranean reservoirs of terrifying cruelty within the human personality just waiting to be tapped. An overly confident retributive outlook on crime and punishment—particularly one that would presume to target deep character—has great potential to tap those resources, and this is why my commitment to a retributive theory of punishment has now become reluctant and cautious.

Judgments about deep character and responsibility for that character go far beyond the mere attribution of intention and other *mens rea* mental states. My worries about such judgments are to some degree applicable at all points in the criminal justice system, but they are most obviously applicable at the time of sentencing—most dramatically in capital sentencing. And it is these judgments—judgments about what Kant called "inner viciousness"—that will, I fear, both exceed our epistemic capacities and risk engaging the cruelty latent in all of us.

Symmetrical obstacles will also be present, of course, if we seek to reward good character—e.g., by imposing less punishment on a criminal who we believe manifests the character virtue of deep and sincere repentance. This problem is obviously logically similar to the problem about punishing inner viciousness, but I tend to find it less practically worrisome because it will have no tendency to engage our capacities for cruelty. I tend to worry more about engaging these capacities than I do about engaging our capacities for trust, generosity, and kindness—in part, I suppose, because I think that there is already too much of the former in the world and precious little of the latter. Excessive generosity can be dangerous, of course, if it leads us to free dangerous people to prey again upon the public. But we can surely accomplish the legitimate goal of just crime control with concepts of blameworthiness and desert that do not, as do ultimate negative judgments of deep character, invite hatred and the denial of the human dignity and worth of even the worst among us.

I realize that closing with expressions of uncertainty and unease is something of a philosophical disappointment. However, such lack of total clarity and comfortable confidence may be a moral and political good. To the degree that we are nervous and unsure of exactly what we are doing when we punish our fellow human beings, then I am inclined to think that to that same degree we will, at the very least, be less cruel.

I know, of course, that there are dangerous, even monstrous, people in the world—both within and outside our national borders—and that they do not become less dangerous or monstrous simply because they are often our creatures—to some degree products of how we have treated or ignored them—ignored them because, as Simone Weil noted, the poor and other outsiders are invisible to most of us unless seen, as they rarely are, with the eye of love. Because of this and our at least partial responsibility for it, we should, of course, seek to correct when we can the conditions that breed such dangerous people. In the meantime, however, we must for the survival of our communities find ways to contain the threats posed by these people; and sometimes criminal punishment—even very severe criminal punishment—will emerge as the method of choice. But even when it comes to that, I think that it is probably wise not to be too charmed by such retributive slogans as "giving them what they deserve" and not to be too enthusiastic in the belief that one is on a righteous retributive crusade. Better, I think, that Nietzsche be given the last word here: "He who fights with monsters should look to it that he himself does not become a monster."

BIBLIOGRAPHY

I have provided a list of the publications of mine on which I have drawn in preparing my presidential address and a list of the works of some other contemporary philosophers (I am sure that I have forgotten many) who have greatly influenced my thinking on the topics covered in the address. Full citations to Kant may be found in (3) below, and full citations to Nietzsche may be found in (7) below.

Works by Jeffrie G. Murphy

1. "Marxism and Retribution," *Philosophy and Public Affairs*, 2, 3 (Spring 1973): 217–43.
2. "Retributivism, Moral Education, and the Liberal State," *Criminal Justice Ethics*, 4, 1 (Winter/Spring 1985): 3–11.
3. "Does Kant Have a Theory of Punishment?" *Columbia Law Review*, 87, 3 (April 1987): 509–32.
4. *Forgiveness and Mercy*, with Jean Hampton. Cambridge: Cambridge University Press, 1988.
5. "Legal Moralism and Liberalism," *Arizona Law Review*, 37, 65 (Spring 1995): 73–94. This essay contains an appendix in which I try to respond to critiques from Jean Hampton and Herbert Morris on the main body of the essay.
6. "Repentance, Punishment, and Mercy," *Repentance—A Comparative Perspective*, edited by Amitai Etzioni, 143–70. (Lanham: Rowman & Littlefield, 1997).
7. "Moral Epistemology, the Retributive Emotions, and the 'Clumsy Moral Philosophy' of Jesus Christ," *The Passions of Law*, edited by Susan Bandes. 149–67. New York: New York University Press, 1999.
8. "Shame Creeps through Guilt and Feels Like Retribution," *Law and Philosophy*, 18 (1999): 327–44.
9. *Getting Even—Forgiveness and Its Limits*. New York: Oxford University Press, 2003.
10. "Law Like Love," *Syracuse Law Review*, 55, 1 (2004): 15–32.

11. "Well Excuse Me!—Remorse, Apology, and Criminal Sentencing," *Arizona State Law Journal*, Vol. 38, No. 2, 371–386, Summer 2006. An expanded version of this essay is chapter 7 of the present volume.

Works by Others

Burgh, Richard. "Do the Guilty Deserve Punishment?" *Journal of Philosophy*, LXXIV, 4 (April 1982): 193–213. Powerful skeptical case against certain forms of retributivism.

Devlin, Lord Patrick. *The Enforcement of Morals*. Oxford: Oxford University Press, 1965. This contains as Chapter 1 a reprinting of the 1959 Maccabaean Lecture "The Enforcement of Morals" and some responses to Hart's critique of that essay.

Dolinko, David. "Some Thoughts about Retributivism," *Ethics*, 101, 3 (1991): 537–59. One of several insightful essays in which Dolinko develops a critique of retributivism.

Dressler, Joshua. "Hating Criminals: How Can Something that Feels So Good Be Wrong?" *Michigan Law Review*, 88 (May 1990): 1448. In this essay Dressler accuses me, with some justice, of exhibiting excessively "macho" attitudes in my defense of retributive hatred in *Forgiveness and Mercy*.

Duff, R. A. *Trials and Punishments*. Cambridge: Cambridge University Press, 1986. Sympathetic treatment of some forms of retributivism while locating them in a framework of more communitarian values.

Dworkin, Ronald. *A Matter of Principle*. Cambridge, MA: Harvard University Press, 1985. Develops the idea that governmental neutrality is central to liberalism.

Feinberg, Joel, "Some Unswept Debris from the Hart-Devlin Debate," *Synthese*, 72 (1987): 249–75. Seeks to meet with a principle of fairness Devlin's critique of Millian liberalism.

Gaita, Raimond, *A Common Humanity*. London: Routledge, 2000. Drawing on Simone Weil and others, Gaita explores ways in which one can retain a sense of the humanity of even the worst among us.

Hampton, Jean. "How You Can Be Both a Liberal and a Retributivist: Comments on 'Legal Moralism and Liberalism' by Jeffrie Murphy," *Arizona Law Review*, 37, 1 (Spring 1985): 105–16.

Hart, H. L. A. *Law, Liberty and Morality*. Stanford: Stanford University Press, 1963. A Critique of Lord Devlin's Maccabaean Lecture "The Enforcement of Morals."

Hart, H. L. A. "Prolegomenon to the Principles of Punishment," *Punishment and Responsibility—Essays in the Philosophy of Law*. 1–27. Oxford: Oxford University Press, 1968. Distinguishes between a distributive question about punishment and a question about punishment's general justifying aim.

Hill, Thomas Jr. "Servility and Self-Respect," *Monist*, 57, 1 (January 1973): 87–104. Links rights and justice to the concept of self-respect.

Moore, Michael. "The Moral Worth of Retribution." In *Responsibility, Character and the Emotions*, edited by Ferdinand Schoeman. 179–219. Cambridge: Cambridge University Press, 1987. In my view, this joins Herbert Morris' "Persons and Punishment" as one of the two most powerful philosophical defenses of retributivism.

Morris, Herbert. "Persons and Punishment," *Monis*, 52, 4 (1968): 475–501. A powerful defense of robust retributivism that almost singlehandedly rendered such retributivism philosophically respectable again.

Morris, Herbert. "Professor Murphy on Liberalism and Retributivism," *Arizona Law Review*, 37, 1 (Spring 1995): 73–104.

Nozick, Robert. *Anarchy, State and Utopia*. New York: Basic Books, 1977. Challenges fairness arguments based on mere receipt of benefits.

Rawls, John. "Two Concepts of Rules," *Philosophical Review*, 64 (1955): 3–13. A generally rule-utilitarian defense of retribution conceived as limiting punishment to the legally guilty.

Chapter 5

Shame Creeps Through Guilt and Feels Like Retribution

INTRODUCTION[1]

The stories of William Trevor often contain, near the end, a single sentence that captures – in one crystalline moment – a core insight toward which the story has been building all along. Near the end of his novel *Death in Summer*, the following sentence occurs: "Her compassion faltered: shame creeps through guilt and feels like retribution."[2] I believe that my ability to understand the profundity of this sentence, and thus the story in which it occurs, was aided enormously by my reading of the essays of Herbert Morris. And thus, in my essay, I will reflect on the themes present in this sentence and thereby follow, in my own limited way, a path familiar to all those who have

---

1. This paper was presented on April 2, 1999, in Berkeley, California, at the annual meetings of the American Philosophical Association, Pacific Division, at a special session, "The Work of Herbert Morris." I was pleased and honored to be a part of this session, since my own thinking has been greatly influenced and enriched by Morris' work and my life has been enriched by my personal interactions with him. I thus dedicate this paper to him with esteem and affection. I have received useful comments on an earlier draft, for which I am very grateful, from Herbert Morris, Peter de Marneffe, Elaine Yoshikawa, Jerome Neu, Sharon Lamb, Betsy Grey, Dan Strouse, Rebecca Tsosie, and Margaret Holmgren.
2. William Trevor, *Death in Summer* (New York: Viking, 1998), p. 211. In Trevor's earlier *Felicia's Journey* – a novel ultimately of understanding and even forgiveness of the most apparently unworthy of people – a similar function is performed (at least for me) by this sentence: "Lost within a man who murdered, there was a soul like any other soul, purity itself it surely once had been."

read Morris: drawing philosophical inspiration from literature, trying to be open to the moral and spiritual insights latent in dark and mysterious stories and sayings,[3] reflecting on the intertwined emotions of guilt and shame, and seeing – in all of this – implications for punishment and forgiveness, both of self and of others. In Morris' own work, of course, these perspectives are all employed with great human sensitivity – employed by a person whose compassion never seems to falter.

GUILT AND AUTHORITATIVE COMMANDS

I will approach my topic somewhat indirectly by opening with a discussion of John Deigh's quarrel with some of the positions taken by Herbert Morris in the essay "Nonmoral Guilt." I will be drawing on an earlier draft of Deigh's paper "All Kinds of Guilt" (a paper about which we have corresponded in the past), and I write in the realization that he may now have changed some of his views.[4] I think that the positions here discussed are of sufficient intrinsic interest, however, to justify their exploration even if they have now to some degree been abandoned by their author. Similar positions

---

3. Morris' ability to use stories as a basis for deep philosophical reflection is impressive – e.g., his use of Friedrich Durrenmatt's *Traps* at the beginning of "Persons and Punishment" and his anaysis of the story of Adam and Eve in "Lost Innocence." And on the issue of dark sayings: I once chided Morris for quoting, with obvious appreciation, what at the time I took to be a stupidly obscurantist remark by Simone Weil. I have since come to realize that there was more wisdom in Weil's remark and Morris' use of it than in my hasty rejection. (For my exchange with Morris on Weil, see the symposium on forgiveness and mercy in *Criminal Justice Ethics* 7(2)(1988).) Unless otherwise noted, the Morris essays cited in this paper will be found in his collection *On Guilt and Innocence* (Berkeley: University of California Press, 1976).
4. A final version of Deigh's paper appears as "All Kinds of Guilt," *Law and Philosophy* 18 (1999), pp. 313–325. All subsequent quotations are taken from an earlier version of Deigh's paper.

are, for example, to be found in the work of Herbert Fingarette and Jean Hampton. (Indeed, on the theory that something worth saying once is worth saying again, I have adapted for use here a couple of pages from an earlier essay of mine on Jean Hampton.[5]) I have learned a great deal from Deigh's insightful paper and believe that he has told an important part of the story about guilt and bad conscience. I shall argue, however, that an even fuller and richer story will be told if we draw upon some insights from the work of Herbert Morris.

Deigh attributes to Morris the view that guilt is the principal moral feeling expressing bad conscience (he calls this the view that is "now common in moral philosophy") and also attributes to Morris a certain analysis of the moral feeling of guilt. Moral guilt, he claims (both for himself and for Morris), is a self-critical feeling occasioned by disobedience to requirements set by a "governing moral authority." It is "the appropriate feeling one experiences in response to one's having ignored these requirements... *The object of the feeling [of guilt] is one's disobedience*."[6] Deigh then argues that many of the cases identified by Morris as nonmoral guilt should be seen instead as moral guilt since they do involve, in ways that Morris has missed, disobedience of authoritative rules.

But is this Morris' view of guilt? And is this view (whether Morris' or not) correct? These are the questions that I shall now explore.

Morris, like Deigh, has certainly been influenced by a Freudian psychoanalytic perspective and would no doubt agree with Deigh that the development of a moral sense or conscience (a super-ego) at some point involves the internalization of parental commands

---

5. Herbert Fingarette, "Punishment and Suffering," *Proceedings of the American Philosophical Association* 51 (1993), pp. 499–525. Jeffrie G. Murphy, "Jean Hampton on Immorality, Self-Hatred, and Self-Forgiveness," *Philosophical Studies* 89(2–3)(1998), pp. 215–236 – reprinted in Jeffrie G. Murphy, *Character, Liberty, and Law* (Dordrecht: Kluwer, 1998).
6. Italics mine.

perceived as authoritative. But this, of course, cannot be the whole story – as the existence of *critical morality* (which may involve a challenge to parental commands) surely demonstrates. A psychoanalytic account of causal origins clearly has some bearing on the nature of the moral feelings, but it surely cannot represent a full account of those feelings.

What does Morris think? At the outset of "Nonmoral Guilt" he quotes H. K. Lynd's claim that "guilt consists in the intentional transgression of prohibition, a violation of a specific taboo, boundary or legal code, by a definite voluntary act."[7] Of course Morris quotes this passage only to reject at least part of it, for the important kind of guilt he labels "nonmoral" does not require the kind of intentional and voluntary acts spoken of in the passage. But does Morris subscribe to the other elements of Lynd's analysis of moral guilt – particularly to the idea that the essence of guilt is the transgression of an authoritative prohibition?

I think that a case can be made that the answer to this question is *no*. Writing of early childhood development, Morris claims (and here is in agreement with Deigh) that normal development involves "the child acquiring the concept of a rule, his accepting a rule, and in cases of infraction feeling guilt."[8] He also stresses, however, the importance in guilt of *connectedness to other people*. He writes:

> What is valued in a [guilt morality] is...a relationship with others...With guilt we have a conceptual scheme of obligations and entitlements [leading to] the idea of owing something to others...With guilt one's status is intact but one's relationship to others is affected. [Guilt thus leads to attempts at] restoration.[9]

---

7. Herbert Morris, "Nonmoral Guilt," in *Responsibility, Character, and the Emotions*, ed. Ferdinand Schoeman (Cambridge: Cambridge University Press, 1987), pp. 220–240.
8. *On Guilt and Innocence*, p. 60.
9. *On Guilt and Innocence*, pp. 60–62.

It [also] seems clear that we often feel guilty and quite appropriately, I believe, in circumstances where we have not disobeyed the commands of conscience. The damage we do through faulty inattentiveness is often great and there is nothing like the setting of our will against a cognizable command, though we may feel guilty. But even without fault we may do great damage; it may derive from an understandable ignorance or blindness and only after much soul-searching might we discover the harm and our role in it. This may not be moral blameworthiness but the guilt we feel is not pathological. The feeling seems grounded on a sense of our responsibility for damage to what we value, anger at oneself because of it and a disposition to repair.[10]

In the later essay "Nonmoral Guilt," Morris stresses what he calls the value of "human solidarity" as central to many instances of appropriate guilt. However, in this essay, he claims that guilt based solely on human solidarity in the absence of responsible wrongdoing should be conceptualized as "nonmoral guilt."

I think that this choice of terminology is unfortunate, allowing – as it does – a Kantian ethic of principle and voluntary wrongdoing to gobble up the entire domain of morality. However, if there is anything at all to the idea of what is now called virtue ethics, then surely a person who lacks a feeling of solidarity with his fellow human beings (unlike, say, someone who lacks an appreciation of Bach) can properly be said to have a moral deficiency of character. Human solidarity, like compassion, deserves to be classified as a moral feeling; and thus there is a sense in which any guilt that is based upon this feeling, even in the absence of voluntary wrongdoing, may appropriately be classified as a kind of moral guilt. (Evolutionary biologists tend to see

---

10. "Reflections on Feeling Guilty," *Philosophical Studies* 40 (1981), p. 192.

altruism as the paradigm moral feeling, and perhaps – though overstating their case – they are seeing something missed in a purely psychoanalytic perspective.) Mrs. Iveson, in the William Trevor novel, feels guilt in part because "her compassion faltered," and I do not find it illuminating to call this nonmoral guilt. Neither, for reasons I will explore later, do I find it illuminating to call it simply shame. Thus I think that the great insights of Morris' essay would have been better served if the essay had been entitled, not "Nonmoral Guilt," but rather "Two Kinds of Moral Guilt."[11]

At any rate, an idea repeatedly stressed by Morris is the idea that morally mature guilt essentially involves our relations with other people, our concern with them as fellow human sufferers, and our placing high value on their welfare (or at least their freedom from injury). I think that Morris is correct to stress this as an important part of the moral phenomenology of guilt, and I also think that it is an aspect of guilt that we miss if we analyze guilt too heavily in terms of the violation of authoritative commands. I think that Morris realizes this and that he is importantly right in realizing this. For if guilt were solely a matter of violating authoritative commands, how could we account for important aspects of guilt that Morris emphasizes – e.g., the idea that the guilty person owes something to others?

To make this point more clearly, let us consider the kinds of cases that are now (following Thomas Nagel and Bernard Williams) generally referred to as cases of "moral luck." A normal person who drives while intoxicated and kills a child in a crosswalk will, I suspect, be eaten up with intense guilt for a long time – perhaps unto

---

[11]. Deigh and I agree that some of the guilt that Morris identifies as nonmoral should be identified as moral, but our reasons are different. Deigh, seeing moral guilt only where there is rule violation, finds rules (and thus moral guilt) where Morris does not. On my view, the attachment of guilt to certain moral sentiments is sometimes enough to qualify the guilt as moral even in the absence of rule violation.

death. But that same person probably will feel little or no guilt if, through good luck, there is no child in the crosswalk when he speeds through it. In the first scenario the person may spend a lifetime searching in vain for self-forgiveness, whereas in the second scenario the person would hardly see the point of even raising the issue. The difference here can only be explained, I think, by the presence of harm in the one case and the absence of harm in the other. The element of violation of an authoritative prohibition is equally present in both cases.

We typically feel our most intense guilts, not because of abstract and formal violations of authoritative rules, but because we see vividly the harm that we have inflicted on others by such violations. Violation is often part of the story, of course, but it is not always center stage. Center stage is frequently occupied by harm or injury. Robust defiance of major rules will often, in the absence of injury, leave us free – if not of all guilt – at least of the more severe and conscience-burdening varieties of guilt. Knowing or even thoughtless neglect of lesser rules, however, will often generate guilt bordering on self-hatred if we see that such neglect inflicts injury – particularly on those with whom we are intimately involved and about whom we care deeply. The writer A. N. Wilson captures this point nicely in the following passage from his novel *Incline Our Hearts*:

> It is only on those whom I have loved that I have ever knowingly inflicted pain. The guilt of it remains forever, my words selected with such malice and the startled expression on the victim's face as the effect went home. These are the faces which return during nights of insomnia, forever hurt in my memories, and inconsolably so... Sometimes in spells of profound depression, it is these moments alone which surface in the memory. Everything else is a bland, misty background against which these figures stand out

sharp and clear – women in tears, or my uncle, drawing back the corner of his lips and sticking a pipe in his mouth, trying to conceal the extent to which I was hurting him.[12]

Wilson here captures perfectly at least my sense of the paradigm cases where guilt is likely to arise. And these cases would be radically distorted, in my view, if analyzed as centrally concerned with disobedience to authority. To this extent, I think that Melanie Klein has noticed something missed by Freud; and Martin Hoffman has noticed something missed by Piaget.[13]

In correspondence, Herbert Morris has suggested that the feelings of negative self-assessment in these cases of harm to others should perhaps be identified as *remorse* rather than guilt. However, Wilson does use the term "guilt," and – to quote a remark made by Morris himself in his essay "Nonmoral Guilt" – "I am skeptical about any claim of widespread misuse of terms for emotional states, and I am generally disposed to accept first-person reports as accurate."[14] Thus I am presently inclined to continue seeing harm as central to guilt – at least as central as (and sometimes more central than) rule violation.

---

12. A.N. Wilson, *Incline Our Hearts* (London: Penguin Books, 1988/1990), pp. 143–144. Although Wilson speaks here of guilt, I shall later argue that shame must also be an important part of what is being felt here. I recalled the Wilson passage when I read this from psychologist Donald L. Nathanson's book *Shame and Pride*: "Whatever portion of us is revealed during a shame experience causes the unfolding of a process that brings from their hiding places a host of other hidden memories. Our ability to group memories, to order our experience so that it may be handled in some intelligent manner, this very facility that allows us to organize our internal world becomes the source of the very images we would most like to forget. Shame can be triggered by exposure of the self to the view of others. But it triggers further exposure of the self to the self, maintaining and amplifying shame, creating shame-filled moments or even shame-dominated moods." Donald L. Nathanson, *Shame and Pride* (New York: W. W. Norton, 1992), pp. 254–255.
13. I can claim no expert knowledge of any of these writers and am depending heavily on what John Deigh says about them in his essay.
14. Morris, "Nonmoral Guilt," p. 221.

I would even go so far as to suggest that an overemphasis on mere transgression and rule violation would cause us to miss a central element in the greatest story of transgression in our culture, a story from which we may get many of our ideas of guilt, and a story upon which Herbert Morris has written with great insight in his essay "Lost Innocence."[15] I am thinking, of course, of the story of Adam and Eve in the garden.

One would, I think, miss a great deal that is important in this story if one viewed it mainly as a story about the violation of an authoritative prohibition. After all, the discussion between Eve and the serpent focuses not on issues of moral principle, but rather on competing prudential hypotheses. Eve seems concerned, not with God's abstract moral authority, but rather with the question of the reliability of God's promise to sustain her being and promote her interests. She fears to eat from the tree, not because she has some primitive grasp that "Do not eat from the tree" is a categorical imperative, but because God has said that anyone who eats from the tree will die. She is not sure, however, that her fear is justified; and thus the serpent is able to seduce her into disobedience, not by inviting her to replace God's moral authority with her own, but rather by reassuring her about the promised sanction. He says simply, "Of course you will not die," and Eve, alas, believes him.

In my view, what the serpent blinds Eve from seeing is not the majesty of God's categorical moral authority but rather the fact that God the creator knows what is in the best interest of his creatures whom he loves – a point missed by a reading of the story that places too much stress on issues of authority and command. The God of the story is to be obeyed for the very practical and prudential reason that he created human beings and therefore knows what is required in order for them to flourish.

---

15. *Supra*, note 3.

I think that a reading that places too much stress on the violation of authoritative rules also makes us miss an aspect of the story that is even more important for our present purposes – namely, the nature of any guilt that Adam and Eve might feel after their disobedience. If they experience guilt (and the story, speaking only of shame, does not tell us that they do) is this because they have defied an authoritative rule or rather because they have deeply betrayed and disappointed – and thus *hurt* – the Heavenly Father who loves them? I suspect it is in large part the latter. God's response to them strikes me as personal as well; it is largely that of an injured but still loving father whose loving care has been unappreciated, not simply the response of a cosmic policeman who – like Oliver Wendell Holmes Jr. – holds the abstract belief that the law must keep its promises. The story of the garden is a powerful *personal* drama and a powerful *family* drama – something we would miss with too much emphasis on rules and authority and mere disobedience.

I am supported in this hunch by, if I understand him correctly, Bernard Williams. He has argued – in his book *Shame and Necessity* – that Western guilt morality had, at the time of its origins, one great strength: attention to the hurts and claims of victims. He believes that this strength was lost, however, when guilt morality became overly Kantian – i.e., highly abstract, formal, and legalistic.[16] The worry that Williams raises poses serious problems, I think, for any analysis of guilt that places too heavy an emphasis on principle, rule, and disobedience. In such an analysis, the powerful claims of victims – their hurts, their outrages, even their hatreds – drop out in favor of an abstract concept of defiance of law. What drops out as well, I suspect, are the powerful reactive attitudes that seem so naturally a part of either being a victim or reacting to victims but so artificially grafted on

---

16. Bernard Williams, *Shame and Necessity* (Berkeley: University of California Press, 1993), esp. pp. 219–223.

to abstract notions of law. Morris' full analysis of guilt, at least as present in some of his essays as I interpret them, restores the values that Williams finds missing from other modern accounts.

In summary: Although I would not deny that disobedience of authoritative rules is an important element in some instances of guilt, I would not myself stress its centrality to the degree that Deigh does. What is central in many cases – and what tends to cause the most painful pangs of guilty conscience in morally mature persons – is not just wrong but *wrongful injury to others*.[17]

One could, of course, say that what is at issue here is some authoritative rule of the form that others are to be cared for. But this strikes me as perverse. In the best case, what I really care about is *them*. A poor second best is to care about not them, but about some rule that says that they are to be cared for. Most of us cringe when Mrs. Solness (in Ibsen's *Master Builder*) blocks expressions of gratitude from Hilde Wangel by making it clear that there is no kindness or concern involved, only duty. "It is no more than my duty," she says with respect to her gestures of assistance. Mrs. Solness would no doubt feel a kind of guilt merely for failing in such duty, but such guilt is not – I would be inclined to say – the best kind of guilt.[18]

Guilt is simply too complex to be fully captured by notions of authority and disobedience and rules; and it is one of the great strengths of Herbert Morris' writings on guilt that they often reveal deep sensitivity to this complexity. He always starts the story of guilt

---

17. Donald L. Nathanson, a psychologist who has authored several influential studies on shame and guilt, sees that harm plays a role at least equal to rule violation in understanding guilt. He writes: "Guilt is the painful emotion triggered when we become aware that we have acted in a way to bring harm to another person or to violate some important code" (*Shame and Pride*, p. 19). Nathanson suggests here that the harm in guilt does not even have to be from wrongful conduct. Even if I have sufficient reason to subject a child whom I love to a painful medical procedure, I might well – in spite of my realizing that I have done the right thing – experience guilt. Is such guilt pathological or irrational? I am inclined to think not.
18. My thinking about the Ibsen play has been greatly influenced by Peter Winch's essay "Moral Integrity" in his collection *Ethics and Action* (London: Routledge and Kegan Paul, 1972).

with rule violation, but before he ends the story he has usually stressed the one thing that (in my view) gives even these rules their moral point: their tie to certain values, particularly the value of human beings – their rights and their welfare – and the relationships among human beings.

GUILT, SHAME, AND THE PANGS OF CONSCIENCE

Having suggested that guilt (in the best and morally mature cases) involves much more than a negative self-assessment based on disobedience to authority, I would now like to explore Deigh's claim that "guilt is the principal moral feeling expressing bad conscience."

My immediate thought, when I first read Deigh's claim, was "What about *shame*?" Does not this important moral feeling play, along with guilt, a central role in the analysis of moral conscience? And is not the omission of shame particularly surprising on the part of John Deigh – who is the author of one of the most insightful essays on shame in the current philosophical literature?[19]

This first thought remains my present thought. I think that shame is absolutely central to a full understanding of guilt and the pangs of conscience and I think that Herbert Morris, in several of his writings, shows a grasp of this point – this grasp being sometimes obscured for the reader, however, because of Morris' tendency to prefer the *language* of guilt – speaking of "guilt before ourselves" in many cases where the rest of us might speak simply of shame.

In what follows I shall attempt to use insights in several of Herbert Morris' essays to show how shame is required in order for guilt to

---

19. John Deigh, "Shame and Self-Esteem," *Ethics* 93 (1983) and reprinted in *Ethics and Personality*, ed. John Deigh (Chicago: University of Chicago Press, 1992).

become sufficiently self-punishing, sufficiently tied to personal suffering, to deserve characterization as a full-blown bad conscience.

Before beginning my discussion of the kind of shame I shall seek to defend (I shall call it "moral shame") I want to make two preliminary points. First, I am well aware that, at least in our culture, shame is an emotion of toxic potential. When extremely directed toward inappropriate objects – e.g., poverty or social status or appearance – shame can be deeply destructive of personal well-being and even mental health. These consequences can be particularly destructive if they occur when character is being formed in childhood. As the novelist Annie Ernaux remarks of her own shameful childhood of poverty, social ostracism, and family violence: "This can be said about [such] shame: those who experience it feel that anything can happen to them, that the shame will never cease and that it will only be followed by more shame."[20]

I have no desire to defend this kind of shame or to wish it on anyone.

The second preliminary point I want to stress is that the arguments I shall here give in defense of moral shame should not be seen as offering even partial support for the currently trendy movement in American criminal law toward what are sometimes called "shaming punishments." Such punishments (at least as practiced and recommended in America) have been given their best defense by Dan Kahan but have been subjected to what I regard as a nearly fatal critique by Toni Massaro and others.[21] As practiced in America, these punishments (e.g., requiring prisoners to work on chain gangs or

---

20. Annie Ernaux, *Shame*, translated by Tanya Leslie (New York: Seven Stories Press 1998), p. 95.
21. For a defense of shaming punishments, see Dan Kahan's "What Do Alternative Sanctions Mean?" *University of Chicago Law Review* 63(1996), pp. 591–653. For a critique of shaming punishments, see Toni Massaro's "Shame, Culture and American Criminal Law," *Michigan Law Review* 89 (1991), pp. 1880–1944 and "The Meanings of Shame – Implications for Legal Reform," *Psychology, Public, and Law* 3 (1997), pp. 645–704.

wear pink underwear or requiring convicted sex offenders to post notices of their crimes on their houses) have little or nothing to do with moral shame but rather strike me as mainly coercive exercises in humiliation and degradation – a kind of smug and mean-spirited vengeance with tendencies to lapse into arbitrary cruelty. They do not engage and rebuild the core of the moral self but simply add extra punitive burdens and inconveniences (some of them quite grotesque) to the criminal's postconviction life.

Having attempted to indicate the two kinds of shame and shaming I am not concerned to defend, let me now move – with the help of Herbert Morris' writings – to an articulation and defense of what I have called "moral shame" – what I will have in mind in the remainder of the paper when I simply use the word "shame." I shall here be referring to a collision between one's actual self – past or present – and one's internalized and moral ego ideal.

Let me begin with a personal story. In my view, the best way (at least initially) to test a philosophical account of an emotion is to test that account against one's own experience of that emotion. Does the account illuminate or distort? This strategy has its dangers, of course, for one may discover – as one talks with others or reads widely – that one's own experience is highly idiosyncratic or even pathological. Hoping that mine is neither, let me recall what is for me one of the most painful examples of bad conscience that I have ever experienced – a story that, even after many years, can make me almost double over in angst when, in a private movement, it forces itself upon my memory. (When I intentionally recount it in public, the context provides enough psychic distance to eliminate most of the pain.)

When I was a boy, I loved baseball and desperately wanted a baseball glove. Although I was not aware of this, my parents were at that time experiencing great financial distress – such great distress, indeed, that even the cost of a baseball glove was beyond their means. As it happened, the naval base where my father was stationed fielded several amateur baseball teams and these teams sometimes discarded used equipment. My father came across a discarded baseball glove. He tried it on, found that it was still in surprisingly good condition, and – with delight in his eyes – presented it to me when he came home at the end of the day. But my father was, alas, left-handed; and I am right-handed – a difference he had not, at the moment of trying on the glove, brought to consciousness. When I tried it on, my immediate disappointment at its uselessness to me was obvious and I rather contemptuously cast it aside. My father lost his temper, called me ungrateful and selfish, and sent me to my room – behavior on his part that I now see as his way of defending himself against his own hurt and disappointment when one of his rare attempts to do something he found so difficult – show love – misfired.

A small incident, you may well say; but it is one of the more interesting things about human psychology that such small incidents can become life-defining moments for us. They can, though generating no guilt or shame or bad conscience at the time, generate all this to a painful degree when recalled in later life. Ignoring its relevance to Bill Clinton, consider this humorous but profoundly instructive exchange between Simon and his analyst in Donald Barthelme's novel *Paradise* – an exchange that beautifully illustrates the way in which certain childhood experiences can be central in the formation of the self:

> "What was your first sexual experience, Simon?"
>
> He thinks for a moment "I was about ten. This teacher asked us all to make little churches for a display, kind of a model of a church. I made one out of cardboard, worked very hard on it, and took it in to her on a Friday morning, and she was pleased with it. It had a red roof, colored with red crayon. Then another guy, Billy something-or-other, brought in one that was made of wood. His was better than mine. So she tossed mine out and used his."

"That was your first sexual experience?"
"How far back do you want to go?"[22]

But now back to my own story – a story very like the A. N. Wilson memory that I discussed earlier and one that I recall with enough painful guilt to say with confidence that I feel in it the deep pangs of a bad conscience.[23] I of course have other similar stories – we all do – and by no means all of them involved relations with my father or any other childhood experience. Friends, lovers, children, colleagues, students, strangers, and even my dogs would be mentioned in a complete inventory of my occasions of bad conscience. I limit myself to one such story, however, because I think it is representative and because telling more than one would, I fear, strike my reader as a boring and even offensive exercise in self-indulgence on my part. Perhaps, even telling the one, I run such a risk.

Whether in wisdom or stupidity, however, the story has now been told; and I want to understand the bad conscience at the heart of it – the pain generated by the memory of what I did. What is the basis for this pain?

I simply cannot believe that the violation of any authoritative rules was very much involved, so that is not an important part of this particular story.

Certainly the hurt and disappointment that I caused to my father is an important part of the story, but that is not the whole story either. Why? Because there are other cases where I hurt and disappointed him (and have hurt and disappointed others) that have not left me with such self-loathing.

What, then, is left to provide the basis? I think it is a kind of *shame*; because what comes most vividly before my mind in this case, but

---

22. Donald Barthelme, *Paradise* (New York: G P. Putnam's Sons, 1986), p. 19.
23. For another similar story, see William Maxwell's novel *So Long See You Tomorrow* (New York: Knopf 1980).

not in all cases, is this question: "How could I have been the *kind of person* who could have been so insensitive – a person so mired in his own narcissism that he utterly lacked empathy, so unable to recognize gestures of love, and so willing to inflict hurt simply because his own small desires were unmet?"[24]

To raise these kinds of questions – questions about the integrity and value of one's very self – just *is* to feel shame. In psychoanalytic language, these questions point to a conflict between what one is or has been and the image one has of one's ideal self, one's ego-ideal; and, if one's ego-ideal has moral values as constitutive elements, then at least certain moral failures will produce not just guilt, but shame as well. For the difference between "I am sorry I did that" and "I am sorry that I was the kind of person who (for those motives) could have done that" is subtle but important.

Why did I not feel such deep pangs of conscience at the time I hurt my father but came to feel them only later? Is it because I had no clear ego-ideal at the earlier time and had to await its development – and its assumption, for me, of moral properties – in order to feel the relevant kind of moral shame? I am not sure.

One might, of course, respond to my story by saying "Give yourself a break, Murphy – you were just a kid. You should forget all this because your continuing recollection of it and other cases from your past is pathological." Although I cannot here explore all of my reasons for thinking this, I think that such a response is shallow. To disavow the self of one's past – even one's childhood self – blocks, among other things, one's ability to understand the sense in which one may see oneself as having experienced moral growth and the path by

---

24. Not all moral failures raise this worry about the self. Moral wrongs that are *out of character*, for example, may be occasions for guilt (and desires to make restitution, etc.) but not moral shame. Motives – and particularly settled dispositions – matter greatly here. In *On Guilt and Innocence* (p. 63), Morris notes that a shame morality essentially involves, in a way that a guilt morality does not, "concern with motives, with purity of heart, grandeur of soul."

which further moral growth may be possible. And is not all bad conscience directed toward the past?[25]

It is possible, of course, that a legitimate recollection of such cases could, given a certain self-indulgence, transform itself into an obsession with them; and here is where repentance, forgiveness from others (if they are still alive), and ultimately self-forgiveness have vital roles to play. Herbert Morris makes this point forcefully when he writes: "Humility of a certain sort seems essential to a number of distinct conditions: to contrition, to repentance and to forgiveness of oneself... When conscience is at work we must be able to forgo an attachment to a self-inflated image of ourselves that may lie behind continued self-reprobation."[26]

Morris here offers wise counsel against obsession with self, but the existence of pathological cases should not blind us to other cases where attention to the shamed self can be a sign of health and a stimulus to moral improvement – the attempt to mold a better character – through the painful prod that such shame provides. For in my view, it is the narcissistic wound inflicted by shame that causes the greatest suffering, the greatest self-punishment, that we associate with a bad conscience. In short: shame creeps through guilt and feels like retribution.[27]

---

25. "We have no right to let go of so much that shaped us; we shouldn't be allowed to forget." Sue Miller, *While I was Gone* (New York: Alfred A. Knopf, 1999), p. 98. My colleague Peter de Marneffe has put the point this way. "If being a morally inadequate person is a good reason to feel ashamed, way isn't having been a morally inadequate person also a good reason, since one is, in many important respects, the same person?"
26. "Reflections on Feeling Guilty," supra note 10, p. 191.
27. In the Trevor story, this claim is made about Mrs. Iveson, one of the central characters. She learns of the unspeakable horrors contained in the childhoods of those damaged people who stole but then returned her grandchild, and – in the sudden loss of an undesirable kind of innocence – she is struck by an image of herself as a shallow person who has lived in the smug illusions of privilege and wealth and isolation from the sufferings of ordinary people. Like Lear, she sees that she has "ta'en too little care of this."

   I have used the phrase "narcissistic wound" to describe the pain of moral shame, and this may strike some of my readers as odd since I clearly want to regard such shame as legitimate and, in ordinary language, we tend to use the word "narcissism" to describe pathological vanity. For my own usage, I am drawing on Heinz Kohut, one of the leading psychoanalytic

Where did I learn these important lessons about the relationship between guilt, shame, and bad conscience? I believe that I learned them from reading and reflecting upon (without, I hope, too much distortion) the essays of Herbert Morris. Let me quote three representative passages from those essays:

> I do not believe that one can begin to explain the suffering attached to one's disobeying conscience without emphasizing a person's deep attachment to being a person of the sort partly defined by one's conscience. Conduct contrary to conscience is not just disobedience. We are attached to the source of the command and thus disobedience becomes like self-betrayal. With this there is an inevitable loss of self-esteem…[W]e experience a form of fragmentation; there is a breakdown in our sense of wholeness.[28]
>
> And where the maintaining of [a] relationship is an element in one's model identity, when one acts in a way incompatible with the relationship, the shame response focuses on failing to be a worthy person as one conceives it…[29]
>
> …[O]ur failure may be…in doing and failing to do things that, while ultimately involving harm to others, are most directly crimes involving ourselves, crimes that consist in one way or another in failures of integrity, failures to be and to act as our conception of ourselves dictates. There is strong temptation to talk of guilt here – guilt before ourselves – rather than shame, for

---

writers on narcissism. Kohut regards some level of narcissism as healthy – even necessary: "Since the self is, in general, cathected with narcissistic libido, the term 'narcissistic self' may with some justification be looked upon as a tautology." Heinz Kohut, *The Analysis of the Self* (Madison, Connecticut: International Universities Press, 1971), p. 26. When such narcissism reaches a pathological level, Kohut uses the terms "grandiosity" or "grandiose self."

28. "Reflections on Feeling Guilty," *supra* note 10, p. 189. For a rich exploration of the relationship between guilt, shame, and self-esteem see John Deigh's "Shame and Self-Esteem." For reasons I noted earlier, I would not emphasize the ideas of disobedience and command to quite the extent that Morris does in this passage.
29. *On Guilt and Innocence*, p. 61.

fault conditions do obtain in many instances... The impulse to talk of shame [here] comes from the inappropriateness in these cases of alleviating the feelings we have by conduct such as... receiving punishment.[30]

Morris vacillates here between shame and what he identifies as guilt before ourselves, and perhaps he is right to do so. Perhaps the moral phenomenology here is too complex to be captured adequately by either concept. What is important, however, is that he sees the vital role played by the pain of negative assessment of one's very worth – and not just rule violation and not just harm – in a proper account of the sufferings of a bad conscience.

This brings to a close my ruminations on guilt, shame, and bad conscience. With apologies to William Trevor and in deference to Herbert Morris' preferred conceptualization, I will close with a one-sentence summary of my core idea: Guilt before ourselves creeps through ordinary guilt and feels like retribution.

30. *On Guilt and Innocence*, pp. 134–135. In this passage Morris also claims that ascribing shame seems appropriate in these cases to the degree that the asking of forgiveness seems inappropriate. I think that this claim is mistaken, and I think that Morris corrects this mistake elsewhere. In "Reflections on Feeling Guilty" (*supra* note 10, pp. 189–192), Morris sees that forgiveness from others might allow one to attain the kind of humility that allows one to overcome the excessive self-centeredness that is an obstacle to the development of a proper sense of self. Thus one might ask for forgiveness partly in the hope that, if granted, one obstacle has been removed that may stand in the way of moving closer to one's ideal self and thereby overcoming shame. "It seems we need someone to know us *as we are* – with all we have done – and forgive us. We need to tell. We need to be whole in someone's sight: Know this about me, and yet love me. *Please.*" (Sue Miller, *While I Was Gone*, *supra* note 25, p. 261).

I am not even sure that Morris is correct when he says that receiving punishment is inappropriate as a way of alleviating shame. This may depend on the *purpose* of the punishment. If the purpose is purely retributive – to administer the suffering that is properly proportional to one's desert – then Morris is probably right in claiming its inappropriateness to shame. But what if its purpose is reformative – designed, say, to mortify the flesh and humble the will in the hope that a new and better self may emerge form the punitive process? This could, I think, be appropriate as a means of alleviating shame. See Jeffrie G. Murphy, "Repentance, Punishment and Mercy" in Amitai Etzioni (ed.), *Repentance* (Lanham: Rowman and Littlefield, 1997), pp. 143–170, reprinted in Jeffrie G. Murphy, *Character, Liberty and Law* (Dordrecht: Kluwer, 1998).

Chapter 6

Repentance, Mercy, and Communicative Punishment

We should [look at the] example... of the offender who has genuinely repented his crime before he is convicted and sentenced... [Such repentance], however deep and genuine, cannot alter penal desert (unless it is so immediately and intimately connected to the wrongdoing as to alter our understanding of the seriousness of the wrong): the repentant offender deserves no less severe a punishment than the unrepentant offender.

R. A. Duff[1]

Grounding his argument in his well-known communicative theory of punishment, Antony Duff has argued that "mercy involves an intrusion into the realm of criminal law of values and concerns that are not themselves part of the perspective of criminal law: a merciful sentencer acts beyond the limits of her legal role, on the basis of moral considerations that conflict with the demands of penal justice."[2]

---

1. R. A. Duff, "The Intrusion of Mercy," *Ohio State Journal of Criminal Law*, Volume 4, Number 2, Spring 2007, pp. 361–387. Antony Duff is, of course, a man who has made truly significant contributions to criminal law theory. Even when I find myself in disagreement with his claims, I am always stimulated by him and always learn from thinking about those claims. He has also been a valued friend for many years. I dedicate this essay to him with esteem and affection.
2. *Supra* note 1, p. 361.

When Duff claims that mercy—even if grounded in the repentance of the wrongdoer—involves an "intrusion" into the realm of criminal law, he does not mean to suggest that such an intrusion is always unjustified. He means simply that the cases where it is justified are cases in which the values intrinsic to criminal punishment (particularly retributive desert) are being trumped by values from a totally different moral realm. One of my favorite novelists, J. M. Coetzee, may agree with Duff here as David Lurie, the central character in his novel *Disgrace*, explains his unwillingness to provide the university disciplinary board (under which he must defend himself against sexual harassment charges) with the expressions of remorse and repentance that they seek:

> [We] went though the repentance business yesterday. I told you what I thought. I won't do it. I appeared before an officially constituted tribunal, before a branch of the law. Before that secular tribunal I pleaded guilty, a secular plea. That plea should suffice. Repentance is neither here nor there. Repentance belongs to another world, to another universe of discourse... [What you are asking] reminds me too much of Mao's China. Recantation, self-criticism, public apology. I'm old fashioned. I would prefer simply to be put against a wall and shot.[3]

I respectfully disagree with both Duff and Lurie (and perhaps Coetzee also) in this matter. In the present essay I plan to exploit the parenthetical insertion that occurs in the quoted paragraph with which I opened the essay. In so doing I will expand on a suggestion I have made in previous publications: that a significant part (but, of course,

---

3. J. M. Coetzee, *Disgrace*, New York: Viking Press, 1999. pp. 58, 66. Lurie, like Duff, is claiming that repentance belongs to another realm of discourse—one other than the legal realm. He seems to think that the other realm is religious rather than secular, however, and I see no reason to think that this is how Duff would identify the other realm.

not all) of the harm and wrong of many (perhaps all) criminal offenses is the insulting communicative message of contempt conveyed to and about the victim (and the larger community) by the commission of a criminal offense. Duff's parenthetical insertion suggests that this sort of thing happens with such infrequency as to be hardly worth mentioning. I disagree. I will argue that repentance, if a genuine withdrawal of the contemptuous message, lessens the harm and wrong in significant ways and thereby has a direct and significant bearing on the retributive punishment that the offender deserves for the crime.

If I am correct about this, it might still be considered controversial whether a reduction of punishment based on repentance should be conceptualized as mercy or rather as a more finely tuned understanding of justice. In this essay, however, I am not concerned to address this issue in any detail.[4] My concern is simply to argue that giving weight to repentance in sentencing is to give weight to a value that is *in principle* intrinsic to criminal punishment and not the intrusion of a value from a totally different moral realm.[5]

I should perhaps note in passing that I totally agree with Duff that it may sometimes be appropriate to reduce a criminal sentence—and in that sense show mercy—for reasons that are not intrinsic to penal desert itself and that thus represent intrusions into the domain of criminal law. I do not think that this is the case with repentance—

---

4. Since repentance, in my view, to some degree lessens the harm or wrong of the crime, I tend to think it is better to think that counting it as relevant to sentencing is a matter of justice rather than mercy.
5. I say "in principle" because of my belief that there are in the real world of sentencing many practical reasons why one should be skeptical of counting repentance at the time of sentencing—one of them being the difficulty of distinguishing genuine repentance from fake repentance as a strategy on the part of the defendant to get a lighter sentence. Also, there is the worry that one who seeks a lower sentence reveals thereby that he is perhaps not really repentant. I have developed these skeptical arguments at some length—along with a suggestion that such skepticism may be less justified in clemency or pardon decisions. See my "Remorse, Apology, and Mercy," *Ohio State Journal of Criminal Law*, Volume 4, Number 2, Spring 2007, pp. 423–453.

which I regard as intrinsically related to penal desert—but other reasons for reducing a sentence would fall into Duff's category. Kant, for example, imagines a case in which a criminal has so many culpable accomplices that the state itself would dissolve if all of them were punished in accord with their deserts. In a case such as this, Kant believes that the sovereign would act rightly—on consequentialist grounds—in showing mercy that is explicitly at odds with penal desert. This would indeed be an intrusion in Duff's sense—one that, if Kant is correct, would be justified intrusion.[6]

A contemporary example of an extrinsic intrusion into the realm of strict penal justice is the practice of reducing a criminal's sentence because of what are regarded as the criminal's past "good deeds"—honorable service in the military, for example. This practice has been defended by Carissa Hessick in a provocative essay. Among other things, she argues that since we count earlier bad acts (previous crimes, for example) as relevant reasons for increasing sentences, it seems reasonable to count earlier good acts as relevant reasons for decreasing sentences.[7]

Although I do not know if Hessick would agree with me, I think that such a practice—unlike counting repentance—has to be regarded as what Duff calls an intrusion into the values intrinsic to criminal law by values of another sort. Repentance is a direct repudiation of the message of contempt carried by the criminal wrong in a way that previous good acts, not having the crime in question as their object, are not.

---

6. Immanuel Kant, *Practical Philosophy*, translated by Mary J. Gregor, Cambridge: Cambridge University Press, 1996, p. 475.
7. Carissa Byrne Hessick, "Why Are Only Bad Acts Good Sentencing Factors?" *Boston University Law Review*, Volume 88, 2008, pp. 1109–1163. I wonder if the asymmetry that bothers Hessick would be less worrisome if we counted as relevant only previous crimes of the same sort as the crime for which the wrongdoer has now been convicted. It makes more sense (at least to me) to count previous convictions for crimes involving assault in determining the sentence for a current conviction of a crime involving assault than to, for example, count previous convictions for criminal fraud or shoplifting.

I will now develop in more detail my argument that repentance is intrinsic to the idea of penal desert and that it is not, in Duff's sense, an intrusion of values from a totally different context.

There is a tendency for the communicative theory of punishment to focus exclusively on what punishment communicates to and about the criminal offender. Since it is a theory of *punishment*, this is of course not surprising. However, it seems to me worth considering—as part of a larger communicative theory of *crime* and punishment—what message (literal or symbolic) the criminal wrongdoer may be conveying by his wrongdoing. Let me quote what I have previously written about the relevant communication:

> ...One reason we so deeply resent moral injuries done to us is not simply that they hurt us in some tangible or sensible way; it is because such injuries are also messages—symbolic communications. They are ways a wrongdoer has of saying to [the victim] "I count but you do not," "I can use you for my purposes," or "I am here up high and you are there down below." Intentional wrongdoing *insults* [and reveals *contempt* for the victim on the part of the wrongdoer]—and thus it involves a kind of injury that is not merely tangible and sensible. It is moral injury, and we care about such injuries. (As justice Holmes famously observed, even a dog notices and cares about the difference between being tripped over accidentally and being kicked intentionally.[8]) [Normal people] care about what [is thought and expressed] about them—how much [others] think [they] matter. Our self-respect is *social* in at least this sense, and it is simply part of the human condition that we are weak and vulnerable in these ways...
>
> But what if the wrongdoer comes to separate or divorse himself from his own evil act? (True repentance is a clear way of

---

8. Being a passionate dog lover, I have always wondered how Justice Holmes knew this. I hope it was not based on his own experience of kicking dogs intentionally.

doing this.) Then the insulting message [of contempt] is no longer present—no longer endorsed by the wrongdoer. We can then join the wrongdoer in condemning the very act from which he now stands emotionally separated… In having a sincere change of heart, he is withdrawing his endorsement from his own immoral past behavior; he is saying "I no longer stand behind the wrongdoing, and I want to be separated from it. I stand with you in condemning it." Of such a person it cannot be said that he is now conveying the message that he holds [both the victim and the relevant legal norms] in contempt."[9]

In addition to what I have said above about the message conveyed to and about the victim by acts of criminal wrongdoing, I would now like to add the thought that this message extends beyond the immediate victim to all members of the relevant community. A message of disrespect is conveyed to all law-abiding members of the community when the criminal presumes to place his own will (guided by what Kant called the "dear self") above the will of the community as realized in its properly enacted laws.[10]

---

9. Jeffrie G. Murphy (Chapters 1, 3, 5) and Jean Hampton (Chapters 2 and 4), *Forgiveness and Mercy*, Cambridge: Cambridge University Press, 1988, pp. 25–26. I have in the quoted passage replaced the original phrase "attempts to degrade" with the phrase "reveals contempt" since the word "attempt" suggests a level of intention that is misleading. I do not mean to suggest that the wrongdoer must have the *intention* of delivering a message—or even to be consciously aware that this is what he is doing. The person who rapes probably just intends to have coerced sex, just as the person who buys a slave probably just intends to have some cheap forced labor. But surely the act of each expresses, at least symbolically or tacitly, a belief or attitude about their victims that conveys a willingness to use them, in Kant's language, as mere means or things to be exploited for the wrongdoers' own selfish purposes—all without any regard for the victims' rights as persons. A society that does not explicitly condemn such acts—perhaps through such powerful symbolism as criminal punishment—can be said to endorse the same message conveyed by the wrongdoers themselves.

10. My discussion presumes that we are speaking of a just system of laws justly enforced and will ignore the special problems raised by disobedience to law based not on the claims of the dear self, but on principled and justified moral objection to the law in question.

Suppose all of the above is true. One still might ask what it has to do with criminal punishment—with the penal suffering that the criminal deserves. I will now attempt to address that issue.

To punish on retributive grounds is to punish as the criminal *deserves* to be punished.[11] Not all those who advocate retribution as a theory of punishment, however, agree on how the concept of desert is to be analyzed. (The first thing one will want to say, of course, is that desert must be analyzed as culpable wrongdoing. But how is that concept to be analyzed?) I will now run through the six (to me) most plausible accounts of retributive desert and try to show that a communicative theory of criminal wrongdoing and harm fits well into each of them.

1. *Character.* I and others have sometimes distinguished between "grievance retributivists" and "character retributivists"—the former making the punishment a function of the nature and quality of the grievance that the victim (and perhaps society as a whole) has against the criminal, the latter making this a function of the badness or evil of the character of the criminal—focusing on what Kant called

---

11. At one time I was inclined to defend very strong versions of the retributive theory of punishment. My current support for the theory is much more limited and qualified. See my presidential address to the American Philosophical Association (Pacific Division) "Legal Moralism and Retribution Revisited," *Proceedings and Addresses of the American Philosophical Association*, Volume 80, Number 2, 2006, pp. 45–62. This essay also appeared in *Criminal Law and Philosophy*, Volume 1, Number 1, 2007, pp. 5–20. I emphasize retribution in the present essay because of Duff's reliance on penal desert as an important part of his communicative theory of punishment. I also have some serious worries about the communicative theory itself. The more that a particular society is inegalitarian in its distribution of benefits and burdens, and the more that the underlying presupposition that all citizens are in fact regarded as of equal worth and value is not satisfied, then to that degree—in my view—is the communicative theory, however laudable as an aspirational ideal, largely inapplicable to that society. So my paper is in effect of an "if, then" form: *if* one subscribes to a communicative theory, and *if* one believes that penal desert is a central part of that theory, *then* one should count repentance as in principle intrinsically relevant to sentencing.

the "inner wickedness" (*inneren Bösartigkeit*) of the criminal.[12] Since repentant wrongdoers are commonly taken to have better characters than unrepentant wrongdoers, it is fairly easy to see how repentance would count as relevant on the character version of retributivism. Surely the willful violation of the norms of the criminal law and the important individual and community rights those norms seek to protect is at least some evidence of bad character; and repentance of those acts of violation some evidence of a better character.[13]

2. *Grievance.* With respect to grievance retributivism, it might initially seem that repentance could have no significant bearing on this. Why, one might well ask, would the grievance I have against a wrongdoer be less because at some later time the wrongdoer repents and even expresses sincere remorse through an act of apology? The communicative theory of harm and wrong that I have earlier suggested has, in my view, a plausible way of answering this question: to the degree that the wrongful harm is a function of the insulting and degrading message symbolically conveyed by the criminal act, then repentance—by a withdrawal of that message—lessens the wrongful harm and thus (at least in most cases) makes the criminal deserve

---

12. *Supra* note 6, p. 474. One might argue that Kant's phrase "inner wickedness" refers not to character but simply to those mental states (e.g., intention) that constitute the *mens rea* conditions for criminal offenses. Although I will not take time to argue for this here, I believe that the context surrounding Kant's remark supports my character interpretation. I also believe that *mens rea* considerations are not always easy to separate from considerations of character. Consider the *mens rea* conditions for what in American criminal law is generally called "depraved heart murder"—a killing that results from a level of recklessness so extreme as to reveal "a hardened, abandoned, and malignant heart indifferent to the value of human life." There is no canonical usage of much of the terminology that is involved in discussions of retribution. Some writers, for example, contrast character retributivism with choice retributivism. I have not elected to give choice retributivism a separate treatment in the present essay because I think that its essence—we should punish for bad choices not bad character—is captured in several of the accounts I give below.
13. Not everyone agrees with this. Cynthia Ozick, for example, holds the surprising view that repentance is an aggravating and not a mitigating factor. See my discussion of Ozick's view in my "Remorse, Apology, and Mercy" (*supra* note 5, pp. 426–428).

not acquittal surely, but less punishment than the unrepentant criminal.[14]

3. *Free Riding.* Herbert Morris is well known for defending a version of retributivism in which the criminal is said to deserve punishment as a sacrifice that, in fairness, he owes those who have been law abiding.[15] The law abiding have made the sacrifice of self-restraint—voluntarily obeying laws they would often prefer not to—and have thereby made possible the benefits that a cooperative rule of law provides for all. The criminal enjoys these benefits but, unlike the rest of us, has not made the sacrifice of obedience. Thus, by such free riding, he has gained an unfair advantage over the law abiding and owes, as a kind of debt, a comparable sacrifice—a sacrifice that we impose on him in the act of punishment.

Of course one important thing wrong with free riding is its unfairness. I do not think, however, that the deep resentment that most of

---

14. A total acquittal would typically not be proper since a message of contempt is, in my view, only one factor that contributes to the wrong and harm of the criminal conduct and thus the total package of retributive desert. Also, to the degree that the community should be seen as repudiating the message, the most effective way to do this is probably with some amount of actual punishment. Finally, letting the repentant offender off entirely would seem to me to give him too much of a role in what happens to him—as though this is all to be a function of his autonomous choices. It was perhaps excessive claims of autonomy that prompted his criminality in the first place. Herbert Fingarette's idea of law as "humbling the will," which I will discuss later in this essay, is relevant here. I use the phrase "at least in most cases" to leave open the possibility that some crimes and some criminals may be so horrendous that it would be improper to give them, even if repentant, any punishment less than the maximum that the law allows—even death if that is the maximum allowed. Are there such crimes and criminals? I have made a start in thinking about this in my "The Case of Dostoevsky's General: Some Ruminations on Forgiving the Unforgivable," *The Monist*, Volume 92, Number 4, 2009, pp. 556–582.
15. Herbert Morris, "Persons and Punishment," in his essay collection *On Guilt and Innocence*, Berkeley: University of California Press, 1976, pp. 31–58; first published in *The Monist*, Volume 52, Number 4, October 1968, pp. 475–501. It is almost impossible to overestimate the importance of this essay in the philosophy of punishment, since it almost single-handedly brought about a rebirth of retributivism as a major contender as the primary justification of punishment.

us feel toward the free rider is solely a function of the objective unfairness of what he does.[16] It is also, I believe, a function of the arrogant message of superiority that his free riding at least symbolically conveys: "I can claim for myself a degree of self-indulgence that—since I value the benefits made possible by the voluntary sacrifices of the obedient—I would not be willing to extend to others." I, and I think others, might well want to respond to this message in anger with the question, "Just who the hell do you think you are, anyway?"—a question that we would probably not raise if the wrongdoer manifested sincere repentance.

4. Reflective Equilibrium. In a justly celebrated essay, Michael Moore argues that retributivism, once freed from assorted confusions and bad arguments against it, captures better than any other theory of punishment the pretheoretical convictions that most of us have about just punishment and its relation to the concept of desert—and thereby puts us into that state of epistemic contentment that John Rawls called "reflective equilibrium."[17] I believe that many (perhaps most) of us—perhaps particularly those involved in the criminal law—have the conviction that repentance counts as relevant to penal desert, and thus a total refusal to count it would disturb our reflective equilibrium. Consider, as a few examples of this, these comments from various actors in the institution of criminal law—one from a state governor

---

16. Morris once told me that he first got the idea for his theory on a Los Angeles freeway during a period of gridlock. All drivers were waiting in long lines for their turn to enter an exit lane when Morris saw a sports car speed along the shoulder, illegally pass a great many cars, and push itself into the exit lane in front of those who had been legally waiting their turn. He said he became absolutely furious at the arrogance and presumption of the driver of this sports car. His theory came to him as he asked himself the question, "Why does this make me so resentful?"
17. Michael Moore, "The Moral Worth of Retribution," in *Responsibility, Character, and the Emotions*, edited by Ferdinand Schoeman, Cambridge: Cambridge University Press, 1987, pp. 179–219. He does not use the phrase "reflective equilibrium," but I think that this is the best way to characterize his methodology.

denying clemency, one from a prosecuting attorney, one from a sentencing judge, one from a distinguished law professor (Michael Moore), and one from a United States Supreme Court justice:

> Is Williams's [claimed redemption] complete and sincere, or is it just a hollow promise? Stanley Williams insists [against overwhelming evidence to the contrary] that he is innocent, and that he will not and should not apologize or otherwise atone for the murders of the four victims in this case. Without an apology and atonement for these senseless and brutal killings there can be no redemption. In this case, the one thing that would be the clearest indication of complete remorse and full redemption is the one thing Williams will not do.[18]

> Have you observed any repentance by Mr. McCleskey? Has he exhibited to you any sorrow? Have you seen any tears in his eyes for this act that he has done?[19]

> The vicious acts you committed on December 7, 1993, were the acts of a coward. What could be more cowardly than entering a train filled with unsuspecting, homebound commuters and systematically shooting them at point-blank range?...What is even more remarkable is your total lack of remorse.[20]

---

18. This is part of a 2005 clemency decision delivered by California Governor Arnold Schwarzenegger in which he denied Crips founder Stanley "Tookie" Williams executive clemency for his death sentence.
19. These rhetorical questions were raised in 1978 by Atlanta District Attorney Richard Parker as he argued before the jury that Warren G. McCleskey, convicted for murdering a police officer, should be shown no mercy but should be sentenced to death. (He was sentenced to death.) The quoted passage is from the transcript of the 1978 trial.
20. An excerpt from the transcript of Judge Donald E. Belfi's remarks at his sentencing of Colin Ferguson on March 22, 1995, to 200 years in prison for his conviction on six counts of murder and nineteen counts of attempted murder in an attack on commuters on a Long Island Railroad train.

> It is true that all of us are guilty of some immoralities, probably on a daily basis. Yet for most [of us]...the immoralities in question are things like not caring deeply enough about another's suffering; not being charitable for the limitations of others; convenient lies; and so forth... Few of us have raped and murdered a woman, drowned her three small children, and felt no remorse about it.[21]

> [S]erious prejudice could result if medication inhibits the defendant's capactiy...to demonstrate remorse or compassion... In [capital cases] assessments of character and remorse may carry great weight and, perhaps, be determinative of whether the offender lives or dies.[22]

5. *The Humbling of the Will.* In his presidential address to the American Philosophical Association (Pacific Division) Herbert Fingarette argued that retribution should not be seen as a moral thesis but rather as a conceptual requirement—something intrinsic to the concept of law itself.[23] Law sets norms that demand obedience—demand that the individual will of the person be subordinated to the relevant norms. The person who disobeys the norms set by law is presuming to exercise his own will in a way that the norms forbid to him. Because of this, the will of the offender must—to use Fingarette's phrase—be *humbled*. To the degree that repentance shows a will that

---

21. Moore 1987, 188.
22. Riggins v. Nevada, 504 U. S. 127, 143–144 (1992) (Kennedy, J., concurring). Realizing that sentencing agents will naturally think that a criminal lacking in remorse is particularly deserving of the death penalty, Justice Kennedy wants to make sure that an offender's failure to express remorse is truly a function of his actual character and not medication. I quote this opinion mainly as one more example of how many will find reflective equilibrium only in an account of punitive desert that makes room for repentance and remorse. It is also, of course, a good example of assessments of *character* playing a role in sentencing.
23. Herbert Fingarette, "Punishment and Suffering," *Proceedings and Addresses of the American Philosophical Association*, Volume 50, Number 6, 1977, pp. 499–525.

has already been to some degree humbled, then to that degree—in my view—does remorseful repentance (the *agenbite of inwit*) render legitimate a sentence less severe than one deserved by an offender whose arrogant presumption remains intact.[24]

6. *Victim Vindication.* In our 1988 jointly authored book, Jean Hampton—drawing I think on the communicative account I had in an earlier chapter given of criminal wrongdoing—argues that the retributive element in criminal punishment should be understood as *victim vindication*—the righting of a wrongful message about the victim that, absent the punishment, would be allowed to stand unchallenged. She thought, indeed, that this was a way to give some sense to Hegel's puzzling claim that punishment *annuls* the crime:

> This reassertion [through punishment of the victim's equal value] may be what Hegel meant when he said that punishment "annuls the crime." Of course it can't annul the act itself, but *it can annul the false evidence provided by the wrongdoing of the relative worth of the victim and the wrongdoer*. Or to put it another way, it can annul the message, sent by the crime, that they are not equal in value.[25]

If is of course absurd to think that punishment annuls the crime in the sense of making it the case that the crime never happened or now goes away. What does go away, however—and is thus annulled—is the message of disrespect for the victim and, I would say, disrespect as well for the legal order of the relevant moral community. Punishment can thus be seen as a social ritual in which,

---

24. This is my view. Fingarette does not himself make this claim about the relevance of repentance. I use here the phrase "remorseful repentance" (which I regard as redundant since I take remorse to be a component of repentance) to emphasize the painful emotional bite of conscience (the *agenbite of inwit*) that is a part of sincere repentance. I discuss remorse and repentance in some detail in my "Remorse, Apology, and Mercy" (supra note 5).
25. *Supra* note 9, p. 131.

though the symbolism of hard treatment, the message of contempt for the victim—a message that the victim is of less than equal value with the wrongdoer—is emphatically repudiated, and another message—that of the full value of the victim as an equal citizen—is emphatically asserted.

And what bearing might repentant remorse (and perhaps public apology as well) have on this vision of wrongdoing, harm, and punishment? Just this: the wrongdoer, through repentant remorse and apology, is on his own withdrawing the contemptuous message and trying to do what he can to restore equality with the victim and seek reintegration into the moral community that he has (he now sees) wrongfully insulted.

Let me now bring my essay to a close by summarizing the essence of what I have been arguing. I have challenged Duff's claim that repentance, if ever relevant to the reduction of a criminal's sentence, must be seen as an intrusion into the realm of criminal justice (particularly its commitment to penal desert) of values from an entirely different realm of discourse. I have argued that part of the harm and wrong of a criminal act is the insulting message of contempt for the victim and for the moral community itself that is conveyed by the act. Because of this intrinsic connection between the message and the criminal harm and wrong—both intrinsic to penal desert—it seems to me proper, from the perspective of penal desert itself, to count repentance (repudiation of the message of contempt) as a relevant ground for a reduction in criminal sentence. In short: if the communicative theory of punishment takes penal desert seriously, it ought in principle to count repentance as a relevant ground for reduction in criminal sentence.

I await with some trepidation Duff's response to the argument I have presented. I suspect that he will have powerful counterarguments—arguments that may force me to change my own views or leave us in the position where, neither of us being fully persuaded by the other, we must simply agree to disagree. Knowing Duff as a man of kind restraint and humility, I can at least take comfort in the fact that I will probably not have to suffer the response that my friend the late Peter Winch told me he once encountered from Jonathan Bennett. Presenting a paper at the University of British Columbia when Bennett was on the faculty there, Winch received sharp criticism from Bennett. He replied, and received even sharper criticism. Winch said that this increasingly heated exchange went back and forth until he finally said, "I think that you and I will simply have to agree to disagree about this, Jonathan." According to Winch, Bennett at this point replied, "Disagree hell! I refuted you!"

Remorse, Apology, and Mercy

It is commonly believed that legal mercy for those guilty of serious crimes is most appropriately bestowed upon those criminals who exhibit sincere remorse and repentance over what they have done—a remorse and repentance often represented by apologies to victims, survivors, and the community as a whole. As the public interest in the Karla Faye Tucker case demonstrated, many people find these displays of remorse particularly compelling if they are presented as a consequence of religious conversion. In contrast, the word "remorseless" is often used to describe those criminals who are viewed as the worst of the worst and thus as least deserving of legal mercy.

This essay—a modification of some of the author's earlier work—explores the nature of remorse, its relation to religion, the role it plays in the assessment of moral character, and the role that such a character assessment might play in decisions to grant legal mercy—in particular, decisions of judges at the time of sentencing or decisions of executives with the power to grant clemency. The complex relationship that acts of apology bear to the kind of remorse that, at least in the minds of many, makes a criminal a legitimate candidate for legal mercy is also examined. The author, exploring both moral and epistemic issues, will express considerable skepticism toward relying on judgments about offender

I thank Stephanos Bibas, Richard Dagger, Anotony Duff, Stephen Garvey, Alan Michaels, Herbert Morris, Mary Sigler, Eleonore Stump, Margaret Walker, James Weinstein, and students in my jurisprudence seminar for their comments on an earlier draft of this essay. I am particularly grateful to my colleague Michael White, whose comments forced me to think more carefully about my use of J. L. Austin's theory of speech acts, and to my wife Ellen Canacakos for the insights she has provided from her practice as a psychotherapist.

remorse at the time of sentencing, but less skepticism about relying on such judgments at the time of an executive decision to grant clemency.

> [One] night later merciless Grendel
> Struck again with more gruesome murders.
> Malignant by nature, he never showed remorse.
>
> *Beowulf*
> Seamus Heaney translation

> On this third planet form the sun,
> among the signs of bestiality
> A clear conscience is Number One.
>
> "In Praise of Feeling Bad About Yourself"
> Wislawa Szymborska

I. INTRODUCTION

It is commonly even if not universally believed that the very worst of evildoers are those who are utterly without remorse for the evil that they have done—an absence often understandably inferred form their unwillingness to express remorse by apologizing or begging forgiveness or by their not engaging in appropriate nonverbal expressive behavior—seeking out punishment, for example. Such absence of remorse may, in the words of Wislawa Szymborska, be a "sign of bestiality" or, in the phrase of Seamus Heaney, reveal them as "malignant by nature." In the legal world, such judgments can be found at various points in the criminal process—where absence of remorse may be cited as an aggravating factor that legitimately should incline us to greater harshness and certainly not to greater compassion or mercy. Here are a few examples—one from a clemency decision, one from a prosecuting attorney's argument at the sentencing stage of a criminal trial, one from a trial judge justifying a sentence, one from a distinguished legal scholar, and one from a United States Supreme Court decision:

> Is William's [claimed] redemption complete and sincere, or is it just a hollow promise? Stanley Williams insists [against overwhelming evidence to the contrary] that he is innocent, and that he will not and should not apologize or otherwise atone for the murders of the four victims in this case. Without an apology and atonement for these senseless and brutal killings there can be no redemption. In this case, the one thing that would be the clearest indication of complete remorse and full redemption is the one thing Williams will not do.[1]

> Have you observed any repentance by Mr. McCleskey? Has he exhibited to you any sorrow? Have you seen any tears in his eyes for this act that he has done?[2]

> The vicious acts you committed on December 7, 1993, were the acts of a coward. What could be more cowardly than entering a train filled with unsuspecting, homebound commuters and systematically shooting them at point-blank range?...What is even more remarkable is your total lack of remorse.[3]

---

1. Statement of Decision, Request for Clemency by Stanley Williams (December 12, 2005) (corrected version), *available at* http://www.governor.ca.gov/govsite/pdf/press_release_2005/Williams_Clemency_Decision.pdf, signed by California Governor Arnold Schwarzenegger. Governor Schwarzenegger denied Crips founder Stanley "Tookie" Williams executive clemency for his death sentence.
2. These rhetorical questions were raised in 1978 by Atlanta District Attorney Richard Parker as he argued before the jury that Warren G. McCleskey, convicted of murdering a police officer, should be shown no mercy but should be sentenced to death. (He was sentenced to death.) The quoted passage is from the transcript of the 1978 trail.
3. Judge Donald E. Belfi, remarks at the sentencing of Colin Ferguson (March 22, 1995). These remarks were offered by Nassau County Court Judge Donald E. Belfi as he defended the sentence of two hundred years that he imposed on Colin Ferguson, a man convicted on six counts of murder and nineteen counts of attempted murder in an attack on commuters on a Long Island Railroad train.

> It is true that all of us are guilty of some immoralities, probably on a daily basis. Yet for most [of us]...the immoralities in question are things like manipulating others unfairly; not caring deeply enough about another's suffering; not being charitable for the limitations of others; convenient lies; and so forth.... Few of us have raped and murdered a woman, drowned her three small children, and felt no remorse about it.[4]

> [S]erious prejudice could result if medication inhibits the defendant's capacity...to demonstrate remorse or compassion.... In [capital cases] assessments of character and remorse may carry great weight and, perhaps, be determinative of whether the offender lives or dies.[5]

Not everyone, it should be noted, agrees with the common view that the remorseless wrongdoer is worse in the sense of deserving more punishment than the wrongdoer who feels remorse or with the related view that the remorseful wrongdoer should to some degree gain our sympathy as a ground for mercy. After all, if remorseless wrongdoers really are "bestial" or "malignant by nature," they may be seen as standing outside the moral domain in which such concepts as desert or guilt or punishment make clear sense. These creatures seem to be, if not—in fairness to beasts—literally beasts, then, as psychopaths or sociopaths, possessing a trait that Kant called "moral death"—an absence of moral feeling so pervasive as to render them

---

4. Professor Michael S. Moore here uses the example of remorseless killer Steven Judy as grounds for rejecting Jesus' famous "He that is without sin...let him first cast a stone" remark as an objection to retribution and characterizing such a use as "pretty clumsy moral philosophy." Michael S. Moore, *The Moral Worth of Retribution*, in RESPONSIBILITY, CHARACTER AND THE EMOTIONS 188 (Ferdinand Schoeman ed., 1987).
5. Riggins v. Nevada, 504 U.S. 127, 143–44 (1992) (Kennedy, J., concurring). Realizing that sentencing agents will naturally think that a criminal lacking in remorse is particularly deserving of the death penalty, Justice Kennedy wants to make sure that an offender's failure to express remorse is truly a function of his actual character and not medication.

not fully human from the moral point of view. Perhaps, like mad dogs, they are—at least in principle—more candidates for extermination than for punishment.[6]

The writer Cynthia Ozick, for example, was asked by Simon Wiesenthal to consider if the claimed remorseful repentance and plea for forgiveness from Karl, a young dying Nazi SS soldier who had participated in the cruel murder of a great many Jews, should be a ground for forgiving the young soldier or at least thinking better of him. Even on the assumption that the claimed remorse was sincere, Ozick did not consider it a valid ground for softening our judgment of the soldier. Indeed, she thought his repentance was an aggravating factor rather than a mitigating one, a factor that made him worse than an unrepentant murderer. The unrepentant murderer, she speculated, is likely to be simply a thoughtless and ignorant thug or perhaps a sociopath—malignant by bestial nature rather than by choice and thus not fully responsible. The remorseful murderer, however, reveals in his very remorse that he had at the time of his act a moral conscience and knew that he was doing evil. Thus, in order to do the evil, he had to suppress that moral conscience; and this, in Ozick's judgment, makes him worse than the mere thug and thus worthy of the most severe punishment. Should we then forgive or show mercy to him on the basis of his remorse? Certainly not, says Ozick, and on the contrary says this of the dying SS soldier:

> We condemn the intelligent man of conscience because... though at heart not a savage, he allowed himself to become one, he did not resist. It was not that he lacked conscience; he

---

6. For an exploration of the Kantian concept of "moral death" and its implications for responsibility, see Jeffrie G. Murphy, *Moral Death: A Kantian Essay on Psychopathy*, 82 ETHICS 284 (1972), *reprinted in* ETHICS AND PERSONALITY 207 (John Deigh ed., 1992). I no longer endorse all the claims made in this essay, but I would like to think that it still contains some insights.

smothered it. It was not that he lacked sensibility; he coarsened it. It was not that he lacked humanity; he deadened it. The brute runs to feed Moloch because to him Moloch is not a false god, but a Delightful True Lord, the Master who brings him exaltation. In exaltation he shovels in the babies... The intelligent man of conscience also shovels in the babies, and it does not matter that he does it without exaltation. Conscience, education, insight—nothing stops him. He goes on shoveling. He knows what wickedness is... He is a morally sensitive man, and he shovels babies to glut the iron stomach of the idol... A virtuous future as a model of remorse lies ahead of him; he shovels. He shovels and shovels, all the while possessed of a refined and meticulous moral temperament—so refined and so meticulous that it knows the holy power of forgiveness and knows to ask for it... Let the SS man die unshriven. Let him go to hell. Sooner the fly to God than he.[7]

These are powerful words that should pull us up short and provide an opportunity for deep reflection. However, although I think that Ozick is on to something, her observation strikes me as insufficiently nuanced to capture the whole story. Consider the "opportunistic" cooperater in evil. Wilhelm Furtwängler, the eminent conductor of the Berlin Philharmonic during much of the Nazi period, might be an example here. Suppose, as some people have claimed, he remained in Nazi Germany in considerable awareness of the evil of the Nazi regime, knew that his remaining allowed the Nazis to use him as a powerful symbol, and remained there mainly out of

---

7. SIMON WIESENTHAL, THE SUNFLOWER 209–10 (rev. & expanded ed., 1997). In this book Wiesenthal recounts his experience of a dying SS soldier who asked him for forgiveness. Wiesenthal shared that story with various people (writers, theologians, philosophers, etc.) and asked them to write brief essays in order to answer the question of what, in their view, Wiesenthal's response should have been.

ambition and vanity—the fear that, if he left, someone else, the one he contemptuously called "little K" for example, might replace him as the leading star of German orchestral music.[8] Or consider Adolf Eichmann as a much more dramatic example. Suppose that, as Hannah Arendt suggested, he assisted in the Holocaust, not out of much genuine conviction, but mainly as a method of career advancement—thereby illustrating what she famously called "the banality of evil."[9] With respect to people of this nature, I am inclined to sympathize with Ozick and, at least as my first thought, think that had they offered any apologies, expressions of remorse, or pleas for forgiveness (they in fact did not) this might well be regarded, as the saying goes, as "a day late and a dollar short." Why? Because they surely knew full well the nature of the evil enterprise in which they were complicitous and either did not care or culpably deceived themselves about it simply in order to advance their self-interest.

Karl's story strikes me as perhaps a story of a very different sort, however. Given his youth and the susceptibility of youth to peer pressure, given the fact that he came to his adolescence at a time when most people in Germany were being charmed by National Socialism, and given that membership in the Hitler Youth was at that time almost socially mandatory for young German males, it is

---

8. Furtwängler, although perhaps the greatest conductor of his generation, had a petty streak that made it difficult for him to express admiration for any other conductor. (His expressed opinions of Toscanini, for example, were outrageous.) He particularly feared being moved aside by younger German conductors—particularly by Herbert von Karajan, whom Furtwängler contemptuously referred to as "little K" (Furtwängler was quite tall, von Karajan rather short). The Nazis could sometimes get Furtwängler to conduct on occasions with a dramatic Nazi presence (occasions he seemed to want to avoid) by telling him that if he would not conduct, then the authorities would engage von Karajan. A very entertaining way to learn a few basic things about the controversies concerning the degree of Furtwängler's cooperation with the Nazi government is to be found in the play *Taking Sides* by Ronald Harwood. Much of the dialogue of this play (made into a fairly decent film, by the way) is drawn from transcripts of Furtwängler's denazification hearings.
9. HANNAH ARENDT, EICHMANN IN JERUSALEM: A REPORT ON THE BANALITY OF EVIL (1963).

at least possible that Karl was not fully aware at the time he acted that he was advancing evil but did, at a later time and on more mature reflection, lose his "innocence," come to see the evil of what he had done, and become genuinely remorseful. It is not at all clear, at least to me, that he performed his evil actions with full knowledge and out of self-interest. Rather it seems that he may have been acting out of principles—evil principles, to be sure, but ones that he perhaps could not see as evil until he actually saw and participated in unspeakable acts that he had only before thought of in abstract terms. Perhaps, in the moral realm, knowledge by description must sometimes be supplemented by knowledge by acquaintance. Thus I am reluctant to lump him in with Furtwängler and Eichman and simply assume that any remorse he expressed must be morally irrelevant to our ultimate assessment of his character and desert. So, unlike Ozick, I would not so quickly put the fly in front of Karl on the road to God.[10]

Most people would, I suspect, defend—for the reasons given above or for other reasons—a view directly opposed to Ozick's— would argue indeed that repentance and remorse, at least with respect

---

10. Actually, I am increasingly reluctant to endorse any judgments about the final worthlessness of any human being—even the Eichmanns of the world. This is why, in discussing Furtwängler and Eichmann, I said that my *first* (but not necessarily my last) thought was to apply Ozick's dismissive analysis to them. For some of the reasons behind the softening of retributive views I have previously defended in such matters, see my *Legal Moralism and Retribution Revisited*, in 1 CRIMINAL LAW AND PHILOSOPHY 5 (2007). This was my 2006 presidential address to the American Philosophical Association, Pacific Division, and has also appeared in 80 PROCEEDINGS AND ADDRESSES OF THE AMERICAN PHILOSOPHICAL ASSOCIATION 45 (2006). For rich discussions of how we might come to see precious humanity even in those who have performed acts of great evil—discussions to some degree inspired by Simone Weil—see RAIMOND GAITA, GOOD AND EVIL: AN ABSOLUTE CONCEPTION (2d ed. 2004), and RAIMOND GAITA, A COMMON HUMANITY: THINKING ABOUT LOVE AND TRUTH AND JUSTICE (2000). For a rich essay exploring the way in which a "stain on the soul" can remain even on a repentant wrongdoer, see Eleonore Stump, *Personal Relations and Moral Residue*, in HISTORY OF THE HUMAN SCIENCES: THEORIZING FROM THE HOLOCAUST—WHAT IS TO BE LEARNED? 33 (Paul Roth & Mark S. Peacock eds., 2004).

to some individuals, are among the best reasons one could have for granting mercy. Sister Helen Prejean, for example was highly critical of George W. Bush's decision (when he was governor of Texas) not to grant clemency to Karla Faye Tucker—a death row inmate who had converted to Christianity and who seemed to be genuinely repentant and to exhibit remorse for what she had done. Suspecting that Bush's decision in this case revealed that his claim to be a Christian was either ignorant or insincere, she has this to say about him and his decision:

> Here was Karla Faye, a woman who had transformed her life and would have been a source of healing love to guards and prisoners for as long as she lived, yet the iron protocol of retributive justice demanded that she be put to death.... I already knew the substance of Bush's position toward Karla Faye, but [when I heard him say] "May God bless Karla Faye Tucker and may God bless her victims and their families"... my anger at George W. Bush turned to outage... I had to struggle to keep a vow I made to reverence every person, even those with whom I disagree most vehemently. Inside my soul I raged at Bush's hypocrisy... [I tried] to reign myself in, I took a deep breath, said a fierce prayer, looked into the camera and said "It's interesting to see that Governor Bush is now invoking God, asking God to bless Karla Faye Tucker, when he certainly didn't use the power in his own hands to bless her. He just had her killed."[11]

---

11. Sister Helen Prejean, *Death in Texas*, N.Y. Rev. Books, Jan. 13, 2005, *available at* http://www.nybooks.com/articles/17670 (Sister Helen Prejean describing, in a 2005 essay, her earlier futile struggles to save the life of Karla Faye Tucker). I would not presume to speculate on the sincerity of President Bush's claimed commitment to Christianity. It is worth pointing out, however, that Sister Prejean is confused here. One cannot legitimately

Earlier in the same essay, Sister Prejean summarizes the case she had made in favor of merciful clemency for Karla Faye Tucker.

> Yes, [she was] guilty of a horrible crime—she killed two helpless people with a pickax—but she seems genuinely remorseful for her crime; she seems to have undergone a genuine life-changing religious conversion. Even the warden and corrections officers attest that for fourteen years she's been a model prisoner. Couldn't she spend the rest of her life helping other prisoners to change their lives? Is a strict "eye for an eye" always called for?[12]

In this essay, I propose to examine the concepts of apology and remorse, explore some of their moral and epistemic dimensions, and finally discuss whether they have any legitimate role to play in showing mercy. I have previously written about remorse and apology in connection with criminal sentencing, and I will here revisit some of the ideas I presented in those writings—will even steal most of the text from one of them—but will substantially modify (even abandon) some of those ideas and extend some of them into other areas of criminal law where mercy may be thought appropriate—in particular, the area of executive clemency.[13] I will argue that the moral issues

---

infer from the fact that a person believes that a criminal deserves the secular death penalty the conclusion that this person cannot consistently hope for the salvation of the soul of the criminal who is executed—the meaning surely of "may God bless" in this context. Were all judges who closed their sentences of death with "and may God have mercy on your soul" being confused or hypocritical? I think not.

12. *Id.*
13 The essay (a transcript of public lecture) on which I am mainly drawing is *Well Excuse Me!—Remorse, Apology, and Criminal Sentencing*, 38 ARIZ. ST. L.J, 371 (2006). It is an occasion of some embarrassment to me that in the present essay I am correcting a major mistake in an essay that appeared so recently. I am not sure why my insight into the need for a correction did not come earlier, but I am inclined to blame Michael White for not noticing the mistake when he read the earlier essay—a mistake for which he has, of course, to some degree atoned by catching it this time around. (The mistake, to be discussed in detail later,

raised by apology and remorse are roughly the same in both sentencing and clemency decisions, but that the epistemic situation in the two areas may differ substantially.

II. A PRELIMINARY DIGRESSION

Prior to my primary discussion, there are two points I would like briefly to discuss: (1) an ambiguity in the concept of remorse and (2) the difference, not always appreciated, between religious conversion and remorse.

A. *Two Kinds of Remorse*

In an earlier essay, understanding remorse simply to be feelings of guilt over wrongdoing, I characterized repentance in the following way:

> Repentance is the remorseful acceptance of responsibility for one's wrongful and harmful actions, the repudiation of the aspects of one's character that generated the actions, the resolve to do one's best to extirpate those aspects of one's character, and the resolve to atone or make amends for the harm that one has done.[14]

---

concerns the issue of the degree to which apologies are performative utterances.) In the present essay I have also drawn on my *Repentance, Punishment, and Mercy*, in REPENTANCE: A COMPARATIVE PERSPECTIVE 143 (Amitai Etzioni & David E. Carney eds., 1997) [hereinafter Murphy, *Repentance, Punishment, and Mercy*].

14. Murphy, *Repentance, Punishment, and Mercy, supra* note 13, at 147. Purely for the sake of simplicity, I will sometimes in the text use "remorse" and "repentance" interchangeably. Speaking strictly, however, it should be noted that—as indicated here—remorse is only one component (though in my view the most important one) of full repentance. I believe that the resolve to reform oneself and to make amends are also important components of full repentance.

I still think that this analysis of repentance is generally in the right ballpark, but I have now come to realize that the concept of remorse involves a complexity I had not previously appreciated, a complexity that shows that in at least one of its forms it should not simply be identified with guilt. In other words, I will note a way in which the word "remorse" is ambiguous.

Consider the unjustified and unexcused breaking of a reasonably important promise—one of significance to the person to whom the promise has been made, but not one the breaking of which will cause irrevocable harm to that person. In such a case, some nontrivial guilt feelings would surely be expected of a morally serious person, but many would be reluctant to use the word "remorse" to capture these feelings—preferring to reserve the word "remorse" to capture those extremely powerful guilt feelings that are appropriately attached only to grave wrongs and harms. Indeed, for a person to feel and express remorse over wrongs or harms that are less than grave might well strike many not as a sign of moral seriousness, but simply as neurotic—nonneurotic remorse involving great and powerful guilt only in cases where this is proportional to what has been done.

The difference between some cases of remorse and other instances of guilt is not simply a matter of degree, however. This is because I have come to think that a kind of *hopelessness* is essential to the inconsolable bite of conscience—what some medievals called the *agenbite of inwit*—that is the essence of one kind of remorse. This kind of remorse, although having powerful guilt feelings as a component, seems to involve more than guilt—seems to involve the idea that the wrong one has done is so deep, has involved such a wanton assault on the very meaning of a person's human life, that one can in no sense ever make it right again—such a possibility being permanently lost. Breaking a promise is typically not a wrong of this nature. Blinding a person is—as is murdering a person or that person's beloved child. Rape and torture also come to mind as other examples. In these cases one has inflicted such a moral horror on one's victim that he or she may never again have a secure grasp of their place in the world or of the meaning of their lives.[15]

And what would atonement look like in such extreme cases? Certainly not compensation in the sense of a tort law remedy—e.g., financial sacrifice in the payment of damages—since the very idea of making the victims whole again, returning them to status quo ante, may be so obviously impossible that the very suggestion seems obscene. In these cases, the best that one might be able to do in the way of atonement would be an extreme form of penance—e.g., Stavrogin's suicide (in Dostoevsky's novel *The Devils*) or Father Sergius' cutting off his finger with an axe (in Tolstoy's story "Father Sergius").[16] Even then, however, even if one tried to impose on oneself some "eye for an eye" suffering as intense as the suffering one has caused, could one ever put the wrong fully behind one and honestly say, "Now I have made it up, can forget about it, and simply get on with my own life"? Probably not. This may be in part because whatever suffering one imposes on oneself is a result of one's own choices—something that victims cannot say of themselves with respect to the suffering imposed on them. Even in extreme self-imposed penance, penance of great suffering, one still retains an autonomy that one has denied to one's victims. Thus, no matter what one might do, one could never fully get right with victims of this

---

15. The concept of "moral horror" has been richly explored by Robert Merrihew Adams in his book FINITE AND INFINITE GOODS (2003), and the related concept of "horrendous evil" has been richly explored by Marilyn McCord Adams in her book HORRENDOUS EVILS AND THE GOODNESS OF GOD (1999).
16. I do not mean to suggest that the sole explanation of Stavrogin's suicide is an expression of remorse and an attempt at penance. Some competing Nietzschean fantasies of heroic will are also at work in this complex and troubled character. I am grateful to Stephanos Bibas for discussion of this novel.

nature.[17] (Whether one could ever get right with God after such atrocities is a different matter.[18])

The points I want to make in the main body of this essay will rarely require my distinguishing between the two kinds of remorse that I have highlighted, and—unless otherwise noted—I will generally use the word "remorse" in such a way as to elide the distinction. When there is an ambiguity in our language, however, as I have suggested there is with the word "remorse," this sometimes points to a difference in concepts. Thus the distinction between two kinds of remorse seems to me worth making if only in the interest of total conceptual clarity. Even if the distinction will not do much work in the present context, it might do considerable work in another and will thus be useful to keep at least in the back of one's mind.

B. Religious Conversion, Repentance, and Remorse

It is very commonly thought that religious conversion is closely linked to remorse over and repentance of criminal wrongdoing—perhaps even a necessary condition for the latter two or even equivalent to them.

17. "[I]n the case of remorse, 'there are no set ways to remedy evil.' One has destroyed an object of value and this destruction may be, precisely, irremediable." Alan Thomas, *Remorse and Reparation: A Philosophical Analysis*, in REMORSE AND REPARATION 127, 130 (Murray Cox ed., 1999). Thomas is quoting from John Deigh's important essay "Love, Guilt, and the Sense of Justice" from Deigh's essay collection THE SOURCES OF MORAL AGENCY: ESSAYS IN MORAL PSYCHOLOGY AND FREUDIAN THEORY (1996).

18. Our secular concepts of repentance and remorse no doubt have at least part of their origin in religion, but the secular meaning of those concepts can differ substantially from at least some religious meanings. From a purely secular perspective, it does indeed seem odd to think that remorse might legitimately attach to both trivial wrongs and serious wrongs. From some religious perspectives, however, all sins might be viewed as affronts to God and thus equally serious and demanding the same level of remorse. Also God's ability to forgive may be infinite in a way that it would be unreasonable to think likely for mere human beings. So even if getting right with my neighbor may sometimes be impossible, no matter how much remorse I feel, getting right with God may still be regarded as possible. Indeed, to believe otherwise is often regarded as the unforgivable sin of despair.

This way of thinking is mistaken. A genuine religions conversion would surely lead to remorse over and repentance of one's sins, but this does not entail that the concept of sin involved will be equivalent to criminal wrongdoing. Suppose someone of a totally secular frame of mind becomes a terrorist engaged in the criminal killing of innocent people as a way of supporting Palestinian liberation—a cause he supports for purely secular political reasons. Further suppose that at some later time he converts to radical Islamic fundamentalism. It is likely that, rather than repenting of his acts of terrorism and feeling remorse over them, he will be even more convinced than before that he has been engaged in a righteous cause—a cause now viewed as righteous on both secular and religious grounds. This example should show that the concepts of religious conversion and repentance/remorse, although sometimes and perhaps even often causally linked, are not equivalent. Nor is one a necessary or sufficient condition for the other. Sincerely religious people can be utterly unrepentant for (at least some of) their crimes, and some sincerely repentant people can be totally nonreligious or even antireligious.

A related point I will here state simply as a guess since I am not sufficiently studied in evangelical Christianity to have an expert opinion on the matter: Many evangelical Christians speak of their conversion experiences as being "born again" and describe themselves as starting with a clean slate, as "beginning again." On one interpretation of this way of talking, it seems to me that one might be encouraged not to spend much time looking to or thinking about the past (and remorse involves rather consuming thinking about the past) because, having now been saved by perceiving the direct intervention of Jesus into one's life, one is now in some sense a "new person"—not the same person who committed those terrible past criminal acts. Indeed, an excessive brooding over one's past sins, particularly if it results in the kind of hopeless and inconsolable remorse I discussed above, may approach the sin of despair, the sin of believing that God's forgiveness and love are forever lost. This sin, very likely the one exhibited by Judas when he hanged himself, is the one sin that is often regarded as unforgivable.

But perhaps all my example shows is the mysteriousness—even incoherence—of "new person" talk if such talk is taken at all literally.

Now that these two preliminary points are out of the way, let me move to the primary question of my essay: What legitimate role, if any, should remorse or apology on the part of the wrongdoer play in the administration of legal punishment and legal mercy?

III. REMORSE AND THE CULTURE OF APOLOGY

Must successful apology always be linked with remorse? Surely not. For small wrongs, the mere verbal formulae "I apologize" or "I am sorry" or "Forgive me" or "Excuse me" are generally adequate since their only function is to keep oiled the wheels of civility and good manners. What works for small wrongs is likely to be quite unacceptable for wrongs of greater magnitude, however. For grave wrongs, we—both victims and spectators—normally expect more than a verbal formula—perhaps nothing as extreme as Stavrogin's suicide or Father Sergius' cutting off his finger with an axe, but we expect something more than mere apology as a formality. Here we normally expect such things as repentance, remorse (in at least one of its forms), and atonement; and we are interested in apologies only to the degree that we believe that they are sincere external signs of repentance and remorse and reliable external signs of future atonement.

One of the things I intend to do in this essay is to explore the relationship between apology and these others states. Herbert Morris once published a wonderful essay with the title "The Decline of

Guilt"[19] and an alternative title for my essay could have been "The Decline of Remorse"—a decline that I believe is revealed, paradoxically enough, in the increasing prevalence and even celebration of public apology that we find in early twenty-first century America. We now live in what has been called the "new culture of apology"[20]—a cultural movement so pervasive that at least one novelist, Jay Rayner, has found it worthwhile to write a satirical novel (*Eating Crow*) about it—a novel that begins with an apology for the book itself:

> I am sorry you bought this book. If it was given to you as a gift, then technically I am not required—or even entitled—to apologize to you. My apology should go to the original purchaser and they, in turn, should say sorry.[21]

Some people, of course, find the growing culture of apology a very good thing, whereas others—and I count myself among them—fear that it may be little more than a sign of what theologians have called "cheap grace." Those who defend the development will typically see it as advancing general social utility and progress, goals that will be retarded if we remain stuck in the past. "Let bygones be bygones, says Werner von Braun" as the old Tom Lehrer song has it.

Bad people, it should be noted, are often quick studies of social trends that can be used to their advantage, and so it is now not uncommon to find such phrases as "it is time to get this all behind us and move forward" or, more recently, "let's not play the blame game" shamelessly and almost instantly on the lips of wrongdoers—often those in high political office. And those who speak this way—or buy it from others who speak this way—either do not notice or do not

---

19. Herbert Morris, *The Decline of Guilt*, 99 ETHICS 62 (1988), reprinted in ETHICS AND PERSONALITY, *supra* note 6, at 117.
20. Nicholas Mills, *The New Culture of Apology*, DISSENT, Fall 2001, at 113.
21. JAY RAYNOR, EATING CROW 1 (2004).

care that this way of responding to wrongdoing gives no weight at all to such values as truth or justice or genuine character reformation. Indeed, the more that people lap up this sort of thing, the more are wrongdoers tempted to celebrate their own corruption. Mindful of the old proverb, "It is hard to beg forgiveness, but not as hard as asking permission," these wrongdoers may even take delight in their opportunity to apologize—as revealed in this *New Yorker* cartoon:[22]

"*Hi, hon. Guess who's going to be on national television apologizing to the American public.*"

Such a celebration of form over substance is not always defended merely on grounds of progress and general utility, however. It may also be defended on moral or religious grounds or on grounds of mental health.

Here, for example, is a piece of idiocy about apology—one that deprives it of any useful meaning—cloaked in the language of idiotic theology. I quote it from the magazine *The Living Church*, self described as "An independent weekly serving Episcopalians." In a column devoted to "Advent Preparation," this theological gem occurs in what is supposed to be a commentary on the readings for the first Sunday in Advent:

22. © *The New Yorker Collection* 2000 Charles Barsotti from cartoonbank.com, published in The New Yorker on Oct. 16, 2000. All Rights Reserved. Used by Permission.

> We're prepared to meet the Lord to the extent that we live out his kingdom's values here and now. We're to honor and respect one another without qualification. We're to apologize when we offend the sensibilities of our sisters and brothers, even when they know we haven't done wrong.[23]

Surely we should ask a few skeptical questions before pledging our allegiance to this piece of treacle. If I have done nothing wrong, then what exactly am I supposed to be apologizing for? "Offending their sensibilities," it would seem. But what if they are *wrongly* sensitive, being offended by what is simply honest criticism—as (for example) poor students often are, desperately wanting some explanation other than their own lack of ability or preparation for their failures? I should be apologizing to them? I think not. The suggestion that I should is simply some mixture of mushy sentimentality and political correctness masquerading as theology and morality. I am reminded here of the way that *The Living Bible*, often an unintended source of theological humor, renders "Judge not that ye be not judged" at Matthew 7:1 as "Don't criticize, and then you won't be criticized."

Added to arguments of social utility and theology are, as we might expect in our present therapeutic culture, arguments grounded in trendy notions of mental health where such gems of psychobabble as "closure" and "a time for healing" are the order of the day. So sloppy, indeed, is the current state of theology and morality that these shibboleths of pop psychology sometimes simply pass *as* theology and morality. Even Bishop Desmond Tutu, generally a man of wisdom and charm, frequently heaps praise on the spiritual and mental health he sees exhibited by those who accept the "reconciliation" offered by the South African Truth and Reconciliation Commission—perhaps

---

23. The Living Church, Nov. 28, 2004, at 4.

without realizing that this seems to suggest, at least by implication, that those who do not wish to reconcile with those who victimized them may suffer from some kind of moral and psychological failing. And this is not even a failure on their part to accept an apology, since the guards and jailers who appeared before the commission were not required to apologize as a condition of amnesty for their atrocities—for example, the torture and murder of those imprisoned by the apartheid government.

My reader can certainly see by now that I am inclined to throw something of a wet blanket over the hasty and undue celebration of apology that is current in our culture, and in what follows I will attempt to develop, to the degree that topic and space limitations allow, a more careful and nuanced discussion of what I have so far merely sketched.

IV. REMORSE, REPENTANCE, AND PUNISHMENT

Since this is a symposium that is focused on the possible roles of mercy in the criminal law, I will obviously not be able to explore all the current important cultural issues with respect to apology and remorse. I will not, for example, explore the odd fact—called to my attention by both Herbert Morris and Margaret Walker—that the mania for public apology in legal and other institutional settings coexists with a frequent unwillingness of people to apologize in the setting of intimate personal relationships. I will not even explore all the current important legal issues—many of which emerge in tort law[24]—and some involving the very complex matter of groups apologizing and express-

---

24. Lee Taft, *Apology Subverted: The Commodification of Apology,* 109 YALE L.J. 1135 (2000). Taft's skepticism about apology in tort law inspired me to turn my own skeptical eye to apology in criminal law.

ing remorse to other groups. I will confine myself to criminal law and even here my discussion will be limited in the main to remorse and apology with respect to serious felonies. I have no hope of settling anything in a brief essay, but I will offer a few observations in the hope that they might stimulate productive thought and conversation. A detailed argument in defense of an expanded role for apology in all aspects of criminal law can be found in a recent essay by Stephanos Bibas and Richard A. Bierschbach,[25] and I have—earlier in this essay—cited some real-world examples in which apology or remorse (or their absence) have had legal relevance in the criminal law, either as arguing for mercy or arguing against mercy. I will begin my discussion here, however, by taking an example from a work of fiction.

David Lurie, the central character in J. M. Coetzee's novel *Disgrace*, has admitted sexual harassment of a student but could save his job if he simply apologized and expressed the kind of repentance and remorse demanded of him by the university disciplinary board that has punitive authority over him. In refusing to give them what they went, he says the following:

> [W]e went through the repentance business yesterday. I told you what I thought. I won't do it. I appeared before an officially constituted tribunal, before a branch of the law. Before that secular tribunal I pleaded guilty, a secular plea. That plea should suffice. Repentance is neither here nor there. Repentance belongs to another world, to another universe of discourse.... [What you are asking] reminds me too much of Mao's China. Recantation, self-criticism, public apology. I'm old fashioned, I would prefer simply to be put against a wall and shot.[26]

---

25. Stephanos Bibas & Richard A. Bierschbach, *Integrating Apology and Remorse into Criminal Procedure*, 114 YALE L.J. 85 (2004). This is the most detailed and persuasive case for an expanded role for apology in criminal law that I have encountered.
26. J.M. COETZEE, DISGRACE 58, 66 (1999).

What I find most interesting in this passage is Lurie's identification of the mechanism of legal or quasi-legal punishment as *secular* and his claim that talk of repentance, remorse, and apology has no business in such a secular context. His point, presumably, is that these concepts—particularly the concepts of remorse and repentance—are at their core *religious* concepts and that their introduction into a secular context is radically misplaced.

Why might one think this? One possibility is the belief that repentance and remorse are conditions of one's very soul and that the secular state acts wrongly—perhaps even impiously—in presuming to inquire into such private matters and to make secular punishment depend on secular guesses about when these states of character or soul are present. These are, one might think, private religious or spiritual matters between a person and one's God, matters that might be corrupted if the outcome of legal proceedings could depend on them. Indeed, desires for legal leniency might tempt one into *sin*—into confusing genuine repentance with soul-damaging fakery, hypocrisy, and self-deception. So concerned was ancient Jewish law to avoid such temptations to sin, indeed, that even confessions, and not just apologies and expressions of remorse, were inadmissible in criminal proceedings.[27] It has also been argued that our own constitutional protections against self-incrimination may have some similar religious foundations.[28]

Another related consideration here is that issues of deep character are matters about which the state is probably incompetent to judge—it cannot even deliver the mail very efficiently, after all—and which, for that reason and others, might well be regarded as simply none of the state's business. On one fairly traditional understanding of the liberal state, for example, it is legitimately concerned with prohibiting

---

27. Creyle G. Bader, "*Forgive Me Victim for I Have Sinned*": *Why Repentance and the Criminal Justice System Do Not Mix—A Lesson From Jewish Law*, 31 FORDHAM URB. L.J. 69, 70 (2003).
28. Rebert S. Gerstein, *Privacy and Self-Incrimination*, 80 ETHICS 87 (1970).

acts that are not in conformity with its public rules but treads on dangerous ground if it seeks to inquire too deeply into the private attitudes that offenders have when they manifest nonconformity. The liberal state might legitimately explore such *mens rea* conditions as intention, since these define the prohibited act itself; but inquiring into deep character, perhaps even motive on some understandings of that concept, may be viewed as going into matters beyond its legitimate scope.

It is not just liberals and secularists, however, who worry about the issues raised above. Queen Elizabeth I, for example—hardly a liberal and hardly a secularist—surely had some of these concerns in mind when, in imposing the Religious Settlement that stabilized the Church of England, she said, "I would not open windows into men's souls." Elizabeth's primary worry was no doubt prudential—her realization of how speculations about the interior lives of various of her subjects could easily become hostage to disruptive political factionalism. Her worries might have been religious as well, however, since deeply religious people who place great weight on the religious significance of repentance and remorse or other inner states of character might oppose blending such matters with criminal law not because they do not value them but rather because they value them so very much—so much that they do not want to risk having them tainted by secular legal mechanisms. Such blending might work out splendidly in Dostoevsky novels but work far less splendidly in the messy real world of actual criminal law, a world in which what passes for justice is administered by always fallible, often fearful, and sometimes cruel and corrupt human beings. You will not, I suspect, find very many contemporary American criminal prosecutors who, like Dostoevsky's Porfiry Petrovich, have a deep, honest, and informed concern with the spiritual reclamation of the criminals whom they must pursue, arrest, and bring to trial; and I am not at all sure that our society would or should welcome anyone who would presume to be such a prosecutor.

Let us grant, then, that Coetzee has, through his character of David Lurie, revealed some spiritual and even political dangers that can be present when religious concepts of remorse and repentance are brought into secular tribunals. To the degree that he is suggesting that all concepts of remorse and repentance are religious in nature, however, then it seems to me that he is simply mistaken.

Remorse (as bad conscience) is, as I have argued elsewhere, often best understood as the painful combination of guilt and shame that arises in a person when that person accepts that he has been responsible for seriously wronging another human being—guilt over the wrong itself, and shame over being forced to see himself as a flawed and defective human being who, through his wrongdoing, has fallen far below his own ego ideal.[29] Shame should provoke repentance—the resolve to become a new and better person—and guilt should (where this is possible) provoke atonement—embracing whatever personal sacrifice may be required to restore the moral balance that one's wrongdoing has upset and to vindicate the worth of one's victim, a worth that one's wrongdoing has symbolically denied. This may be a sacrifice of liberty or even life (a punishment in proportion to the wrong one has done) or it may be a sacrifice of resources—e.g., the paying of restitution. "Put your money where your mouth is" is, I think, a cliché with legitimate bite, since the willingness to make sacrifices is a relevant if not conclusive test of sincerity.

Why, one might ask, are such remorse and repentance of value and worthy of our respect? One of the reasons is, of course, found in those religious perspectives previously discussed but is not limited to them. Even the atheist can believe that the person who is sincerely remorseful and repentant over his wrongdoing exhibits a better and more admirable character than a wrongdoer who is not repentant.

---

29. *See* Jeffrie G. Murphy, *Shame Creeps through Guilt and Feels Like Retribution*, 18 LAW & PHIL. 327 (1999).

Cynthia Ozick to the contrary, most of us probably believe that simply having a character properly connected to correct values, even if late in coming, is an intrinsic good—something worthy of our respect quite independently of any external consequences it may have. Remorseful persons can also serve as "models of remorse" (to use Cynthia Ozick's phrase against her)—models of what is humanly possible in the realm of self-transformation, models that will perhaps make us less discouraged in our hopes for our own moral and spiritual progress.[30]

Remorse and repentance may also have useful social consequences, and these may matter as well. It is often said, for example, that people who are remorseful and repentant are less dangerous, less likely to do wrong again, than those who are unremorseful and unrepentant. I hope that this is true, but I am not sure. The wrongdoer can be self-deceptive or just honestly mistaken about the sincerity of his own repentance, and even the sincerely repentant wrongdoer can suffer from weak will. It is not for nothing that the term "backsliding" plays a role in both our moral and religious vocabularies, and the concept of weakness of will (*akrasia*) has produced a vast body of philosophical and religious writing. Surely Jesus' disciples were sincere when they promised to stay awake and keep watch while he prayed at Gethsemane, but he found them asleep and could only observe, "The spirit is willing but the flesh is weak."

Another external consequence worth noting is one that may have its most meaningful impact on victims. As I have argued elsewhere,[31] a wrongful act is, among other things, a *communicative* act. When one is wronged by another, a nontrivial portion of the hurt may be the

---

30. I am grateful to Ellen Canacakos for this insight about the way in which seeing self-transformation in others may assist us in gaining confidence for our own attempts in this regard.
31. Jeffrie G. Murphy, *Forgiveness and Resentment*, in FORGIVENESS AND MERCY 14–34 (1988); JEFFRIE G. MURPHY, GETTING EVEN: FORGIVENESS AND ITS LIMITS (2003).

receipt of an insulting and degrading symbolic message delivered by the wrongdoer, the message, "I matter more than you and can use you, like a mere object or thing, for my own purposes." The repentant person repudiates this message, stands with his victim in its repudiation, and acknowledges moral equality with the victim—an equality denied by the wrongdoing. It is for this reason that repentance may open the door to forgiveness. If one forgives the unrepentant wrongdoer, then one risks sacrificing one's own self-respect through complicity in or tacit endorsement of the insulting and degrading message contained in the wrongdoing. A repentant wrongdoer, however, eliminates at least this one obstacle to forgiveness. To the degree that the whole community, and not just the individual victim, is a victim of criminal wrongdoing, then repentance on the part of the wrongdoer can have symbolic significance for the community as well.

But even if repentance is a great moral and spiritual good—one carrying both actual and symbolic significance—it does not follow, given the limitations of the secular state, that it should play any significant role in the criminal law. Repentance may make victims feel better, and rightly so, but it is by no means clear to what degree, if any, the system of criminal law should be driven by the goal of victim satisfaction. Perhaps it should be, but that—as revealed in the leading victim impact statement cases—is controversial.[32]

Another real problem here is not theoretical but is practical, and how one deals with it may depend on one's general attitude toward the human world—on whether that attitude is largely trusting or largely suspicious. The practical problem is obvious—namely, the perpetual possibility of self-serving fakery on the part of wrongdoers. As Montaigne observed, there is "no quality so easy to counterfeit as

---

32. In the 1987 case *Booth v. Maryland*, 482 U.S. 496 (1987), the United States Supreme Court ruled that the use of victim impact statements in capital sentencing is unconstitutional. In 1991, *Booth* was overruled in *Payne v. Tennessee*, 501 U.S. 808 (1991). The various judicial opinions on both sides (in both cases) reward study and reflection.

piety"[33]—an observation echoed, so I have been told, by a Hollywood mogul who said this of sincerity: "Sincerity is the most precious thing in the would. When you have learned to fake that, you've got it made."

So a practical problem with giving credit for remorse and repentance is that they are so easy to fake; and our grounds for suspecting fakery only increase when a reward (e.g., a reduction in sentence, clemency, pardon, amnesty, etc.) is known to be more likely granted to those who can persuade the relevant legal authority that they manifest these attributes of character. To the degree we give rewards for goodness of character, then to that same degree do we give wrongdoers incentives to fake goodness of character. One might even suspect, indeed, that the truly remorseful and repentant wrongdoer—particularly one whose remorse is of the second kind noted previously—would not seek a reduction in punishment but would rather see that punishment as one step on a long and perhaps endless road of atonement. Although this is not necessarily the case, the person who asks us to go easy on him because he is repentant may reveal, in that very request, that he is *not* repentant. And to the degree that we hand out rewards to those who fake repentance and remorse, then to that same degree do we cheapen the currency of repentance and remorse—making us less likely to treat the real article with the respect it deserves.

Worries about fakery and inducements to fakery might have been among the reasons that prompted those who designed the South African Truth and Reconciliation Commission (TRC) not to require apology or expressions of remorse from those seeking amnesty through the commission. All that was required was full disclosure of wrongdoing and acceptance of responsibility for that wrongdoing. Since the commission's design was under the strong influence of Anglican Bishop Desmond Tutu, we may be confident that he—as a

---

33. Michel de Montaigne, *Of Repentance*, in THE COMPLETE ESSAYS OF MONTAIGNE 617 (Donald M. Frame trans., 1958).

Christian clergyman—did not leave out apologies or expressions of remorse because he did not value them. More likely, he simply did not want to give incentives to fakery, increase cynicism about such expressions, and thereby devalue the general currency of repentance and remorse. Coetzee, a South African novelist, may well have had that country's TRC in mind when he told the story of David Lurie's refusal to apologize or express remorse before the secular tribunal that had him in its punitive power.[34]

---

[34] In commenting on an earlier draft of this essay, Alan Michaels called to my attention the fact that the distinction between acknowledging wrongdoing and the further steps of either repentance or apology may be found, not only in the workings of the South African TRC, but also in the United States Federal Sentencing Guidelines. The most common method by which an offender lowers his "offense level" under the guidelines is through "Acceptance of Responsibility" under Section 3E1.1 of the FSG. Pleading guilty is almost always both a necessary and sufficient condition for acceptance of responsibility (though technically, it is neither necessary nor sufficient, since the sentencing judge is said, with no clear explanation of what this means, to have some discretion). Remorse, repentance, or apology, as opposed to acknowledgment of wrongdoing, are not formally required, or even expressly made relevant. Perhaps this approach of federal law is because of the difficulty of determining the sincerity of repentance and remorse and the likely outcome of the cheapening of apology that might follow from their mere rote offering. On the other hand, there are (as I will note later) some reasons—from both a utilitarian and retributive perspective—why remorse or apology might merit a lower sentence, making federal law's failure to capture these reasons interesting. Of course, it may simply be that the guidelines are not attentive to many of the distinctions and evaluative judgments noted in this essay. The single mention of remorse in the commentary is this: "This [downward] adjustment [for acceptance or responsibility] is not intended to apply to a defendant who puts the government to its burden of proof at trial by denying the essential factual elements of guilt, is convicted, and only then admits guilt and expresses remorse." The use of the word "remorse" is interesting here since simple admission of guilt (absent remorse) will normally earn a downward adjustment pretrial, and all the remorse in the world added to posttrail acceptance of responsibility will not result in a downward adjustment. This gives rise to the suspicion that the guidelines give credit only for pretrial acceptance of responsibility (with or without remorse) because the "mercy" the defendant receives in return is really nothing more than a quid pro quo for saving the government and the witnesses the social costs of a trial, one benefit that is not gained by posttrial acceptance and one that is not a value that we normally associate with mercy when we think of mercy as a moral virtue. The relevant guideline and commentary may be found at 18 U.S.C.S. app.§ 3E1.1 (2006), available at http://www.ussc.gov/2005guid/3e1_1.htm.

The degree to which expressions of repentance and remorse are to be welcomed as grounds for legal mercy will, of course, depend to a substantial degree on the reasons that incline one to favor criminal punishment in the first place. All of my readers are, I am sure, familiar with the main justifications frequently offered for criminal punishment—deterrence, rehabilitation, and retribution—so let me briefly explore how repentance and remorse might or might not fit into each of these.

If one thinks that the main purpose of punishment is special deterrence, then one will favor counting repentance and remorse if one believes that remorsefully repentant people are less likely to commit future crimes—a controversial claim, surely. Such people may also seem to need less in the way of incapacitation. If one places greater weight on general deterrence, however, one may reasonably believe that this is to some degree undermined if it becomes known that one way to avoid serious punishment is to express repentance and remorse.

What about rehabilitation? This is not much talked about these days, alas, in our rather vindictive and stingy society. If what used to be called "the rehabilitative ideal" does return, however, and if we begin seeking to design penal practices with rehabilitation as a goal, we will probably, as Antony Duff has argued,[35] want to structure these practices in such a way that penance, remorse, and repentance will be encouraged and rendered more likely—something not likely at all, of course, in the present barbaric conditions found in many American jails and prisons, where such horrors as gang rape are the order of the day.[36]

---

35. R.A. Duff, Trials and Punishments (1989); R.A. Duff, Punishment, Communication, and Community (2001).
36. See Mary Sigler, *By the Light of Virtue: Prison Rape and the Corruption of Character*, 91 Iowa L. Rev. 561 (2006), for an argument, based in virtue theory, that our acceptance of such a high incidence of prison rape corrupts the characters of inmates and may reveal corruption in the characters of those of us who tolerate it or, in some cases, even make or enjoy jokes about it.

Some have suggested that *religion* could be a crucial element in the rehabilitation of criminals. Such "faith-based" programs might, however, face some serious constitutional and political problems. Constitutionally, they might run afoul of the Establishment Clause of the First Amendment. Politically, those who initially favor religion in prisons because for them religion is identical with evangelical Christianity may not be happy to support religious programs of rehabilitation where the religion involved is, say, the Nation of Islam—*that* kind of repentance and rebirth not being *their* kind of repentance and rebirth. Also as I noted earlier, religious conversion may not always foster the kind of remorse and repentance that is to be hoped for in a secular system of criminal law.

Suppose for the moment that these objections can be overcome and that serving one's sentence in the right sort of penal environment is indeed a route to a valuable kind of remorse, repentance, and rebirth. In such a case, we should I think be particularly skeptical about letting claims of remorse and repentance influence us toward leniency at the time of sentencing, since in the world we are now imagining we will be sentencing people to a kind of punishment that, though it will of course involve the hardship of deserved loss of liberty for them, will also offer them a great good: the possibility of becoming better people. And why would we want to allow the present vice of fake remorse and repentance to deprive us and criminals of the future benefit that a genuinely rehabilitative penal system might confer—the benefit of their becoming better people and better citizens? So, ironically enough, the more that one stresses the reformative value of systems of punishment that will encourage genuine remorse and repentance, the more should one be on one's guard against anything—fake remorse and repentance, for example—that might allow the criminal improperly to avoid such a system or improperly to cut short his time in it.

With respect to clemency decisions, however, the situation in a properly designed rehabilitative world will be quite different. If the goal of the system is itself rehabilitation, and if rehabilitation is thought to be present when remorse and repentance are present, then—when faced with a truly remorseful and repentant prison inmate—it can be seen that the system has done its work and release from criminal custody will clearly be in order. This point only holds in theory for an imagined world of pure rehabilitation, of course, since in the actual world rehabilitative goals, however laudable, will likely compete with other values—deterrence, for example.

But suppose that one is not inclined to defend punishment in terms of either deterrence or rehabilitation but is instead a retributivist—one who claims that the purpose of punishment is to give criminals the punishment that they deserve. This claim immediately forces us to ask "what exactly is *desert*?" If one thinks that desert is a function of the wrongdoing itself and the legitimate *grievance* that it creates for individual victims and for society at large (grievance retributivism), then one might find it hard to see how grievance is lessened by subsequent repentance.[37] If someone assaults me and thereby creates in me a legitimate grievance against him, how is that grievance lessened if the wrongdoer later finds Jesus and repents? *He* may, of course, be a better person because of this, but is *my own* grievance any less? Is society's? If one thinks that the grievance is in part based on the symbolic message of insult and degradation contained in the wrongdoing, then—for reasons earlier discussed—one might indeed think that a grievance is less after repentance, which represents the wrong-

---

37. "Retributivism has a distinct temporal orientation. It looks backward. This simple point has important consequences if the basic goal of the penalty phase is to impose deserved punishment. From a retributive perspective, the punishment a defendant deserves is, to put it somewhat metaphorically, fully congealed at the time of the crime." Stephen P. Garvey, "*As The Gentle Rain from Heaven*": *Mercy in Capital Sentencing*, 81 CORNELL L. REV 989, 1029–1030 (1996). Subject to the qualification about symbolic messaging that I will soon note, this claim seems correct for grievance retributivism. There are forms of what I will later call character retributivism, however, that would challenge this claim.

doer's withdrawal of the endorsement of that message. However, to the degree that one thinks that grievance is based on much more than this symbolic message—as it might well be for very grave wrongs and injuries—then repentance simply might not be enough.

Suppose one it not a grievance retributivist but rather subscribes to *character retributivism*—that is, one believes, with the philosopher Immanuel Kant, that the purpose of punishment is to give people the suffering that is properly proportional to what Kant called their "inner viciousness."[38] Most of those holding this view (but not the Ozickian holdouts) will be strongly inclined in theory to count repentance and remorse in favor of the criminal, since these states of character, if truly present, will be viewed as revealing an inner character that is much less vicious than the character present in the unrepentant criminal.

Even for the character retributivist, however, there will still be the practical problem earlier discussed of distinguishing the genuine article from the fake. Also, if one is going to count one's judgments about good character in favor of the criminal, then it would seem—in symmetry—one ought also be willing to count judgments of bad character against the criminal. It is interesting in this regard, however, that—at least in my experience—many of those who want to count expressions of repentance and remorse in the criminal's favor are first in line to condemn the use in assigning punishment of claims that the criminal's character is "cruel, heinous and depraved" or reveals a "hardened, abandoned, and malignant heart"—phrases that have appeared in death penalty and other American homicide cases.

Is this lack of symmetry logically inconsistent or irrational in some other way? One might argue that humanity and decency require that one be willing to run more risks on behalf of gentleness rather

---

38. *See* Jeffrie G. Murphy, *Does Kant Have a Theory of Punishment?*, 87 COLUM. L REV. 509 (1987).

than on behalf of harshness—a sentiment in line with the venerable slogan that it is better to let guilty people go free than to punish innocent people. I have great sympathy with this line of thought, but it—like the venerable slogan itself—is not self-evident and thus should not be accepted without argument.[39]

Where, then, do I personally stand on the issue of remorse and repentance as grounds for mercy in criminal law? Given that my own nature (alas) tends to be more cynical and suspicious than trusting, my current inclination—although I am still conflicted about this—is *not* to give much weight to expressions of remorse and repentance at the sentencing stage of the criminal process. I simply see too much chance of being made a sucker by fakery.

With respect to clemency decisions, however, it strikes me that judgments about remorse and repentance may have a much more legitimate role to play. The same noted moral and political values—deterrence, rehabilitation, retribution—are at stake here as are present with respect to sentencing, but the epistemic problems seem—at least to me—less worrisome. Why? Simply because we will have a more reliable evidential foundation upon which to base judgments of sincerity. The writer Florence King, commenting on the Karla Faye Tucker case, gives her reasons for believing that Tucker's conversion was sincere:

> Faith, hope, and snobbery aside, I believe Karla Faye's conversion was sincere, in part because the Born Again stance is so

---

39. Stephen Garvey has suggested to me that another way of explaining the noted asymmetrical treatment of good and bad character is to claim that neither is relevant in determining the punishment that the defendant deserves but that both are relevant in decisions to grant or withhold mercy. Since mercy can by nature only result in an actor receiving a lighter sentence, the effect of considering character is necessarily asymmetrical: if the decision-maker decides to grant mercy, the defendant gets a lesser sentence; if the decision-maker decides to deny mercy, then the defendant gets the sentence he deserves. This line of argument assumes, of course, that character is never relevant to desert—an assumption that, as I noted earlier (*see* Garvey, *supra* note 37), would be granted by some forms of retributivism but not by all.

exhausting that no one could fake it for very long. Remember, she was saved in 1985 and spent 12 years witnessing, praising, and thumping, not to mention perfecting the Pat Robertson art of smiling, laughing, and talking at the same time. "Protestantism," said Mencken "converts the gentle and despairing Jesus into a YMCA secretary, brisk, gladsome, and obscene." Without the lube job of sincerity working in mysterious ways she would have dislocated her jawbone.[40]

And here, in addition to the reasons previously quoted, are some of the other reasons given by Governor Schwarzenegger for *not* granting clemency to Stanley Williams:

> [A] close look at Williams' post-arrest and post-conviction conduct tells a story that is different from redemption. After Williams was arrested for these crimes, and while he was awaiting trial, he conspired to escape from custody by blowing up a jail transportation bus and killing the deputies guarding the bus. There are detailed plans [although never executed] in Williams' own handwriting.... The dedication of Williams' book "Life In Prison" casts significant doubt on his personal redemption. This book was published in 1998, several years after Williams claimed redemptive experience. Specifically, the book is dedicated to "Nelson Mandela, Angela Davis, Malcolm X, Assata Shakur, Geronimo Ji Jaga Pratt, Ramona Africa, John Africa, Leonard Peltier, Dhoruba Al-Mujahid, George Jackson, Mumia Abu-Jamal, and the countless other men, women, and youths who have to endure the hellish oppression of living behind bars." The mix of individuals on this list is curious. Most have violent pasts and some have been convicted of heinous murders, including

---

40. Florence King, *Misanthrope's Corner*, Nat'l Rev., Mar. 9, 1998, at 72.

the killing of law enforcement. But the inclusion of George Jackson on this list defies reason and is a significant indicator that Williams is not reformed and that he still sees violence and lawlessness as a legitimate means to address societal problems.[41]

Although Florence King is being her usual cynical and funny self, and Governor Schwarzenegger is being sober and deliberate, they are both making some similar and important points (whatever one may think of the conclusions drawn from those points in the cases at issue): Those making clemency decisions have a lot more time and a lot more information upon which to base their decisions than would ever be possible given the time and evidential limits imposed on a criminal trial that culminates in a sentence. Mistakes are still possible in clemency decisions—there is never an ironclad guarantee against being deceived by fakery—but the probability of such mistakes is surely reduced by a nontrivial degree.[42]

Do these factors weigh differently in death penalty cases than in cases where serious but not lethal punishment is present? I find this a

---

41. *See* Statement of Decision, *supra* note 1. George Jackson was an extremely violent individual—his violence including murder—who, it seems, embraced and celebrated his violence rather than repenting it.

42. Maimonides distinguished coerced from deliberative repentance. The former arises when the conditions for indulging in sinful behavior are no longer present. He called coerced repentance "imperfect" because it does not guarantee a sincere change of heart on the part of the wrongdoer. As such it is contrasted with "perfect" repentance that can only be seen in an environment where it is still possible for the wrongdoer to succumb to the relevant temptation. It is thus hard to see how, on this theory, incarceration could ever provide more than an opportunity for imperfect repentance and thus less than conclusive evidence that the wrongdoer is genuinely repentant. However, if the only way to get conclusive evidence is to put the wrongdoer in an environment in which he could again commit his crime, there are obvious reasons why we would not want to get certainty at this high a price and would rather settle for the best evidence we can get from cases that are imperfect in Maimonides' sense. It would be quite irresponsible, for example, to put—unsupervised—a convicted child molester in an environment of small children in order to make sure that he has his pedophilia under full control. *See* PINCHAS H. PELI, SOLOVEITCHIK ON REPENTANCE (1984). This is a treatise on Rabbi Soloveitchik's teachings on Maimonides.

difficult question. On the days (and for me these are most days) when I oppose the death penalty, I tend to oppose it in part because of my own moral and religious convictions about the deep value of remorse—called by Kierkegaard an "emissary from eternity." I want criminals to have sufficient time for remorse, repentance, and rebirth and do not want to foreclose this possibility by killing them. The days on which I tend to favor the death penalty, however, are days on which I recall Samuel Johnson's observation that nothing is more effective at concentrating the mind than the prospect of being hanged in a fortnight. Remember the Tim Robbins film *Dead Man Walking*—often taken and probably intended to be a sermon against the death penalty? What many people seemed to find most moving in the film was the apparent moral transformation of the death row inmate played by Sean Penn. But would this inmate have attained this transformation had he not realized he was facing execution? And would he have retained this transformation if he had at the last minute received clemency? Focusing on this aspect of the film (and on the book by Sister Helen Prejean on which the film was based) one might, somewhat ironically, see the film as making a rather good case in *favor* of the death penalty.[43]

V. APOLOGY AND MERCY

I have up to this point been focusing on remorse and repentance as possible grounds for mercy. Apology has, however, been lurking in

---

43. Consider also Tolstoy's famous novella *The Death of Ivan Ilych* and ask yourself this question: If, at the last minute, a miracle cure had been provided for Ivan's terminal illness, would the spiritual transformation that he experienced when he accepted that he was dying remain intact? See also the short story *A Good Man Is Hard to Find* by Flannery O'Connor in which an escaped criminal, called The Misfit, says this after an old lady has a moment of grace and redemption just before he shoots her: "She would have been a good woman if it had been somebody there to shoot her every minute of her life."

the background of my discussion up to this point, but I think that the time has come, in what will be the essay's closing section, for me to say a few more explicit and direct things about it and the role that it might play in decisions to grant or withhold mercy.

The initial point I want to make is to note that apology is something *quite different* from remorse and repentance. Remorse is an internal mental state and repentance is an internal mental act, both aspects of character that often have external manifestations but are not themselves external. Apology, however, is more complex. In some cases an apology is nothing but a public linguistic performance, a purely external performance that tells us nothing at all about mental states. In other cases, however, an apology is something much more than this—a public linguistic performance, to be sure, but one that leads listeners to form legitimate expectations concerning the presence in the apologizer of certain mental states or mental acts, in particular remorse and repentance.

When I first (and, alas, quite recently) wrote on the topic of apology, I suggested that all apologies are what philosopher of language J. L. Austin called "performative utterances," ways of "doing things with words."[44] I have now come to think that this view is mistaken—that only some apologies are performatives in Austin's sense.[45]

According to Austin, if one says "I apologize" or "I am sorry" in the appropriate circumstances—circumstances largely defined by conventional linguistic and social rules—then *one has apologized*, end of story. In this way "I apologize" is like "I promise" or "I do" (in a

---

44. J. L. AUSTIN, HOW TO DO THINGS WITH WORDS (1962).
45. I owe my enlightenment on this issue mainly to conversations with Michael White, whose knowledge of Austin's philosophy of language is far greater than mine. I have also been influenced by the argument that Lee Taft makes in repenting his earlier view that all apologies are Austinian performatives. See his stimulating essay *On Bended Knee (With Fingers Crossed)*, 55 DEPAUL L. REV. 601 (2006).

wedding ceremony). These words are not representing any mental states—this is the very thing that makes them performative and not descriptive—and thus "I apologize" carries with it no commitment to genuine remorse.

Some apologies are, of course, exactly this and nothing more. These are the kinds of apologies that are appropriate for trivial wrongs and social gaffes—for example, accidentally bumping into someone in a crowded hall. Here one says "I apologize"—or, more likely, "Excuse me" or "I'm sorry"—merely as counters in social rituals of civility. Indeed, it would actually be quite nuts to feel genuine remorse over something so trivial, and the person who receives and accepts the apology does not expect such remorse—would actually be quite nuts if he did. Can anyone imagine a normal human being in normal circumstances stopping someone who just said "I'm sorry" after a light bump in the hall and conducting an inquiry into the issue of whether the person was sincerely sorry? Surely not.

Of course, if the apologizer visibly crosses his fingers or says "I'm sorry" in an openly sarcastic way, then the "apology" misfires and fails to be an apology since one of what Austin calls the "felicity conditions" of a successful apology performance is that the public performance not include public behavior normally associated with insincerity. But to require, as a condition of successful performative apology, the absence of public behavior normally associated with insincerity is a far cry from saying that a mental state of actual remorse is being described or represented. So in the kind of trivial social contexts here described, I quite agree with Austin that apologies are mere linguistic performatives.

When we come to the context of serious harms and wrongs, however, I now believe that Austin's analysis leads us astray since in these cases our expectations for apologies tend to be far more than linguistic in nature. In these contexts, because of social rules and conversational implicatures, we take both promises (at least significant ones) and apologies to involve the representation that one sincerely means what one says—that one really is sorry, remorseful, and repentant in the case of apologies and that one really does plan to do what one says one will do in the case of promises. Here one must, in other words, represent that one is sincere. Indeed, in these cases, what we call "the apology" invariably involves not merely saying "I apologize" or "I am sorry," but also telling a *story* about one's behavior—a story in which one acknowledges how terrible it was, explains it without seeking to justify it, and conveys the depth of one's sorrow or even self-loathing over it. We would be quite shocked, I think, if a person attempted to apologize for a grave wrong merely by saying "I apologize" and nothing more. That, we would say, was really no apology at all.[46]

It is interesting that Austin missed the importance of seriousness of context with respect to apologies and thus failed to see the distinction between apologies as mere linguistic performatives and apologies that must represent sincerity. In discussing excuses in his famous essay *A Plea for Excuses*, he noted that certain excuses—e.g., "I did it inadvertently"—that work just fine with respect to fairly trivial matters simply will not do when the matter is serious. He wrote:

> [G]iven, I suppose, almost any excuse, there will be cases of such a kind or of such gravity that "we will not accept" it. It is interesting to detect the standards and codes we thus invoke. The extent of the supervision we exercise over the execution of any act can never be quite unlimited, and usually is expected to fall within fairly definite limits ("due care and attention") in the case of acts

---

46. When we promise we invite people to count on us—sometimes in very significant ways—and this in part explains why promises typically create moral obligations. It is hard to see how promises could function in this way if they were not taken to be sincere expressions of intent. Apologies, with respect to serious matters, typically invite wronged parties to think better of the wrongdoer and perhaps even to forgive him and restore relations with him. It is hard to see how apologies could function in this way if they were not taken to be sincere expressions of remorse.

of some general kind, though of course we set very different limits in different cases. We may plead that we trod on the snail inadvertently: but not on a baby—you ought to look where you are putting your great feet. Of course it *was* (*really*), if you like, inadvertence: but that word constitutes a plea, which is not going to be allowed, because of standards. And if you try it on, you will be subscribing to such dreadful standards that your last state will be worse than your first.[47]

As Austin said of excuses, so too—I now think—for significant apologies. In my discussion from now on, I will be concerned with apologies in a context of seriousness (serious wrong, serious harm) and will thus use the word "apology" in the way I take appropriate to such a context.

One of the reasons that apologies sometimes misfire is because the person supposedly apologizing fails to represent the right kind of sorrow—e.g., saying that he is sorry that you interpreted his (presumably innocent) remark in such a way that your (probably overly sensitive) feelings were hurt. This fails as an apology because, in mislocating the proper object for the sorrow, it fails to acknowledge the genuine wrongdoing that a genuine apology would address. (Although Stanley Williams expressed some general regrets with respect to his previous life of crime, he did not express regrets—much less apologize or express remorse—with respect to the crimes of which he had been, in the judgment of Governor Schwarzenegger, rightfully convicted. Thus even the expressed regrets, having the wrong target, were judged by the governor to be irrelevant to the clemency decision.)

As I write this essay, the news is filled with reports of another misfired apology—this time from actor Mel Gibson. It is not surprising

---

47. J. L. Austin, *A Plea for Excuses*, in PHILOSOPHICAL PAPERS 142–143 (1961).

that his first apology for the anti-Semitic tirade he delivered when being arrested for drunken driving was regarded by many to be insufficient since he merely expressed general regrets for having said things that (so he claimed) he does not really believe. Small wonder that Abraham H. Foxman of the Anti-Defamation League rejected this apology as "unremorseful and insufficient."[48] Of course this simply initiated the apology dance that has become so common in America— Gibson (perhaps coached by his agent) making a second apology that actually mentions anti-Semitism and claims that he is not anti-Semitic, the Anti-Defamation League giving a reluctant and qualified partial acceptance of that apology, discussions of possible cooperative projects of healing, and so on it goes.[49] The shelf life of this dance will surely expire in about another week and will probably have as its primary public value the production of some great comedy. Not since the person shot by Vice-President Dick Cheney in a hunting accident publicly apologized to Cheney for causing him and his family distress have Jay Leno, Jon Stewart, and Steven Colbert had something so choice to work with. (I still recall with pleasure a gem about the Cheney incident that came from Jon Stewart: "Just imagine how powerful you have to be if when you shoot somebody he apologizes to you.") Perhaps comedy is the way that some of us get "closure" from the suffocatingly boring and shallow apology dances to which we are now so often exposed.

Even when representations of remorse and repentance are directed to the proper object, however, it is important to remember that representations are simply representations. They are not the same as actual remorse and repentance. The convincing fraud who

---

48. Press Release, Anti-Defamation League, *ADL Says Mel Gibson's Anti-Semitic Tirade Reveals His True Self: Actor's Apology "Not Good Enough,"* at http://www.adl.org/PresRele/ASUS_12/4861_12.htm (last visited November 2, 2006).
49. Allison Hope Weiner, *Mel Gibson Seeks Forgiveness From News,* N.Y. TIMES, August 2, 2006, at E1.

makes an insincere apology really has apologized in the Austinian sense, but in a context of seriousness we normally take an apology to be something more than an Austinian performative. We take it to represent sincere remorse, and so we may reject the apology as an insulting piece of mere acting—one sense of "performance"—if we believe that there is in fact no remorse, that the representation is nothing but a representation.

Is apology in the absence of genuine sincerity enough so long as it represents sincerity? I think that it sometimes is and sometimes is not. It all depends on what one wants out of an apology. If one wants admission of and acceptance of responsibility, a properly constructed apology provides that—although, as the South African TRC reveals, one can also get that without apology. How? Simply by having the wrongdoer explicitly disclose facts that establish wrongdoing and accept responsibility for what he has done. An apology does that but, in also representing remorse, it does more than that.

There are also some retributive satisfactions that can be gained even from—perhaps especially from—an insincere public apology. To force someone to make a public apology is to subject that person to a social ritual that can be painfully humiliating for that person—particularly, I should think, if that person is *not* sincerely sorry. Some victims of wrongdoing might not care about the sincerity of the apology, however, so long as the making of the apology is painful to the right degree for the person who must deliver it. That it causes deserved suffering might be satisfaction enough for those who are retributively inclined. Thus the public disclosure of wrongdoing, required by the TRC as a condition for amnesty, may have had more retributive bite than Bishop Tutu—who likes to think of the TRC as "restorative justice" rather than "retributive justice"—likes to admit. For at least some people it must be quite painful, even if one does not apologize or express remorse, simply to acknowledge in public—including before one's friends and family and fellow parishioners—

that, for example, one of the tasks performed as a government police officer was to torture and sometimes even kill suspects or prisoners. Mere humiliating public disclosure without apology can sometimes provide retributive satisfaction to victims—the reason why truth commissions (such as Chile's) that do not publish names of wrongdoers often seem less satisfying to victims than those (such as South Africa's) that do. But if mere disclosure without apology can provide retributive satisfaction to victims, it might be the case that requiring an apology as a condition of amnesty or clemency, even if that apology is insincere or suspected to be so, might provide even more retributive satisfactions to those victims.

Many, of course, might regard the retributive satisfactions afforded some victims by rituals of humiliation—particularly if those rituals require what may be insincere apologies and expressions of remorse—as bought at too high a moral and political price. This is perhaps why, in the Coetzee novel, David Lurie compared the demand that he make a public apology to the humiliating rituals of Mao's China during the Cultural Revolution.

I am personally conflicted about this matter. Sometimes I favor public humiliation as a punishment and have even suggested, for example, that a good punishment for a student or faculty plagiarist is to force that person to apologize in front of the entire academic community of which he is a member and to endure the shame that is his due. There are other times, however, when I share David Lurie's reservations and think that the self that desires the humiliation of others, even in a just cause, is not my better self.

Even if one can imagine a place for public apology as a shaming punishment in the academic world, however, it is not at all clear that one should welcome this in the realm of legal punishment. An academic community may be presumed, without I hope too much self-deceptive fiction, to be bound together by shared values—to be, in short, a genuine community. I fear that many of those who advocate a greater role for apology and expression of remorse in American criminal law may overestimate the degree of actual community present in our large and complex society with its massive social class and racial and cultural divisions. Such advocates often speak warmly of the capacity of apology to lead to reconciliation and reintegration with the larger community—an idea that makes perfect sense where there is a genuine community but is ludicrous when applied to persons who are so alienated that they have never felt a part of the larger community in the first place.[50] Apology advocates may also have too rosy a picture of the nature of the communitarian society that would make talk of deep reintegration and reconciliation through apology rituals genuinely possible. What was Mao's China, after all, except what might be called communitarianism on steroids?

VI. CONCLUSION

It will surely come as no surprise that the skepticism I earlier expressed concerning the possible role of repentance and remorse as grounds for mercy (particularly in sentencing) I now extend to apology as well. A truly sincere apology can be a wonderful, even blessed, thing since it involves the kind of remorse and repentance that often marks a step on the road to moral rebirth, can sometimes provide legitimate comfort to victims, and in the proper sort of cases can indeed lead to a valuable kind of reconciliation. Turn all of that over to the American system of assembly line justice, however, a system starved for resources and staffed by people who are oppressively overworked and in a hurry to clear cases, and we will—I fear—do little more than cheapen the currency of the real thing and add to the cynicism about our system of criminal law, and indeed about our society in general,

---

50. *See* Jeffrie G. Murphy, *Marxism and Retribution*, 2 PHIL. & PUB. AFF. 217 (1973).

that grows greater each passing day. Just recall the shameful spectacle of President Clinton in the Monica Lewinsky matter. So quick and frequent were his apologies that one could use his example to make a case that apologizing can now be added to the list of obsessive-compulsive disorders, and this not surprisingly made him the brunt of a variety of jokes and cynical comments. And recall the cynical *New Yorker* cartoon I quoted earlier and the new novel *Eating Crow* by Jay Rayner. Cynical jokes about public apology are already the order of the day, and I cannot see an expanded role for apology in criminal sentencing as doing anything more than adding to this cynical perspective—a very funny one, indeed, but not in my view one that contributes to a healthy society. As the *New Yorker* cartoon suggests, apology in America may not even be shaming these days—in which case there go even the retributive satisfactions that might, as noted earlier, be gained by victims from an apology even if that apology is insincere and known to be so. Just as bankruptcy has generally ceased to be an occasion of shame and has become instead a business or personal planning tool, so might a willingness to apologize if necessary be little more than part of a rational strategy for maximizing one's self-interest.

As with remorse, however, the role of apology strikes me as less controversial in clemency decisions than in sentencing decisions. My reason for this is the same as given with respect to remorse: less risk of mistakes because of the greater time and more extensive evidential base that clemency decisions make possible. Here the evidence gathered may not simply go to the sincerity of the person making the apology but also to the likely impact, for good or ill, that the apology will have on the victims and on society as a whole.

I am an enemy neither of apology nor remorse; and indeed I have acknowledged, at least in passing, that apologies (particularly when sincerely expressive of remorse) can sometimes have many virtues—both individual and social. In a different social and historical context

I might have wanted more to stress those virtues and discuss them in more detail. Our present intellectual culture, however, strikes me as one in which apology and other expressions of remorse are often located (and often over praised) in the context of a sentimental ideology of therapy and healing rather than, say, an ideology of truth and justice.

As a counter to this sentimental ideology, I have been concerned here mainly to express some skepticism, both substantively and rhetorically, toward the trendy celebration of apology and expressions of remorse and to the uncritical extension of that celebration into criminal law. Mainly for evidential reasons, my skepticism is much greater when remorse and apology are offered as grounds for mercy in sentencing than when they are offered as grounds for mercy in clemency decisions. However, as Governor Schwarzenegger's thoughtful denial of clemency to Stanley Williams suggests (at least to those who do not regard Williams to have been innocent of the murders of which he was convicted), a healthy dose of skepticism is well in order in the domain of clemency as well.

I would not, however, want my qualified sympathy with Governor Schwarzenegger's clemency decision in the narrow confines of that one case to be taken as a sign that I am at all comfortable with the general context in which such decisions must be made. So, as a final point, let me baldly state my view that the whole American system of so-called "criminal justice" has to a great degree become a moral and administrative mess—a great bloated monster driven by competing and sometimes inconsistent values, and sometimes by no values at all but simply by cruelty or indifference or institutional inertia. It calls, in my judgment, for radical rethinking and redesign. Thus I cannot help thinking that spending a lot of time tinkering with the small corners of the present system that might be affected by remorse and apology is rather like, as the saying goes, rearranging the furniture on the decks of the *Titanic*. That, however, is a topic for another occasion.

APPENDIX: REPLY TO CRITICS

Several of my commentators rightly take me to task for not acknowledging that the difficulty of determining the sincerity of remorse and apology may not differ significantly from determining the truth of a variety of other claims at trial and sentencing and that the same mechanisms that lawyers, judges, and juries use to reduce those difficulties will also be available to them with respect to expressions of remorse and apology. As Sherry Colb notes, "a group of strangers making up a jury does a decent job of detecting who is and who is not telling the truth, particularly with the assistance of a prosecutor who can point out weaknesses in the defendant's story and reasons (including his status as a party) to doubt his credibility." My main practical point still stands, however—namely that *much more* is available to minimize mistakes at a clemency hearing.

Moving from a legitimate worry that several of my commentators share, I would now like to respond briefly to a few points made by individual commentators.

Stephanos Bibas claims that I, somewhat surprisingly for someone who is supposed to be a retributivist, undervalue the retributive value of expressions of remorse and apology. I do not think that he is correct about this. I explicitly say that public expressions of remorse and apology, even if insincere, can be painfully humiliating and that this pain can represent retributively deserved suffering. I also say explicitly that such expressions can sometimes lessen the victims' grievances by publicly withdrawing the endorsement of the wrongdoing that might otherwise be allowed to stand.

Bibas also reminds us that "when hateful men murder, angry mobs assault, or bigots burn and desecrate, they have already violated the Millian harm principle [and] no longer deserve immunity from scrutiny," but surely he does not think I would want to deny this. I did not say that such evil actors should be free of *all* scrutiny but merely expressed skepticism that their expressions of remorse and apology should be given much weight at sentencing. A certain amount of scrutiny—*mens rea* inquiries, for example—are vital to the criminal process, but inquiring into remorse and repentance could reasonably be viewed as spiritually intrusive and in that sense beyond the legitimate scrutiny of the liberal state. Forced apologies, as Lisa Griffin notes, may be degrading and dehumanizing for the defendant, and it is not at all clear that the liberal state should be in the business of degrading and dehumanizing any of its citizens.

Susan Bandes has more confidence than I do that the death penalty is special in such a way that remorse and apology should be allowed to play a much more significant role in that context than in any other sentencing or clemency context. She gives two reasons for thinking this. First, she notes that a death sentence is *irrevocable*. This is certainly true, but are not *all* criminal sentences irrevocable simply because *the past* is irrevocable? We cannot give an executed person back his life, but neither can we give a person who has wrongfully served twenty years back those twenty years and erase from his mind the no doubt unspeakable conditions (e.g., gang rape) to which he has been subjected during that period—conditions that may have hardened him to such a degree as to undermine any possibility that he might seek and attain redemption. I sometimes wish that some of the passion directed against the death penalty (a fairly rare penalty, after all) could be redirected toward unspeakable prison conditions—conditions that could easily be regarded by some as a "fate worse than death."

Second, Bandes says that "[a] death sentence is an assertion that the defendant is irredeemable and no longer fit to live." This strikes me as too quick. A justification for a death sentence might acknowledge a belief that the defendant is redeemable but might claim that this value is trumped by some even greater value—the value of victim vindication perhaps. Also, clarity is not served if "the defendant deserves to die" or "deterrence will be served by execution of this defendant" are translated simply as "the defendant is no longer fit to live." One might recall Samuel Johnson's observation that nothing so focuses the mind as the prospect of being hanged in a fortnight and come to think that the prospect of being executed may provide the wrongdoer with the very incentive that he needs to bring him toward repentance and redemption. I raise these points not because I necessarily agree with them but because I believe that many people who are deeply opposed to the death penalty are sometimes tempted, in their zeal, to skip careful analysis and the careful consideration of arguments on the other side in favor of claims that are more rhetoric than sober argument.

Lisa Griffin and Janet Ainsworth insightfully stress, in a way that I neglected to do by my perhaps excessive focus on worries about sincerity, the way in which apopogies might be seen as participation in socially valuable rituals. As Ainsworth puts it, "what is said [at sentencing] serves as an articulation of our collective values regarding the causing of harm to others and an appropriate reaction to the causing of that harm."

I think that this was probably once true with respect to apologies, but I am not sure that it still is. The cynicism spawned in our "culture of apology"—where apologies automatically appear on the lips of people trying to avoid responsibility—may have undercut to a substantial degree the social value of the apology ritual. As I noted in my core text, declaring bankruptcy may now be seen as moving from being an occasion of great shame to being simply a business planning tool. So, too, may a willingness to apologize if caught be increasingly seen, not as a willingness to send a socially useful massage, but rather as simply a strategy for advancing self-interest. So those who apologize may be seen as merely "playing amid the ruins of forgotten languages."

Additional Response to Susan Bandes: "The Heart Has Its Reasons"

There is much wisdom in Susan Bandes' essay. I think that she does, however, sometimes confuse two things that, in the interest of conceptual clarity, should not be confused: questions of empirical explanation and questions of philosophical justification. She notes that "the United States (but no other Western country), and thirty-six of the states (but not the other fourteen), consider the death penalty the 'just desert' for certain categories of murder" and that the unpredictable way in which jurors determine who deserves to die reveals a lack of consensus on such matters. She raises the question of why this is the case, and says that "retributive theory has no good answer to this question."

But, of course, it would not. Surely philosophical retributive theory (Immanuel Kant's for example) is an attempt to articulate an ideal model of how punishment should be determined in a just society—a model that can be used to evaluate actual punitive practices to determine the degree to which they fall short of justice. And such a theory is not, contrary to Bandes' claim, "bloodless and abstract"—unless a passionate commitment to justice and what justice requires is bloodless and abstract. It is the job of the empirical social scientist, not the philosopher, to ask why in application the idea of just deserts may point in a variety of conflicting directions. Maybe jurors are stupid or ignorant or corrupt, or perhaps the concept of just deserts is not properly explained to them (because judges are stupid or ignorant or corrupt)—who knows? Certainly not the philosopher, since this is an empirical matter. And surely the philosophical retributivist will not place too much weight on the presence or absence of social consensus (another empirical matter) because such a theorist will not use social agreement as a test for moral justification. For all I know, there may be an emerging social consensus in America in favor of torture (even if not in favor of calling it "torture") and, if so, the retributivist—like any other morally decent person—will hardly regard that as easing moral doubts about the practice. It will instead raise doubts about the virtue of our citizens and the degree to which their opinions should matter to a rational and moral person.

If the actual process we have in America of determining who gets executed and who does not is arbitrary, random, and unpredictable, this is of course deplorable. But who will be first in line to condemn this? The philosophical retributivist. And why will such a philosopher condemn it? Because it is grossly unjust to support a practice that regularly punishes people *more (or less) than they deserve.*

It might be true, as a conceptual matter, that the concept of retributive just deserts is inherently incoherent (a confused product of confused philosophy) or that it is simply, like much philosophy, too complex, and too likely to be misunderstood to be used in providing useful counsel to those who must determine the sentencing of criminals. The first problem is a philosophical problem and requires philosophical examination. The second problem is empirical and awaits controlled empirical investigation.

It is also possible, as Friedrich Nietzsche warned, that the language of retributive just desserts subconsciously draws on corrupt aspects of the human character—human *ressentiment,* to use Nietzsche's term. If this is true—and establishing it would take some hard psychological work—then this is a powerful reason for avoiding this language in the practice of sentencing—capital or otherwise. This is not a critique of philosophical retributivism, however, since such a theorist would be the first to abandon the practical use of his own language if it had a tendency to lead people to sentence based on malice, envy, cruelty, and spite (the essence of *ressentiment*) instead of just desserts.

In summary: There may, for all I know, be good empirical reasons for avoiding the use of retributive language in the actual practice of criminal sentencing. It is hardly a valid criticism of retributive theory, however, that it is not in a position to assess such empirical claims. Even if the claims are true, indeed, this should not upset the philosophical retributive theorist since he can still take pride in having the very best theory to bring to bear in deploring these very empirical outcomes.

Chapter 8

The Case of Dostoevsky's General: Some Ruminations on Forgiving the Unforgivable

One day a house-serf, a little boy, only eight years old, threw a stone while he was playing and hurt the paw of the general's favorite hound. "Why is my favorite dog limping?" It was reported to him that this boy had thrown a stone at her and hurt her paw. "So it was you," the general looked the boy up and down. "Take him!" They took him, took him from his mother, and locked him up for the night. In the morning, at dawn, the general rode out in full dress for the hunt, mounted on his horse, surrounded by spongers, dogs, handlers, huntsmen, all on horseback. The house-serfs are gathered for their edification, the guilty boy's mother in front of them all. The boy is led out of the lockup. A gloomy, cold, misty autumn day, a great day for hunting. The general orders them to undress the boy; the child is stripped naked, he shivers, he's crazy with fear, he doesn't dare make a peep... "Drive him!" the general commands. The huntsmen shout, "Run, run!" The boy runs... "Sic him!" screams the general and looses the whole pack of wolfhounds on him. He hunted him down before his mother's eyes, and the dogs tore the child to pieces...! Well... what to do with him?... Speak, Alyoshka!

"Shoot him!" Alyosha said softly.[1]

---

1. *The Brothers Karamazov*, translated by Richard Pevear and Larissa Volokhonsky, San Francisco: North Point Press, 1990, pp 242–243. In our joint authored book *Forgiveness and Mercy* (Cambridge University Press, 1988), Jean Hampton began her Chapter 4 by quoting

1. DOESTOEVSKY'S GENERAL AS A PARADIGM

In this famous passage from the "Rebellion" chapter of Dostoevsky's *The Brothers Karamazov*, Ivan tells the story of the cruel and murderous general to his brother Alyosha to test the devout Alyosha's commitment to Christianity as a gospel of love. When confronted with evil of such extreme cruelty, Alyosha finds it impossible—at least as his first reaction—to feel any love in his heart for the general as the perpetrator of this atrocity, to think of him as a neighbor covered by the commandment that we should love our neighbor. Could anyone forgive this moral monster? Could even God?—an issue on which I am incompetent to comment.[2] Here is what Ivan has to say about the possibility of human forgiveness for the general:

---

this passage (in a different translation). After I published my book *Getting Even: Forgiveness and Its Limits* (Oxford University Press, 2003) my forgiveness muse went out on a wildcat strike and I began thinking and writing about other topics. I am grateful to Leo Zaibert, the guest editor of the issue of *The Monist* in which this essay appeared, for inviting me to contribute an essay. Working on the essay has rekindled my interest in the topic. My only regret in writing the essay is that I have not, with three fine exceptions, kept up on the recent literature on forgiveness—leaving me with the fear that what I say here may have been said better or even refuted by others. If so, I apologize to them. Two of the fine exceptions, some influence of which can be seen in my essay, are Charles L. Griswold's *Forgiveness: A Philosophical Exploration* (Cambridge University Press, 2007) and Thomas Brudholm's *Resentment's Virtue: Jean Amery and the Refusal to Forgive* (Temple University Press, 2008)—a book for which I wrote a foreword. The third fine exception is a draft of Laurence Thomas' insightful essay "Forgiving the Unforgivable" that he shared with me some years ago. He and I differ in some important respects. He, for example, places the entire weight of his discussion on contrition (what I call remorse) whereas I give equal weight to penance and atonement as suppressions of the dear self—acts that I regard as having value independent of their evidential role in establishing the sincerity of contrition or remorse. In spite of these differences, however, the influence of Thomas' essay on my own thinking will be obvious to anyone who reads both pieces. Thomas' essay appeared in print in 2003 in *Moral Philosophy and the Holocaust*, edited by Eve Garrard and Geoffrey Scare (Burlington, VT: Ashgate Press) pp. 201–30.

2. In a February 2003 meeting with the clergy of Rome, Pope Benedict expressed the hope that most will be saved but added this: "Perhaps there are not so many who have destroyed themselves so completely, who are irreparable forever, who no longer have any element upon which the love of God can rest, who no longer have the slightest capacity to love within themselves. This would be hell." Quoted in *First Things*, May 2008, p. 74. And consider Elie

I do not, finally, want the mother to embrace the tormentor who let his dogs tear her son to pieces! She dare not forgive him! Let her forgive him for herself, if she wants to, let her forgive the tormentor her immeasurable maternal suffering; but she has no right to forgive the suffering of her child who was torn to pieces, she dare not forgive the tormentor, even if the child himself were to forgive him![3]

In addition to seeing the general as a paradigm of one who should not be forgiven (the mother "dare not" forgive him), Ivan in the passage seems to be embracing a fairly common view about forgiveness—namely, that only the *victim* has a right to forgive the person by whom the victim was wronged. The mother is a victim in her own maternal suffering, collateral damage to the wrong done her son, and she can thus forgive for that (although Ivan seems to believe that she should not). She cannot, however, forgive the wrong done to her son. She lacks *standing* for that. Since the son is the only person with standing and is dead, he cannot forgive; and thus we can perhaps see here one possible sense of the concept of the *unforgivable*. This is not the only possible sense of the concept of the unforgivable, however, and it might be useful at this point to note all the possible senses—or at least all the ones that I can think of.

2. THE CONCEPT OF THE UNFORGIVABLE

It is common for people to use the world "unforgivable" about both *injuries* and *people*, but it is not always clear what this is supposed to mean. Indeed, those with a fondness for dark sayings sometimes

---

Wiesel's prayer at ceremonies marking the fiftieth anniversary in 1995 of the liberation of Auschwitz: "God of forgiveness, do not forgive those who created this place. God of mercy, have no mercy on those who killed here Jewish children."

3. *Supra* note 1.

use the word in a way that may make no sense at all—for example, Derrida's claim that "forgiveness forgives only the unforgivable."[4] This may be very deep and profound, but I cannot help being reminded of Austin's observation that "explanatory definition should stand high among our aims; it is not enough to show how clever we are by showing how obscure everything is."[5] At any rate, I think that "unforgivable" could mean any of the following: (1) logically or conceptually impossible to forgive, (2) causally impossible to forgive, (3) very, very, very difficult to forgive, (4) morally ought not be forgiven, all things considered, or (5) morally ought *prima facie* not be forgiven—a judgment that can be overridden by very weighty countervailing moral considerations. Beverly Flanigan and David A. Stoop both wrote self-help books entitled *Forgiving the Unforgivable*.[6] Pretty clearly they did not mean (1), (2), or (4). If they meant (1) they would condemn their books to being total nonsense—rather like writing books on how to be a married bachelor. If they meant (2) they would be identifying the task of their books as so pointless as to be a nontask—rather like writing a book on how to jump to the moon with a pogo stick. If they meant (4) they would admit to writing a book giving advice on how to do something absolutely immoral.

Regarding the general as unforgivable by the boy because the boy (the only one with standing to forgive him) is dead would be to make the claim that forgiveness in these circumstances is logically or conceptually incoherent, since on this view a necessary condition for the

---

4. Jacques Derrida, *On Cosmopolitanism and Forgiveness* (London: Routledge, 2001) p. 32.
5. J. L. Austin, "A Plea for Excuses." *Philosophical Papers* (Oxford: Clarendon Press, 1961) p. 137. He closes the paragraph with this wonderful sentence: "Clarity, too, I know, has been said to be not enough: but perhaps it will be time to go into that when we are within measurable distance of achieving clarity on some matter."
6. Beverly Flanigan, *Forgiving the Unforgivable* (New York: Wiley, 1992) David A Stoop, *Forgiving the Unforgivable* (Ventura, CA: Regal Books, 2005).

meaningful application of the very concept of forgiveness is that it is a response that makes sense only if coming from the victim.[7]

I used to embrace this view that forgiveness can come only from the victim—that only the victim has standing to forgive; but I have now come to think that this view, unless properly qualified, is mistaken. I do think that victim forgiveness is the primary sense of forgiveness, but I now think that third-party forgiveness is also coherent—at least as a secondary or parasitic sense.

If one embraces, as I once did, Bishop Joseph Butler's view that forgiveness is essentially the overcoming of the emotion of *resentment*, then it does seem analytic that forgiveness can come only from the wronged person since resentment does seem, by definition, to be the reactive attitude that is felt by victims. We have another word, "indignation," to capture a similar reactive emotional response from third parties.[8]

But one should not, I now think, fully embrace Butler's claim that forgiveness is simply the overcoming of resentment. Even if resentment is the most common response to being wronged (and

---

7. The boy is of course the primary victim, but the mother could be regarded as a secondary victim. Perhaps the range of secondary victims could be expanded even more—a point to be discussed later in the paper. Several persons who wrote essays for Simon Wiesenthal's book *The Sunflower* (Revised and Expanded Edition, New York: Schocken Books, 1997) expressed outrage that the discussed dying Nazi solider, who had participated in the massacre of many Jews, presumed, on his deathbed, to ask forgiveness for this simply by having a Jew selected at random brought to him so that the Jew could bestow forgiveness on him. My colleague David Kader tells me that Judaism does not allow the forgiveness of murder since forgiveness must come from the victim and in murder the victim is, of course, dead.
8. In using the word "resentment" Butler meant something much stronger than what is suggested in our contemporary use of the word. We would now find it absurd to the point of being comical if we imagined a victim of, say, rape and torture saying to the rapist and torturer, "I really resent that." (Noel Coward nicely captures this comic absurdity in his song "The Stately Homes of England": "There's the ghost of a crazy younger son/Who murdered, in thirteen fifty one,/An extremely rowdy nun/Who resented it.") In my view, Butler's use of the word seeks to capture what I have elsewhere called a "vindictive passion"—a desire to strike back or get even for wrongs done. See Joseph Butler's sermons "Upon Resentment" and "Upon Forgiveness of Injuries" in his *Works*. Volume 2, edited by W.E. Gladstone (Oxford: The Clarendon Press, 1896) pp. 136–167.

I am no longer sure that it is), victims also often feel emotions other than resentment at being wronged—such emotions as sadness, disappointment, insecurity, anger, and even hatred or loathing, for example, and it makes perfectly good sense to attribute these emotions to third parties as well as to victims.[9] Thus, even if I cannot (for purely semantic reasons) properly be said to feel resentment of the general for what he has done to the boy, I can certainly claim—with no misuse of language—to *loathe* him for it and want him hurt in return. And I now see no deep problem in saying, if I overcome this reactive attitude, that I have forgiven the general.

In short, I think that it is important here to be attentive to our ordinary language, since I think that this should be our first word if not always our last word.[10] Along with Herbert Morris, "I am skeptical about any claim of widespread misuse of terms for emotional states, and I am generally disposed to accept first-person reports as accurate."[11] It is very common for people to talk of themselves as forgiving or not forgiving when they are not themselves victims (consider talk about self-forgiveness), and—absent some very powerful argument to the contrary—I am inclined to take their speech at face value.[12] So if a person who is not a victim says that he could never

---

9. I came to see the inadequacy of regarding forgiveness simply as the overcoming of resentment from some email exchanges with Eleonore Stump and from Norvin Richards' essay "Forgiveness," *Ethics*, Volume 99, Number 1, October 1988, pp. 77–97.
10. "Our common stock of words embodies all the distinctions men have found worth drawing, and the connexions they have found worth marking, in the lifetimes of many generations: these surely are likely to be more numerous, more sound, since they have stood up to the long test of the survival of the fittest, and more subtle, at least in all ordinary and practical matters, than any that you or I are likely to think up in our arm-chairs of an afternoon—the most favoured alternative method." J.L. Austin, *supra* note 5, p. 130.
11. Herbert Morris, "Nonmoral Guilt" in *Responsibility, Character, and the Emotions*, edited by Ferdinand Schoeman (Cambridge University Press, 1987) p. 221.
12. People often seek what they call self-forgiveness. They are surely not seeking to overcome resentment they feel toward themselves, and it is by no means necessary that they be thinking of themselves as having victimized themselves—although in cases such as addiction this element may be present. I think that people who seek self-forgiveness are typically

forgive someone such as the general (or that he could), and seems to think that this is a perfectly acceptable use of the word "forgive," I have no inclination to correct him. If he does claim to forgive the general, his forgiveness cannot, for reasons noted, be *for* the boy. He could not overcome the resentment or any other negative reactive attitude that only the boy could feel.

Third parties can, however, coherently claim to have (or not to have) overcome such reactive attitudes as disgust and loathing that were understandably occasioned by seeing the general as a moral monster. These reactive attitudes would very likely include an unwillingness to welcome the general into human society and perhaps even an unwillingness to regard him any longer as a human being—something suggested by the word "monster"—and thus no longer possessed of the dignity that confers human rights upon him. The Nazi judge in the film *Judgment at Nuremberg*, when he brings to full consciousness the evil in which he has been complicitous, says, "I have turned my life into excrement." We might well say of the general that he has forfeited his humanity and turned his life into excrement.[13]

The remainder of my essay does not depend on whether or not it is proper to use the word "forgiveness" in this context (although I now think it is) since the real project of the essay is to grapple with this *moral* question: Under what circumstances, if any, is it morally permissible (or perhaps required) to seek to overcome our natural loathing of such people as the general and our natural inclination to join Ivan (and Alyosha, at least initially) in vowing never to forgive them—to never abandon

---

attempting to overcome some self-loathing occasioned by their past wrongdoing—particularly wrongdoing that has harmed people. See in this regard Norman Care's *Living With One's Past* (Lanham, MD: Rowman and Littlefield, 1996).

13. Although regarding persons such as the general as monsters or vermin or excrement may be a natural first response, I will later argue that it should not be our considered judgment. I will argue that even if we legitimately regard such a person as unforgivable, this should not be confused with regarding that person as lacking in the basic human dignity that confers on him basic human rights.

our loathing of them? Eleonore Stump has published a wonderful essay (which has influenced my own thinking) in which she explores this question: If Goebbels (one of Hitler's closest and most influential subordinates) had lived, would it ever be legitimate for anyone to relate to him again with anything but loathing—to, for example, do such a simple thing as welcoming him into one's home for dinner?[14] I think that one could see her essay as about the possibility of forgiving Goebbels (in the sense explained above) without falling into nonsense.

To find *him* forgivable is not, of course, to find what he *did* forgivable; and, indeed, I am not sure that I understand what it even means to speak—as is often done—of a forgivable or unforgivable *injury* unless this expression is interpreted as a shorthand expression for a more complex thought. Repentant wrongdoers quite naturally say "Forgive *me*"—not "Forgive what I did"—and I am, indeed, tempted to think that when people speak of "unforgivable injuries" this is their way of saying that the *persons* who inflicted the injuries are not forgivable. Otherwise they may be using the term "unforgivable" as equivalent to "irreparable"—and some injuries really may indeed be beyond any possibility of repair. Job may think he was made whole again when he gets new children to replace the ones who had been killed, but the idea that one's beloved children are in this sense fungible surely strikes most modern readers as so primitive as to be beyond belief.

3. A RETURN TO THE GENERAL

Drawing inspiration from Eleonore Stump's thought experiment about Goebbels, I will now proceed to discuss a similar moral question about the general. I am now inclined to regard this as a

---

14. Eleonore Stump, "Personal Relations and Moral Residue," *History of the Human Sciences*, Volume 17, Numbers 2/3, August 2004, pp. 33–56.

question about the moral appropriateness of our forgiving the general—or, from a virtue perspective, of our being persons with characters disposed to forgive the general—but nothing depends on this. Thus even those who wish to retain the constraints that I have abandoned with respect to the concept of forgiveness can, I hope, find my discussion of this question of interest. At any rate, the reader should note that when from now on in the paper I talk of forgiveness, I will—unless otherwise explicitly noted—be talking about the kind of forgiveness that I now think it is possible for third parties (and not just primary victims) to bestow.

One possibility, of course, is that the general is too mentally ill to be held responsible and be an intelligible object of moral hatred. In the Dostoevsky passage quoted, I omitted this sentence: "I believe the general was later declared incompetent to administer his estates." All we have is this single sentence, and the story does not tell us if the general was mentally ill in a way that might have a bearing on his responsibility for the murder of the boy. Inability to manage one's property is no doubt an indication of mental illness of a kind that might explain such things as a failure to pay one's property taxes on time. It seems unlikely, however, that this alone could explain or excuse murder—to render the general, in the language of the American *Model Penal Code's* rendering of the insanity defense, lacking in "substantial capacity" to restrain himself from murder or to "appreciate" that murder is wrong.[15] If he was mentally ill in a way that totally undermined his moral and legal responsibility, he would seem a legitimate object of *excuse* (and pity) but not of forgiveness, since the possibility of forgiveness is typically thought to be present only with respect to responsible wrongdoing, where blame and not pity is appropriate. It has to be admitted, however, that forgiveness is

---

15. American Law Institute *Model Penal Code and Commentaries*, Official Draft and Revised Comment, Part I: General Provisions (1985) Section 4.01.

sometimes identified with excuse—as, for example, in "Father forgive them for they know not what they do" or "To understand all is to forgive all." I used to think that these expressions were simply confused, but now I am inclined to wonder if the distinction between forgiveness and excuse is not always as sharp as I have in the past assumed—a point on which I will expand a bit later.

Assuming that the general was a responsible agent—evil and not simply crazy—should he ever be forgiven?[16] This is the question of the present essay. I should also note at the outset, however, that it is my view that questions such as the one I here raise cannot be answered with definitive finality. All one can really do, in my view, is to put forward one's own "take" on the issue in the hope that others will find it illuminating in some way—that it will at least advance the conversation by providing something worth reacting to. Nietzsche claimed that all philosophy is a part of the psychological autobiography of its author, Thomas Nagel claimed that "philosophical ideas are acutely sensitive to individual temperament and to wishes," and Iris Murdoch claimed that the first question that one should ask of any philosopher is, "What is he afraid of?" I lack the competence to judge if these claims are true for all branches of philosophy (although

---

16. If one literally conceptualizes the general as vermin or excrement at the time he acted, this would seem to remove him from the category of responsible agents and preclude his being blameworthy for his acts. If like the Nazi judge portrayed in the film, his acts turned him into excrement, this would be more complex—leaving him responsible for his acts but perhaps not at a later time sufficiently a responsible agent to be legitimately punished. Conceptualizing him as a monster is equally complex. Even if this would render him nonhuman, it might not remove him from the category of responsible agents. Is Grendel (in the poem *Beowulf*), for example, a responsible agent? One can think of arguments on both sides of this question. All this shows some of the potential confusions and dangers in this context of employing the concepts monster, vermin, and excrement. For an argument that a certain kind of irrationality might be present in the general that would reveal him as both evil and crazy, see Harry Frankfurt's "Rationality and the Unthinkable" in his *The Importance of What We Care About* (Cambridge University Press, 1988) pp. 177–190. We might regard the general as crazy simply because he could effectively will such a thing as the slaughter of a boy as a response to a minor injury to a dog. It is a separate question, of course, if this way of being crazy precludes responsibility.

I suspect they are not), but I firmly believe that they have important (although certainly not dispositive) application to the kinds of issues in moral psychology that I here explore. So, if being truly honest, I should probably say that the question my essay seeks to address is this: "Under what circumstances, if any, might *I* be inclined to forgive the general—to abandon harsh reactive attitudes to him and perhaps even willingly have him as a guest in my home, for example?"

There are surely some who will not have, as their initial reaction to creatures such as the general, loathing or hatred and an inclination to regard such people (from the moral point of view) as evil incarnate. I suspect, however, that many people will join me, at least initially, in having such reactions. It would be very odd for someone to claim that he values a great painting and not react with loathing to a (sane) person who defaces the painting. So too, I suggest, for those who truly value the dignity—even sanctity—of the human being who has been the innocent victim of atrocity.

Why is this? There are, I think, at least two reasons. First, such reactions are emotional testimonies to our allegiance to value—perhaps not the only possible testimonies, but common and natural ones that seem to have at least a *prima facie* legitimacy.

Second, it is hard not to take *personally* behavior that to some degree undermines the pride we might otherwise take in our species membership—our status as human beings. When the poet starts with "what a piece of work is a man...," we expect to find this phrase followed with an impressive list of human excellences—attributes that make it not unreasonable to take considerable pride in ourselves as members of a species that is indeed "the crown of creation." People such as the general, however, make us see that the piece of work that man is can be a *nasty* piece of work. It is of course probably valuable to have our exalted view of humanity to some degree humbled, but people such as the general can make us feel not simply humbled, but *humiliated*—ashamed of our very species membership. Reflecting on the Holocaust—just one dramatic example of the depths of evil human beings can reach—philosopher Robert Nozick draws a very disturbing conclusion:

> [Of course there have been other earlier and later large scale atrocities, but] the Holocaust alone would have been enough, all by itself [to have stained our species]. Like a relative shaming a family, the Germans, our human relatives, have shamed us all. They have ruined all our reputations, not as individuals—they have ruined the reputation of the human family ... we are all stained.... Humanity has desanctified itself.[17]

If the numbers count, events such as the Holocaust may cast shame on the human family to the greatest imaginable degree. But, even if this is so, would not a single event, such as the general's wanton act of cruel murder, cast shame to *some* degree?[18] (What is an act of historical and cultural shame if it is not a large number of acts of individual shame?) And might not knowing the evil depths to which even one member of our species can sink make us feel less comfortably at home in the world—insecure and even filled with self-doubts about our own capacities for evil? After a period of reflecting on these questions, we might even come to think of all members of our species as in some extended sense victims of the general's act—thereby illustrating the truth that may be contained in John Donne's claim that "any man's death diminishes me, because I am involved in all mankind."[19]

---

17. Robert Nozick, *The Examined Life: Philosophical Meditations* (New York: Simon and Schuster, 1989) pp. 237–39. For an argument that the numbers killed (or not saved) may not always make the moral difference we tend to think, see John M. Taurek, "Should the Numbers Count?" *Philosophy and Public Affairs*, Volume 6, Number 4 (Summer 1977) pp. 293–316.
18. If people can take cultural pride in, for example, Beethoven (one man) then surely there can be cultural shame in one man.
19. John Donne, *Meditation XVII: No Man Is an Island*. Even if we do come to regard third parties as victims in some secondary sense, it is important to remember that this is a secondary sense and nowhere close in gravity to what has happened to the primary victims.

But would the *general's* death diminish me? After all, if I have come to think of the general as a monster, and not as a fellow member of the human race, then I might quite properly welcome or at least not lament his extinction. I might, indeed, come to see this as an event of no greater moral significance than euthanizing a mad dog or—since even mad dogs engage my dog-lover sympathies—as an event morally on a par with simply throwing out the garbage or (recalling the Nazi judge in *Judgment at Nuremberg*) with flushing excrement down the toilet.

Of course, if I am going to be open to the possibility of forgiving the general, I must be open to abandoning all these thoughts about how the general should be regarded and treated—no matter how natural and legitimate these thoughts might have initially seemed. But—and here I briefly introduce a thought that I will expand later in the chapter—*I should abandon these thoughts about the general even if I can never forgive him.* To refuse to forgive him is to refuse to regard him as anything but a loathsome human being—perpetually soiled by what Eleonore Stump (following Aquinas) calls "a stain on the soul" and so tainted that I would not wish him in my presence.[20] But a loathsome human being is still a human being, and that status should protect even the "moral monster" from a violation of his basic human rights. His human dignity should be recognized even though he has soiled it. So when I consider the question, "Should the general be regarded as unforgivable?" I am considering the possibility that it may be legitimate to hate and shun him as long as one lives—but not that he may legitimately be regarded as something

---

Indeed, it is perhaps better to regard most third parties as tertiary victims rather than secondary victims, since they surely cannot be so psychologically identified with the primary victims as, for example, the mother of the boy murdered by the general—for whom the designation "secondary victim" should perhaps be reserved. When tied by love to another person, the level of identification with that person as a "second self" is so great that harm to that person is felt as harm to one's self.

20. *Supra* note 14.

less than a human being and treated accordingly—by being tortured, for example.

Should the general be regarded as unforgivable? I will explore this question under two different scenarios. In the first scenario, I will consider the possibility of forgiving the general if he undergoes certain transformations in his character—becomes *repentant*, filled with *remorse*, for what he has done, for example. In the second scenario, I will consider the possibility of forgiving him in the absence of any such transformations of character—imagining that he continues to take the same wanton delight in his murder as he did at the time he committed it. It is probably easier to imagine forgiveness in the first than in the second scenario, but even the first is not without its problems.

It is common to regard remorse (called by Kierkegaard an "emissary from eternity"[21]) as a central component of repentance and an important character change that can open the door to forgiveness.[22] Why is this? I can think of four reasons: (1) It is simply intrinsically valuable, an aspect of personal moral virtue, to be connected to correct values. To the degree that remorse manifests such connection, it is a good thing and merits appropriate acknowledgement. (2) Remorseful people may be less inclined to commit wrongs again—something quite relevant from a social control point of view—although self-deception and backsliding are constant worries here. (3) From a retributive point of view, one might regard the painful suffering of remorse (the *agenbite of inwit*) as part of the deserved suffering that the wrongdoer should endure, and may even tempt us at some point to think "he has suffered enough." (4) Remorse and

---

21. Søren Kierkegaard, *Purity of Heart Is to Will One Thing*, translated by Douglas V. Steere (New York: Harper and Row, 1948) Section 2 ("Remorse, Repentance, Confession: Eternity's Emissaries to Man") pp. 38–52.
22. See my "Remorse, Apology, and Mercy," *Ohio State Journal of Criminal Law*, Volume 4, Number 2, Spring 2007, pp. 423–53.

repentance may lessen the sense of injury that the wrongdoing has imposed. Part of the injury, at least for certain wrongs, is the receipt of a degrading and insulting symbolic message—the message that others count less than the wrongdoer and can be used by the wrongdoer simply as a means to his own gratification. The remorseful wrongdoer repudiates the message, stands now with us in rejecting it, and thus to some degree lessens the harm. Given all these good reasons to respect remorse and repentance, it would strike many people as churlish for victims and aggrieved third parties not to count remorse and repentance as powerful reasons to forgive.[23]

Not everyone, however, agrees with this common view. Simon Wiesenthal asked the writer Cynthia Ozick, a contributor to his book *The Sunflower*, to consider the case of a young dying Nazi SS soldier, now apparently repentant and filled with remorse, who sought forgiveness for the atrocities against Jews in which he had participated. Should he be forgiven? Absolutely not, says Ozick, and indeed argues that his repentance (which she accepts as genuine) should be regarded as an *aggravating* factor, not a mitigating factor. Let me quote what she has to say:

> We condemn the intelligent man of conscience because... though at heart not a savage, he allowed himself to become one, he did not resist. It was not that he lacked conscience; he smothered it. It was not that he lacked sensibility; he coarsened it. It was not that he lacked humanity; he deadened it. The brute runs to feed Moloch because to him Moloch is not a false god, but a Delightful True Lord, the Master who brings him exaltation. In exaltation he shovels in the babies.... The intelligent man of conscience shovels in the babies, and it does not matter that he does it

---

23. See my discussion of the symbolic and communicative nature of injury in my *Forgiveness and Mercy* and my *Getting Even: Forgiveness and Its Limits, supra* note 1. *Forgiveness and Mercy* was coauthored with Jean Hampton.

without exaltation. Conscience, education, insight—nothing stops him. He goes on shoveling. He knows what wickedness is.... He is a morally sensitive man, and he shovels babies to glut the iron stomach of the idol.... A virtuous future as a model of remorse lies ahead of him; he shovels. He shovels and shovels, all the while possessed of a refined and meticulous moral temperament—so refined and meticulous that it knows the holy power of forgiveness and knows to ask for it.... Let the SS man die unshriven. Let him go to hell. Sooner the fly to God than he.[24]

These are powerful words that should at least pull us up short and provoke some second thoughts before we continue to count remorse and repentance as obvious reasons in favor of forgiveness. But should these second thoughts be our final thoughts? In seeking to answer this question, we will probably have to draw some distinctions based on the gravity of the wrong, the nature of the character that led to that wrong, and the kind of remorse and repentance that the self-transformation produces.

Consider a serious but not really grave injury caused by morally culpable negligence. For example: A man's young son falls off a bicycle that a neighbor loaned to him—the neighbor not remembering that he had failed to tighten the screws on the handle bars that he knew to be loose. The boy receives a noncompound fracture of his arm. Here the harm is not crippling (either physically or spiritually) and the man's character defect, though surely morally culpable, is not nearly as wicked as others that might produce injury—malicious cruelty, for example. After all we can all imagine ourselves becoming inattentive and thereby causing injury, but most of us like to think (falsely no doubt) that malicious cruelty could never be a feature of our characters; and we tend to be sympathetic to faults that we think we

---

24. *Supra* note 7, pp. 213–20.

could manifest. Here remorse (expressed in a sincere apology to the boy and his father) accompanied by payment of any medical expenses (and a nice gift to the boy perhaps) would probably strike most of us as quite adequate to justify forgiving the wrongdoer. The father, son, and neighbors might adandon negative reactive attitudes and continue to act in welcoming ways—e.g., inviting the wrongoder to meetings of the neighborhood association and to social gatherings. Those who do not forgive in such circumstances might even be legitimately regarded as rather small-minded.

If the negligent wrongdoer here described can be regarded as at one end of a moral continuum, then surely the general (and those who perpetrate any atrocity) can surely be viewed as at the other end.[25] For these people should remorse and repentance—even if accompanied by compensation—be regarded as sufficient to open the door to forgiveness? I am inclined to think not—and here I find insight in Ozick's observation. Insincerity and self-deception are common in the realm of claimed remorse and repentance, and even if sincere they often do not last very long. So in these cases of extreme evil, a *fully changed life* should—at least from my perspec-

---

25. Is the general one of Ozick's "brutes" or is he "an intelligent man of conscience"? We would need to know much more about the general to feel confidence in any answer to this question, but from what we are told in the story it seems plausible to see him as the former—in which case, according to Ozick, he would be more worthy of forgiveness than another general we might imagine who performed the same deed with calm and deliberate rational planning and even tried to justify the act to himself. But perhaps the general did try to justify the act—saw his treatment of the boy simply as just retribution, for the harm caused to the general's dog. This is no doubt an irrational justification, but is it any more irrational than the justification the young SS man probably gave to himself for setting on fire a locked house full of Jews? It is hard to be certain of our judgments in cases like this—something that should teach us humility with respect to attempting to judge the deep character or worth of another. In this regard, see my "Moral Epistemology, the Retributive Emotions, and the 'Clumsy Moral Philosophy' of Jesus Christ," *The Passions of Law*, edited by Susan Bandes (New York: New York University Press, 1999) pp. 149–67, and "Legal Moralism and Retribution Revisited," 2006 Presidential Address, Pacific Division, *The Proceedings and Addresses of the American Philosophical Association*, Volume 80, Number 2. 2006, pp. 45–62, and also in *Criminal Law and Philosophy*, Volume 1, Number 1, 2007, pp. 5–20.

tive—be a condition of forgiveness for people of this nature. "Call no man happy until he is dead," said the ancient Greeks, and I am inclined to think—in the case of people such as the general—"Call no man repentant until he is dead," although a bit excessive, might be at least in the right ballpark. What is legitimately sought here, I think, is what is sometimes called *penance* and *atonement*—actions that seek, to the degree that it is in one's power, to make the world and oneself, if not right again, at least much better than one's evil had left them, and to do this at a significant cost to desires generated by what Kant called "the dear self."[26] This can typically not be accomplished by a single act—even something as dramatic as Tolstoy's Father Sergius cutting off his finger with an axe as a response to a sinful act or even suicide prompted by self-hatred—because such acts can easily be little more than dramatic acts of moral egoism that assert the very kind of autonomy that requires being humbled. Given that one's evil resulted from the replacement of the demands of morality with the pulls of the dear self, one needs to seek a life that subdues the dear self. As Herbert Fingarette has argued, it is important that wrongdoers—particularly those guilty

---

26. See, for example, the beginning so Section II of *Groundwork of the Metaphysics of Morals* in Immanuel Kant, *Practical Philosophy*, translated and edited by Mary Gregor (Cambridge University Press) p. 62 (4:407 in the Royal Prussian Academy edition). When Kant speaks of the "dear self" he does not simply mean acting on desires that are selfish in the ordinary sense—desires for personal pleasure, for example—although these are certainly included. He means any desire—including desires generated by commitment to corrupt principles (Nazi principles, for example)—that one arrogantly presumes to act on, as acts of self-will, without subjecting those desires to appropriate moral scrutiny (found in the categorical imperative, according to Kant). I tend to conceptualize repentance as the remorseful acceptance of responsibility for one's evil and a commitment to change the aspect of oneself that led to the evil, atonement as doing what one can to "make up" for the evil, and penance as subjecting oneself to hardship or suffering or accepting in the right spirit such hardship or suffering if legitimately imposed by others. All these four—remorse, repentance, atonement, and penance—are, of course, closely related and can overlap. Sometimes, for example, the best way to atone is to undergo penance. For a stimulating argument that criminal punishment can sometimes be seen as atonement, see Stephen P. Garvey, "Punishment as Atonement," *UCLA Law Review*, Volume 46, 1999, pp. 1801–58.

of grave wrongs—have their wills and egos humbled;[27] and one who is angling for forgiveness is exhibiting a kind of self-assertion or autonomy that shows inadequate humbling.

To illustrate some of these points, let me recount a true story told by Eleonore Stump to outline behavior that would incline her to forgive (in the sense of welcoming back) those who act in evil ways[28] The story concerns a Japanese man who was in Hiroshima during the atomic bombing of that city. Fleeing the city after the attack, he noted several people who had fallen in the streets begging for help—particularly for a drink of water. (Radiation exposure apparently creates extreme thirst in victims.) The man considered stopping but decided to ignore the plight of these people and continue his escape from the contaminated city. At a later time he reflected on what he had done, was overcome with self-loathing at the dominance of self-love in his thought processes, built a shrine to the bombing victims, and then lived humbly and devoted the rest of his life to service of others. Professor Stump said that she not only would welcome him into her home but would feel honored by his presence—something that might apply as well to a totally remorseful and repentant Goebbels after years of self-denying service to others or some other behavior that revealed a long-standing repression of the dear self.

Service to others is not the only way, of course, that the dear self may be repressed and denied. The influential priest Father Marcial Maciel, founder of the Legionaries of Christ, had faced numerous charges of sexual abuse during his long career in the church. Pope Benedict, after studying the results of a Vatican investigation into

---

27. Herbert Fingarette, "Punishment and Suffering," 1977 Presidential Address, Pacific Division, *Proceedings and Addresses of the American Philosophical Association*, Volume 50, Number 6, pp. 499–525.
28. I heard Professor Stump recount this story at a conference at Harvard in response to a question on a lecture based on her paper cited earlier, *supra* note 14.

these charges, instructed Father Maciel to renounce all public ministry and to retire to a monastery for a life of prayer and penance. This surely involved at least a brief repression of the dear self (Father Maciel died shortly after the Vatican ruling) and—on a certain theory of petitionary prayer—may also have involved service to others.[29]

Up to this point, I have imagined what it might take for me to at least consider forgiving the repentant general: a transformed life that reveals, over a great time, a conversion from the claims of the dear self to the claims of morality—a conversion that may be illustrated in a life of humble service to others (what Father Sergius was perhaps ultimately able to approximate) or in some other kind of withdrawal from the world and all the satisfactions that such a world provides for the dear self. Since what the general did is obviously much worse than what the Japanese man did—since the Japanese man gave way to the fear and weakness of the moment—a life of humble service, at the very least, is what the general would need to do by way of penance and atonement (following his repentance and remorse) but he surely would, given the gravity of his evil and his cruelty, need to do much more.[30] He might well start this process by seeking severe

29. *Vatican communique on Legionary Founder: Father Marcial Invited to Renounce All Public Ministry.* Vatican City, May 19, 2006 (zenti.org). The difference between mandated versus chosen atonement is interesting and worthy of more exploration. The translator's choice of the word "invited" is interesting, but I assume that an invitation of this nature—unlike an invitation to a dinner party—is not one that one is free to refuse without great cost. Even so, many might regard this sanction—and the penance it imposed—as insufficiently severe given the gravity of the wrong. But surely this kind of sanction must have been very humiliating for an ecclesiastical celebrity of the stature of Father Marcial. Those who, like Kant and orthodox Christians, believe that there is radical evil in human nature, will recognize that it is never possible for a person immersed in what seems to be a life of self-denial to be totally sure that this immersion is not itself in response to a call of the dear self. Father Sergius can never be fully confident that his humble service is not a kind of self-pleasing spiritual pride—feeding a narcissistic desire to be spiritually superior to others. This was also the worry of Beckett in Eliot's *Murder in the Cathedral.* Was he accepting martyrdom out of genuine love of and duty to God or because, out of pride, he rather fancied the idea of being a martyr?

30. Many might regard the Japanese man's total life transformation as an excessive—even pathologically excessive—response to what was a moment of ordinary human weakness. Trying

punishment—enduring suffering as he made others endure it, never seeking pardon from the punishment once administered, not begging for forgiveness, and then in the jail environment (presumably the only environment now open to him) dedicating himself to a life of service, contemplation, and prayer. Then, just maybe, if he lived long enough, he might be able to do enough to justify the abandonment of the loathing and shunning that his previous evil had earned for him.[31]

But what if the general, given plenty of time to become remorseful and repentant, does *not* move in the direction of self-transformation at all but instead remains totally content with what he has done and who he is. Have we here finally found a case where it would be justified never to forgive—to take loathing as one's final considered response to him? I am inclined to believe that the answer to this question is *yes*. I am inclined to think that the retention of loathing and shunning would be a fitting response to a man of such unrepented evil. But how far can we let such loathing and shunning take us? There is, I fear, a strong temptation to let this loathing and shunning carry us all the way to regarding the unremorseful general as less than human—as *literally* a monster or a piece of excrement. Can we then treat him in any way we wish—torture him, degrade him, mutilate him—since we now regard him as unprotected by the values of human dignity and human rights?

---

to see it from what might have been his point of view, however, we might imagine that—as a member of a culture often said to have a shame morality—giving in to this kind of weakness filled him with a shame that shook his ego-ideal to its very foundations.

31. I say "just maybe" since one could not be certain that such welcoming is, all things considered, the right thing to do simply because the general has done everything in his power to do. One also would, for example, have to consider other relevant factors such as effects on third parties. What if there is evidence that permanently shunning people such as the general—never letting them back into full membership in the human family—would give others incentives never to act as the general acted? There might, of course, be competing evidence that a posture of permanent exclusion might give out the message that attempts to improve oneself (and perhaps thereby become less dangerous to others) are futile. These are complex empirical issues.

4. A DIGRESSION ON HUMAN DIGNITY[32]

Tempting as it is to answer a resounding *yes* to this question (think of Hitler, or Pol Pot, or Stalin, or a serial rapist and murderer) one would surely want to at least pause before adopting a position of such moral gravity. Do we really want to say that it is ever permissible to regard any member of the biological human species—even the unrepentant general—in this way?

We might find here some interesting differences between a religious and a secular way of approaching this question. Christians, for example, would surely answer the question with a resounding *no* since they are committed to the view that *all* members of the species—even the general and those like him—are precious because created in God's image. But can one really see preciousness in creatures such as the general? Perhaps only if we view them with the eye of *love* as Simone Weil (and, more recently, Raimond Gaita) have said—a thought captured in Weil's observation that "love sees what is invisible."[33] Perhaps the invisible that one at least thinks one sees through love is a capacity for redemption, no matter how vile the wrongdoer's past. Or perhaps it is to believe that one sees some decent core of the person through all its layers of corruption. "Lost within a man who murdered, there was a soul like any other soul, purity itself it surely once had been," as the novelist William Trevor says of the serial killer who is the central character of his novel *Felicia's Journey*—a moving sentence by a writer of great moral and spiritual sensitivity.[34]

---

32. This section is adapted from my essay "The Elusive Nature of Human Dignity," *The Hedgehog Review* Volume 9, Number 3, Fall 2007, pp. 20–31.
33. See Raimond Gaita, *A Common Humanity—Thinking About Love and Truth and Justice* (London: Routledge, 2002) and his *Good and Evil: An Absolute Conception*, Second Edition (London: Routledge, 1999). Gaita is greatly influenced by Weil, and the Weil quotation is from Gaita.
34. William Trevor, *Felicia's Journey* (New York: Viking, 1995), p. 212. Jean Hampton believed that her Christianity required her to believe in a core of goodness in each person but admitted that living up to this requirement was generally beyond her power. See *Forgiveness and Mercy*, supra note 1, Chapter 4.

However, even those who feel the emotional pull of this sentence, or of the spiritual idea of seeing through the eye of love, will surely have to admit that such a point of view has no clear rational foundation. So perhaps it can be adopted only within a framework of radical religious *faith*—a faith that would allow a believer to see the neighbor even in the general and thus be able to extend the command to love one's neighbor as oneself even to him. Kierkegaard, indeed, found human beings so intrinsically unlovable—"our unpoetic neighbors" he called them—that he thought that one could love them only if one accepted a divine command to do so.[35] Thus one who accepts a divine command to love one's neighbor, and regards every member of the human species as a neighbor, has a perfectly adequate ground for abandoning any degree of dismissive hatred that might lead to seeing the unrepentant general as vermin or a monster or a piece of excrement lacking in all human dignity.

But what is the nonbeliever to do? Should the person incapable of radical religious faith feel free to regard the general and his kind as less than human, as devoid of dignity, and thus as mad animals or monsters that merit no respect and can thus be treated in any way that one might desire?

Even for complete secularists, who are unlikely to recognize any absolute reasons of principle here, there are at least powerful *historical* and *pragmatic* reasons that should give them pause before utterly abandoning the idea of human dignity for people such as the general. The twentieth century, for example, gave us many demonstrations of the terrible dangers that can arise when individual human beings or their governments presume to discard as not really human—and thus treat as monsters, animals, or vermin—members of their own species. These dangers are not merely the terrible

---

35. Søren Kierkegaard, *Works of Love*, edited and translated by Howard. V. Hong and Edna H. Hong (Princeton: Princeton University Press, 1995) Section IIA, pp. 17–43.

things that acting on such a view can bring about to those deemed nonhuman, but also the terrible things that acting on such a view can bring about in the souls of those who would presume to treat others as nonhuman. To guard against these dangers, it is always a good idea to keep vividly in mind Nietzsche's wise counsel that "Whoever fights with monsters should see to it that in the process he does not become a monster. And when you look long into an abyss, the abyss also looks into you."[36]

Nietzsche's counsel is, like all prudential counsel, consequential in nature since it warns of what might happen to the world and to us if we felt free to draw and then act upon the human/nonhuman distinction if applied to members of our own species. It is not strictly utilitarian, however, because it is concerned not merely with social consequences to the general welfare but also with negative influences on our own virtue of character.

Important as these consequential considerations are, the case against embracing and acting on a human/nonhuman distinction applied to members of our own species is not limited to those considerations. To those considerations I would also add what I will call considerations of *moral humility*. If we can overcome our comforting self-deceptions about our own wisdom and goodness, we will surely realize how limited are our cognitive powers to read the heart of another and how great is our own potential for evil—realize that perhaps we do not know enough and are not good enough to presume to dismiss any other human being from the dignity club. A Christian will think here of Jesus' remark "Let him who is without sin among you be the first to cast a stone," but the insight in that remark as a check to human pride as unjustified self-confidence in one's own virtue can surely be embraced by even the most secular of

---

36. Friedrich Nietzsche, *Beyond Good and Evil*, translated by Walter Kauffman (New York: Vintage Books, 1989), p. 89.

readers—an insight that might even incline such a reader to accept Auden's counsel to "love your crooked neighbor with your crooked heart."[37]

"But wait a minute," the secular skeptic might say, "I have never had my dogs rip a child apart or committed any other atrocity—have never raped, have never tortured, have never murdered. So surely I am without sin in the relevant sense and can feel free to cast as many stones as I like at the general and his kind—even the stone of refusing to regard him as possessing human dignity. My heart may be a little bit crooked—I was rude to my secretary yesterday, for example—but not so crooked that I must consider loving the general or even according him the kind of respect as a human that he, being a monster and not really a human, does not merit. He is moral excrement, and excrement pretty clearly lacks dignity."

This response strikes me as too hasty and shallow as a response to the insight expressed in Jesus' remark. This remark, as I interpret it, invites those of us who have been virtuous and law-abiding to ask ourselves *why* this has been the case. Is it, as we would like to think, because our characters are splendid all the way down? Or is it perhaps because our circumstances—of upbringing, of need, of temptation, and of all the other things that John Rawls has called "our luck on the natural and social lottery"—have been favored?[38] And might it not be even possible that we are virtuous and law-abiding simply

---

37. W.H. Auden, from "As I Walked Out One Evening," *Collected Poems* (New York: Vintage Books, 1991) p. 135.
38. John Rawls, *A Theory of Justice* (Cambridge, MA: Belknap Press of Harvard University Press, 1971). In Sections 12 and 13 (pp. 65–90) Rawls uses the idea of a lottery in the distribution of natural and social advantages to reject what he calls "liberal equality" in favor of "democratic equality." Liberal equality is rejected because (in Rawls' view) it unjustly allows natural and social advantages, which are morally arbitrary because simply a matter of luck, to influence the formation of a principle of distribution as part of the basic structure of a society.

because we are *afraid* of the consequences of disobedience? Kant puts these worries this way in his *Religion*:

> We call a man evil, however, not because he performs actions that are evil (contrary to [moral] law) but because these actions are of such a nature that we may infer from them the presence in him of evil maxims. Through experience we can observe actions contrary to [moral] law, and we can observe (at least in ourselves) that they are performed in the consciousness that they are [morally] unlawful; but a man's maxims, sometimes even his own, are not thus observable; consequently the judgment that the agent is an evil man cannot be made with certainty if grounded on experience.... [People] may...picture themselves as meritorious, feeling themselves guilty of no such offenses as they see others burdened with; nor do they ever inquire if good luck should not have the credit, or whether by reason of the cast of mind which they could discover, if they only would, in their own inmost nature, they would not have practiced similar vices, had not inability, temperament, training, and circumstances of time and place which serve to tempt one (matters that are not imputable) kept them out of the way of these vices. This dishonesty, by which we humbug ourselves and which thwarts the establishing of a true moral disposition in us, extends outwardly to falsehood and deception of others. [This dishonesty] is an element of the radical evil of human nature, which (inasmuch as it puts out of tune the moral capacity to judge what a man is to be taken for, and renders wholly uncertain both internal and external attribution of responsibility) constitutes the foul taint of our race.[39]

---

39. Immanuel Kant, *Religion Within the Limits of Reason Alone*, translated by T. M. Greene and Hoyt H. Hudson (New York: Harper, 1960) pp. 33–34. If Kant's concerns here and Rawls' concerns about luck on the natural and social lottery (as arguments for moral humility in judging others) constitute grounds for forgiveness, this suggests that the forgiveness/

Imagine yourself possessed of Gyges' ring—a ring that, in the stories told by Herodotus and Plato, makes its wearer invisible. Imagine yourself possessed of such a ring and then try to answer honestly what you might do under such circumstances. I suspect that for most of us an honest answer will be an important lesson in moral humility, a lesson that might incline us—surely not to condone what the general has done or to free him from all blame and even severe punishment—but at least to resist the temptation to distance ourselves from him too far—so far that we would give in to an abandoned hatred of him that would presume to dismiss him from the human race and attribute to him no human dignity at all and thus make him a target of whatever cruelty we might desire to inflict on him.[40] The question "Who am I to presume to make such a judgment?" combined with the worry "There but for the grace of God go I" should make us at least go partway down the road sketched for us by Walt Whitman in his poem "You Felons on Trial in Courts" as he speaks of himself:

> Beneath this face that appears so impassive
>   hell's tides continually run,

---

excuse distinction may not be as sharp as I once thought. When one says of a wrongdoer, "It may have been so much more difficult for him, given the obstacles posed by his nature and circumstances, to avoid evil than it would have been for me," it strikes me as arbitrary to insist that this must be either an excusing insight or a forgiving insight but not both. It probably serves the interests of clarity to begin by insisting on a sharp excuse/forgive distinction but then to note that, in some cases, these two bleed into each other. Otherwise we may achieve little more than what Herbert Hart once called "uniformity at the price of distortion."

40. The Eighth Amendment of the United States Constitution bans "cruel and unusual punishments." This in theory, if not always in practice, shields even the worst of criminals from treatment such as torture or mutilation—treatment that would assault their dignity as human beings and would compromise the dignity of those who would inflict such punishments. Unfortunately, the Eighth Amendment provides little protection against torture of inmates in some American detention facilities, since this will often be characterized as something other than punishment or even as something other than torture—harsh interrogation techniques used, not on convicted criminals, but on those regarded as enemy combatants, for example.

Lusts and wickedness are acceptable to me,
   I walk with delinquents with passionate love,
I feel I am of them—I belong to those convicts and
      prostitutes myself,
And henceforth I will not deny them—for how can I deny
      myself?[41]

It will, of course, always remain very tempting to adopt the view that the world's great evils are the work of just a few people of great nastiness—people nothing like us. However, books such as Christopher R. Browning's *Ordinary Men*, though not without their critics, provide at least some reason to resist that comforting temptation.[42] It is also useful to think about the phenomenon of psychic distance and the way in which it encourages self-deception. A person who might not be able to put a pistol in a baby's face and blow its brains out might easily be able to drop bombs from thirty thousand feet that will blow the brains out of many babies. (During the Vietnam War the *Doonesbury* cartoon strip would sometimes portray bomber pilots dropping napalm and being struck by the beauty of the little puffs of light and color they saw below them.) Perhaps even those who cannot imagine joining Dostoevsky's general and sending dogs to kill a small boy can—alas—imagine themselves being another kind of general who, in time of war, might without cruelty order a bombing raid on a village while knowing full well that many small boys and many innocent others will be torn to bits—all the while hastily justifying this carnage to himself with slogans about "foreseen

---

41. Walt Whitman, *Leaves of Grass* (New York: Vintage Books/The Library of America, 1992) p. 511. My brief exposition of the idea of moral humility and its relevance to judgments of what I call the "deep character" of wrongdoers and of their worth as human beings is a summary of thoughts I pursue at length in the two essays of mine cited *supra* at note 25.
42. New York: Penguin Books, 2001.

but undesired collateral damage."⁴³ Hannah Arendt claimed (whether correctly or not I cannot say) that Adolf Eichmann prided himself on not being a cruel man—on not seeking or taking any pleasure in the suffering of the Jews whose transportation to death camps he arranged and in justifying his actions by a truly bizarre reading of Kant's categorical imperative.⁴⁴ And even Dostoevsky's general may have in a perverse sense acted on principle—thinking that he was simply inflicting just punishment for the injury to his dog and in that sense not being merely an unreflective thug. But are the reflective and no doubt self-deceiving wrongdoers such as Eichmann and perhaps the general, as Qzick suggested, *worse* than unreflective thugs who delight in cruelty? If so, this poses a worry for all of us in a way that the agent of psychopathic cruelty might not, since it is easier for us to distance ourselves from wrongdoers of the latter sort than the former sort. Eichmann had friends and seemed to many a decent sort and perhaps, in other contexts, the general appeared this way as well—as did surely many of those in Nazi Germany, Russia under Stalin, and apartheid South Africa who, in spite of being fine husbands and fathers and lovers of dogs, were capable—given the right context—of doing truly terrible things.⁴⁵

5. AN INCONCLUSIVE CONCLUSION

Let me now bring to a close this somewhat rambling set of free associations. I have tried to develop a case for the relevance of the virtue

---

43. It is not my intention to suggest that there are no legitimate uses of the doctrine of double effect but rather to note how easy it is to manipulate this doctrine in such a way that one deceives oneself about the evil of what one does.
44. Hannah Arendt, *Eichmann in Jerusalem: A Report on the Banality of Evil*, New York: Penguin Books, 1977.
45. "If there was one thing I had learned in the war it was that decent, law-abiding family men were capable of the most bestial acts of murder and brutality." Philip Kerr, *The One from the Other*, New York: G. P. Putnam's Sons, 2006, p. 118.

of moral humility in refusing to exclude wrongdoers, even ones as terrible as the unrepentant general, from the range of those regarded as having human dignity—refusing to exclude them from the basic human rights that respecting their human dignity generates. I have also, however, argued that including such people within the orbit of human rights is consistent with never forgiving them—with forever regarding them with loathing, contempt, and shunning. I have not claimed that one has a duty to respond to such people in a totally unforgiving way and shunning them utterly—simply that such a response may be morally legitimate and should not be condemned as a lack of respect for human dignity and human rights.

I must confess, however, that I am not totally happy with this view as thus far expressed. I cannot imagine ever wanting the unrepentant general to be freed from punishment and the suffering that such punishment, in addition to giving him what he deserves, might (one hopes) contribute to his moral transformation.[46] But should I be morally content just so long as he is (for example) fed, provided with basic medical care, and not subjected to cruel and unusual punishment (e.g., torture)? Is respecting his human rights and dignity fully satisfied by operating within such constraints? If so, does operating within such constraints exhaust what is involved in recognizing the general as a fellow human being?

Consider this case: the unrepentant general is suffering greatly but his suffering is occasioned, not as his just deserts for his wrongdoing, but by something unrelated to that—and does not result from any violation of his human rights. Suppose, for example, that the general,

---

46. On the possible role of punishment as a contribution to character reformation, see my essay "Christian Love and Criminal Punishment" in *Christianity and Law: An Introduction*, edited by John Witte Jr. and Frank S. Alexander, Cambridge: Cambridge University Press, 2008, pp. 219–235. See also R. A. Duff's essay on punishment as penance in his "Penance, Punishment, and the Limits of Community," *Punishment and Society*, Volume 5, Number 3, July 2003, pp. 295–312.

while in prison, becomes overwhelmed with grief because he learns that his deeply beloved child is dying of a long and painful illness. I would not for this reason want him freed from his deserved punishment, and—if he ever was released from prison—I would certainly not want to have him over for dinner in my home, or go to the movies with him, or play tennis with him. I hope, however, that—were I his jailer, for example—I would to some degree at least grieve with him and seek to comfort him with respect to his beloved child and, if his warden, would see if some way could be arranged to have him visit his child in the hospital. Why? Simply because he is, after all, a fellow human being or, at least, because it is both lacking in virtue and dangerous not so to regard him. My pity may thus be in competition with my loathing and indeed, in my more Platonic moments, I might even think that of all sufferers the unrepentant general is most deserving of pity since he has perhaps irreparably damaged his very soul.[47]

As a real-world example, consider the capture of Saddam Hussein. When I saw the films of Saddam Hussein crawling out of the rat hole where he had been hiding for a very long time, I found that I did not (at least at that moment) see him as the architect of great evil that he was but rather simply as a pitiful and scared old man. Rather than thinking that he was simply getting what he deserved—the evil bastard—I felt sorry for him. Several of my friends said that they had a similar response to the films. Perhaps this was to see him as a fellow human being, as a neighbor in the Christian sense.[48]

Before my friends and I congratulate ourselves on our refined moral and religious sensibilities, however, it is worth noting this: perhaps our ability to see Saddam Hussein in this way was because it had been our good fortune never to have been one of his victims or

---

47. See Peter Winch, "Ethical Reward and Punishment," in his *Ethics and Action*, London: Routledge and Kegan Paul, 1972, pp. 210–228.
48. See Peter Winch, "Who Is My Neighbor?" in his *Trying to Make Sense*, Oxford: Basil Blackwell Ltd., 1987, pp. 154–166.

someone who loved one of his victims—or even to have seen up close the mutilated body of one of his victims. Given the psychological trauma with which victims of atrocity must struggle, I am not inclined—from my posture of comparative security—to add to their burdens by telling them that they must pity or show compassion to or concern themselves with the moral and spiritual transformation of those who victimized them. There are generally significant psychological differences between victims and third parties, and these differences have moral significance.[49]

Once I as a third party open the door to this kind of pity, however—and begin thinking about the fate of the general's own soul—it may be hard not to open that door a bit wider. What if I come to think that by repressing my loathing and shunning of the general, and welcoming even such as he into some kind of human fellowship, I might make a contribution to his ultimate moral and spiritual reclamation— giving him at least the opportunity to see a ray of hope for such reclamation? If there are duties of love, then might this not be a good candidate for one of those duties? When Jesus and Paul counseled that we visit those in prison—even those who clearly deserve to be there— were they not in part concerned to show even very evil people that we share a common humanity with them and are not giving up on them— in the hope that they will not give up on themselves and the possibility of their own moral rebirth (or, in religious terms, their own salvation)?

If there is genuine insight in the counsel of Jesus and Paul with respect to prisoners, and if my earlier discussion of moral humility (inspired by such diverse writers as Kant and Whitman) has insight, then recognizing one as a fellow human being—as a neighbor— involves more than merely respecting his basic human rights. Surely the general does not have any right that I comfort him in his grief

---

49. I owe this insight to Thomas Brudholm (from reading the manuscript of his book, *supra* note 1) and to conversations with Lucy Allais.

and *a fortiori*, could not legitimately complain that indifference from me would be a violation of the kind of basic human rights that Amnesty International seeks to protect. Such comfort for the general would be more expansive than this and would involve the kind of forgiveness I have explored in this essay—forgiveness as the abandonment of total loathing and shunning—and the forgiveness would be offered to a person whom many would plausibly characterize as unforgivable.[50]

Having opened the door enough to allow some forgiveness for even the unrepentant general, I remain reluctant to open it all the way. Loathing and shunning are matters of degree, after all, and my extending some human fellowship to the general that goes beyond the mere respect of his basic human rights does not have to be without limits. Without significant limits, indeed, extending fellowship to the general might be disrespectful to victims and their legitimate grievances. I cannot, for example, imagine myself saying (or even thinking) this to the mother of the boy murdered by the general: "I agree that what he did was really terrible and I feel your pain, but I really cannot let that interrupt my project for the general's reclamation. So you can expect to see me playing tennis with him and inviting him to the tennis club's restaurant on a regular basis. I

---

50. In correspondence Nigel Biggar has suggested a distinction between forgiveness-as-absolution and forgiveness-as-compassion—the latter being the only kind of forgiveness appropriate for the unrepentant general. But should we even show him compassion? Jennifer Geddes once suggested to me that allowing the general to remain in the unrelieved torment of grief and despair over his dying child might be defended as representing nearly perfect retribution for his own wanton cruelty to a child and particularly to that child's mother—a piece of wonderful moral symmetry, something that might even be called cosmic justice. "Let this paradigm of moral depravity feel exactly what the mother felt and thereby get nothing more than what he deserves" one might say—and there are days when I am inclined to think this very thing myself. There are other days, however, in which I am inclined to think that—as I indicated earlier—I ought to transcend thinking about what he "deserves" and reach out to him in a limited way in some spirit of common humanity in spite of all that he has done and the evil that he represents. I am deeply conflicted here.

know that you are a member too, and I am sorry for any pain that this may cause you."

The reader can now surely see why I called my conclusion "inconclusive." There are no simple formulas or decision procedures on issues of this nature. I have suggested that recognizing the general's humanity, even if he is totally unrepentant, goes beyond merely respecting his basic human rights. It must also involve a willingness, based on a strong sense of one's own fallibility coupled with a desire to open doors of self-transformation for the general, to seek—if one is in a position to do so—some kind of human fellowship with him. But I have also argued that drawing relevant moral distinctions (the distinction between repentant wrongdoers and unrepentant wrongdoers, for example) and maintaining human solidarity with the victims of the general's evil will place significant limits on the extent of the fellowship. There are, in short, many values that must be balanced here—but, alas, no decision procedure to tell us exactly how the balance should be stuck.[51]

---

51. Many people kindly provided very helpful comments on earlier drafts of this manuscript, and some of those comments raised such significant issues that I have not been able to deal with them here except in a perfunctory way. I would like to thank the following: Susan Bandes, Nigel Biggar, Thomas Brudholm, Ellen Canacakos, Richard Dagger, Antony Duff, Eve Garrard, Sandra Marshall, David McNaughton, Herbert Morris, Kirsten Pickering, Mary Sigler, Eleonore Stump, Michael White, and Leo Zaibert.

Chapter 9

Response to Neu, Zipursky, and Steiker

INTRODUCTION

When Julie van Camp called to inform me that the American Philosophical Association Committee on Law and Philosophy planned to schedule a session on my work, I had mixed feelings. On the one hand, I was pleased and honored that colleagues whom I respect thought that my work was worthy of such attention. On the other hand, I realized that sessions of this nature are normally scheduled for people whose careers are perceived to be winding down if not essentially over. Although I am conducting a serious flirtation with turning 70, I do not just yet want to think of myself as having acquired the status of an old academic fart.

When I learned who the chair and panelists for the session were going to be, and when I read the papers of the panelists, good feelings moved aside all such reservations. I was honored that some of these colleagues were willing to travel considerable distance—never an

[This paper has been prepared as a response to papers by Jerome Neu, Benjamin Zipursky, and Carol Steiker for the session "The Work of Jeffrie Murphy" held at the meetings of the American Philosophical Association, Pacific Division, on March 22, 2008. My response is directed to these papers as they were presented at the meeting and it does not take account of any changes that may have been made in the papers at a later time. I am grateful to those who organized and participated in this session and to those who read and commented on previous drafts of my response: Svetlana Beggs, Ellen Canacakos, Kirsten Pickering, Mary Sigler, and Michael White.]

easy experience in the contemporary world of air travel, particularly on a weekend when air travel is unusually heavy. To hear so many kind words expressed about my work from people whom I hold in esteem pleased me to the point of embarrassment, and the substantive criticisms and questions raised gave me much worth thinking about—so much, indeed, that I cannot possibly do these criticisms and questions justice in the brief time I am allowed for a response.

Given the limits of time and space here, I will simply select one important issue from each paper presented and will comment on that—leaving open, of course, the possibility that other issues will be raised in later discussion. I will discuss the three papers in the order in which they were presented and will thus begin with Jerome Neu's work.

RESPONSE TO JEROME NEU

Neu is worried, and rightly so, about the degree to which acquiring, extinguishing, or modifying our emotions is really in our power. I have conceptualized morally justified forgiveness as the overcoming of resentment for moral reasons; and I have offered, as an example of such a reason, the recognition of sincere repentance on the part of the wrongdoer. But it seems, alas, that one might recognize sincere repentance, believe that this now renders forgiveness appropriate and perhaps even obligatory, and yet still be filled with resentment—thus finding that forgiving in such a case is simply not in one's power, not in one's voluntary control. There may be simple steps to overcome or constrain some emotions—count to ten before losing one's temper, for example—but this does not seem to work for resentment and for other emotions such as love. Neu here reminds us of Kant's famous distinction in the *Groundwork* between practical and pathological love—the former being in our power (acting as love requires), the latter not in our power (feeling the emotion of love.).[1] And so, too, Neu suggests, for overcoming resentment. It is in our power not to *act* on our resentments—by not taking revenge, for example—but is it in our power to extinguish or even limit our *feelings* of resentment?

At this point I want to draw a distinction between direct and indirect control, and to draw the distinction in a way that seems right and has made me see a mistake (at least a mistake of emphasis) that has often occurred in my earlier writings on forgiveness. The mistake is in thinking of forgiveness primarily as a specific kind of *act* (the mental act of changing one's heart) whereas it should, at least frequently, be thought of as a disposition of *character*—a *virtue* in something like the Aristotelian sense. Like most people, I cannot immediately overcome resentment to forgive the person who has wronged me simply by seeing that I have adequate moral reasons to do so and then commanding myself to forgive right now. There is no direct control here. I can, however, work over time to develop a *forgiving character*—a character that is disposed to constrain resentment within reasonable and moral bounds. This can often give me indirect control over resentment in that I choose now (a matter of direct control) to set myself on a future course that in the long run I have reasonable grounds to believe will make it likely (to paraphrase Aristotle) that my resentments will be at the right time, directed at the right person for the right reason, proportional to the gravity of the wrong and the culpability of the wrongdoer, and weakening or even coming to an end when this is appropriate. Aristotle called the process of indirect control *habituation*, and—depending on the general world view of the person seeking an improved character—this can take many forms: prayer, spiritual counseling, philosophical reading, conversing with wise friends, or psychotherapy, to give a few examples.

---

1. Immanuel Kant, *Groundwork of the Metaphysics of Morals*, 4: 399. All Kant citations are to the Royal Prussian Academy edition of Kant's works. Most English translations of Kant's works provide the academy pagination in the margins.

Even Kant, interestingly enough, thought that this kind of indirect control is possible and even morally mandatory. In his *Doctrine of Virtue*, for example, there are passages that will surprise those who think that his sole view on the control of emotions is to be found in the famous distinction between practical and pathological love. I offer two such passages, the first specifically on forgiveness, and the second on the cultivation of love (or at least empathy)—an emotion that can lead to forgiveness.

> It is...a duty of virtue not only to refrain from repaying another's enmity with hatred out of mere revenge but also never even to call upon the world-judge for vengeance—partly because a man has enough guilt of his own to be greatly in need of forgiveness and partly, and indeed especially, because no punishment, no matter from whom it comes, may be inflicted out of hatred. —Hence men have a duty to cultivate a *conciliatory spirit*.... But this must not be confused with *placid* toleration of injuries..., renunciation of the rigorous means...for preventing the recurrence of injuries by other men.[2]

> [I]t is an indirect duty to cultivate the compassionate natural...feelings in us.... It is therefore a duty not to avoid places where the poor, who lack the most necessary things, are to be found; instead, it is a duty to seek them out. It is a duty not to shun sickrooms or prisons and so on in order to avoid the pain of pity, which one may not be able to resist. For this feeling, though painful, nevertheless is one of the impulses placed in us by nature for effecting what the representation of duty might not accomplish by itself.[3]

---

2. Immanuel Kant, *Doctrine of Virtue*, 6:460–61.
3. *Id.*, 6:457.

Kant seems to be suggesting that there are tendencies of sympathy and compassion latent in all normal people. These are often repressed because it can be both painful and inconvenient to have them, but they can be engaged with a sustained pattern of the right kind of experiences and behaviors.[4]

Finally, let me close this section with a quotation from the essay "The Idea of Perfection," by Iris Murdoch. In this essay Murdoch portrays a woman who feels that it is her duty to develop better feelings toward her initially rather despised daughter-in-law. Her behavior toward her daughter-in-law has always been impeccable—displaying no external signs of how she feels inside—but the woman seeks a change of heart as well. And she seeks—and eventually attains—such a change of heart through something rather like the therapeutic process that cognitive psychotherapists (whose distant ancestors were the Stoic philosophers) call "cognitive restructuring":

> A mother, whom I shall call M, feels hostility to her daughter-in-law, whom I shall call D. M finds D quite a good-hearted girl, but while not exactly common yet certainly unpolished and lacking in dignity and refinement. D is inclined to be pert and familiar, insufficiently ceremonious, brusque, sometimes positively rude, always tiresomely juvenile.... Time passes, and it could be that M settles down with a hardened sense of grievance and a fixed picture of D, imprisoned (if I may use a question-begging word) by the cliché: my poor son has married a silly vulgar girl. However, the M of the example is an intelligent and well-intentioned

---

4. Sympathetic and compassionate feelings can be inconvenient in that they may prompt us to take steps to minimize the suffering of others and these steps may cost us time and resources–time and resources that the "dear self" would prefer to expend on itself. A *New Yorker* cartoon of many years ago portrayed two very rich men sitting in soft leather chairs and smoking cigars in a classy private club. One says to the other, "I too once wanted to do something for my fellow men, but I could not think of anything that would not have put me to some inconvenience."

person, capable of self-criticism, capable of giving careful and just *attention* to an object which confronts her. M tells herself: "I am old-fashioned and conventional. I may be prejudiced and narrow-minded. I may be snobbish. I am certainly jealous. Let me look again." Here I assume that M observes D or at least reflects deliberately about D, until gradually her vision of D alters.... D is discovered to be not vulgar but refreshingly simple, not undignified but spontaneous, not noisy but gay, not tiresomely juvenile but delightfully youthful, and so on.[5]

Kant's virtuous person sets a course—by no means an easy or a quick one—to engage the potential for love, empathy, and forgiveness so that these can come to the fore and feelings of resentment and hatred can correspondingly be diminished—not in a sloppy, sentimental way but in accord with a rational moral view about what the proper balance of values and considerations must be in a properly cultivated "conciliatory spirit." The mother described by Murdoch comes to feel differently about her daughter-in-law—replacing contempt with affectionate appreciation—by trying to see her (and ultimately actually seeing her) in a new way, under new concepts. Each writer thus illustrates one way (certainly not the only way) that one can develop a character disposed to appropriate forgiveness. A person who has developed such a character can then, of course, find it easier to perform appropriate acts of forgiveness.

Neu has focused mainly on my writings on forgiveness and resentment. Benjamin Zipursky and Carol Steiker have focused mainly on my writings on punishment, retribution, and the role that resentment might legitimately play. Zipursky wants me to be more robust and

---

5. Iris Murdoch, *Existentialists and Mystics: Writings on Philosophy and Literature* (New York: Penguin Books, 1998), 312–13. I am grateful to Svetlana Beggs for reminding me of this passage from the Murdoch essay.

systematic in my defense of retribution. Steiker, while noting that I have retreated substantially from my earlier defenses of retribution, wants me to retreat even more. I will first turn to Zipursky.

RESPONSE TO BENJAMIN ZIPURSKY

Woody Allen once said that his only regret in life was that he was not somebody else. In spite of all the kind and appreciative things that Zipursky says about my work, and in spite of the various interesting detailed points he makes, I cannot help thinking that he wishes that I were somebody else. He finds my work "confessional," expressive of "a desire for self-purification," and filled with "hedges"; and he expresses the desire that I finally "come clean"—by which, I gather, he means that I should stop being so vague and tentative and finally provide, in accord with my solid education as an analytic philosopher, clear and final analyses of the concepts that I explore. I should either lay bare in a systematic way the "semantic, epistemological, and metaphysical" underpinnings of my various claims or give an account of why my doing this is unnecessary. He speculates that I am a closet "new self-respect based contractarian retributivist" and he wants me to come out of the closet and avow and then systematically defend this view. (If I understand what this unwieldy label means, by the way, I am pretty sure that I am not one of these characters—closeted or otherwise.[6])

---

6. I am not sure where Zipursky gets the idea that I have been a contractarian in my defenses of retribution. In 1985 I published an essay in which I explicitly argued that liberal versions of contractarianism would not lead to the adoption of any but the most minimalist versions of retributivism. Rawls, a liberal contractarian if anyone is, does not embrace a nonminimalist version of retributivism. (By a "minimalist" version of retributivism I mean one that sees the dominant purpose of punishment to be crime control but will constrain that goal by such retributive principles as "punish only the guilty.") See my "Retributivism, Moral Education, and the Liberal State," *Criminal Justice Ethics* 4, no. 1 (Winter/Spring 1985): pp. 3–11.

In short, although I think that Zipursky has some legitimate concerns—no doubt shared by others—about my philosophical methodology or the lack thereof, I find myself in the awkward predicament of realizing that I can deal with these concerns only with more confessions and hedges (or a defense of confessions and hedges) and with an admission (that should embarrass me) that I could not deal systematically and in depth with issues in semantics, epistemology, and metaphysics if my very life depended on my so doing. (I think that at most I have a vague recollection of what was going on in these branches of philosophy when I was in graduate school, and I suspect that all of this is now regarded as hopelessly out of date.) Let me then briefly lay out how, for better or worse, I do philosophy. Some will already be aware of this, others not.

I am essentially an *essayist* with, at any given time, about a forty-page attention span. (Most of my books have been either explicit essay collections or thinly disguised essay collections.) I think mainly in terms of the big picture, not of details, and I generally paint impressionistically in rather broad strokes. In each essay I conduct a conversation with myself and share that conversation with others in the hope that they might find their own thinking stimulated by mine. It has been many years since I have attempted anything systematic and final—my Rawlsian-inspired Kantianism (or was it my Kantian-inspired Rawlsianism?) now being long behind me. Since those days I have tended, rather like Aristotle in ethics, to think and write in the spirit of "on the one hand, but then on the other hand"—attempting nothing final but only to "advance the conversation," to use Richard Rorty's fine phrase. I share what I am thinking at the time of the essay and generally do not give much detailed thought to what I might have said on the same topic in previous essays. To the degree that there are deep systematic connections among my various writings, this is generally not something at which I have consciously aimed and it would probably—if it is there—come as news to me.

I think, however, that there is a *temperamental* connection that unites a great deal of my work: I am, to some nontrivial degree, driven by a Socratic irritation at most smug, settled convictions—and thus I often write not to offer a final positive view, but rather to show virtues in views currently being rejected. And so I found positive things to say about blackmail when there was universal agreement that it was a unique evil that should be a felony; I said highly critical things about the role of psychiatry in criminal law when I felt that an overly therapeutic view of social deviance was having a tendency to undermine beliefs in human responsibility—beliefs on which beliefs in human dignity are partly based; I said positive things about retribution when most philosophers of punishment were dismissing all but the most minimalist versions of retributivism and justifying punishment with some version of utilitarianism; I said positive things about resentment and negative things about forgiveness when people such as Bishop Desmond Tutu, psychologist Robert Enright, and pop psychologists in the self-help and recovery movements were condemning resentment and claiming that only those who forgive exhibit moral and spiritual health. Most recently, I have said some positive things about legal moralism and some negative things about retribution (including my own early defenses of it) when many philosophers seem to think that Herbert Hart killed legal moralism once and for all in his attack on Lord Devlin, and when both public opinion and our current criminal justice system are dominated by the rhetoric of retribution—something that at one time I might have taken as a victory for my then extreme retributive views. The mention of Bishop Tutu, Robert Enright, pop self-help psychology, and our current system of criminal law is significant, by the way, because in recent years I have been increasingly concerned to write not merely for professional philosophers and legal scholars but also to address concerns in the larger culture that, in my view, raise interesting philosophical issues and might benefit from nontechnical philosophical exploration.

One of Noel Coward's most famous songs contains these lines: "I believe that since my life began/the most I've had is just a talent to amuse."[7] I believe that, for many years now and to the degree I have any talent at all, my talent is—as I have indicated—to write essays that might advance the conversation a bit on issues that interest me. In writing these essays, because they involve my thinking out loud, I draw on what has influenced me, what has inspired me, what worries me, what I am currently feeling, and on conflicts between my various beliefs and attitudes; in that sense my essays are admittedly confessional. I hope, however, that this is not merely narcissistic self-indulgence on my part but that it provides some intimacy with my readers. However, I realize that some people, intrigued by the topics of my essays, will respond when reading them in the manner feared by T. S. Eliot's Prufrock: "That is not it at all/That is not what I meant, at all."

I do not know if Zipursky's primary intention was to force me to think about my philosophical methodology, though I am glad that he has given me a chance to reflect on these matters and on the kind of modest contribution I hope that my way of working can make to moral and legal philosophy. I can only stand in admiring awe of those, such as John Rawls, who have the genius to develop in ethics systematic theories of depth and analytical rigor—theories that will be discussed as long as there is philosophy. This is not me, however. I think that much of our moral life is well captured in such phrases as "muddling through" or "stumbling along," and I would like to think that the sort of thing I do might sometimes be even more helpful than grand theory in assisting the muddling and the stumbling.[8]

---

7. Noel Coward, "If Love Were All," in *Bitter Sweet*, produced at His Majesty's Theatre, London, 1929.
8. Zipursky suspects that I have used the term "fitting" in a moderately technical way (when I have characterized resentment as a fitting response to being wronged) and suspects that this commits me to thinking that people who are wronged *ought* to resent. I fear, however, that I meant nothing very theoretically deep by the word "fitting." I never meant to suggest that

Let me now move to the "prudential reconsideration" of retribution that Carol Steiker urges on me.

RESPONSE TO CAROL STEIKER

"Philosophy," wrote Karl Marx, "stands in the same relation to the study of the actual world as masturbation stands to sexual love."[9] This passage came to my mind as I read Steiker's rich essay, since she—like Marx—reminds us that those of us who do academic writing can often deceive ourselves about the degree to which this writing connects in any useful way to the actual operations of our dominant social institutions and might even unintentionally provide those institutions with covering rationalizations for unspeakable practices. There is no doubt, as Steiker points out, that in our society retributive language is now often used merely as a cover for the advocacy of harsh and even cruel treatment of criminals. Indeed, it is not uncommon to hear people express indifference to such barbaric prison conditions as gang rape by describing this deplorable situation as criminals getting no more than they deserve.

Anyone who fully understands classical philosophical retributivism will, of course, realize that such claims are a perversion of legitimate retributive doctrine. No civilized retributivist (Kant, for example) would ever claim that criminals deserve to endure repeated forced sodomy and would indeed vigorously protest such prison

---

"fitting" means "uniquely fitting"—that resentment is the *only* fitting response to being wronged. (I do admit, however, that those who do not resent being wronged make me not only suspicious but wanting some evidence that they are saints and not merely servile.) In speaking of resentment as a fitting response to being wronged. I was mainly concerned to oppose those who believe that resentment is an *unfitting* response to being wronged.

9. Karl Marx, *The German Ideology*, ed. Christopher John Arthur (New York: International Publishers, 1970), 103.

conditions by condemning them as unjust because far in excess of what any criminal deserves. Kantian retributive doctrine is built on respecting the dignity of responsible autonomous human agents, and such respect should protect them from all cruel and unusual treatment. It should also protect them from being severely punished—or indeed punished at all—for actions that should never have been criminalized in the first place or at most treated as less serious offenses. So the environment of radical overcriminalization and often absurdly excessive punishments—the environment in which we in America live—would be condemned by any genuine retributivist. (I say "often absurdly excessive punishments" rather than "always absurdly" because it strikes me that some criminals—some white collar criminals, for example—tend to be punished with excessive leniency.[10])

I do not think that Steiker would deny the importance of desert, and indeed I think that at some abstract theoretical level she is herself committed in principle to retributivism because her appeal for more mercy is largely *pragmatic*: it is based on the idea that we need some corrective value to ratchet down the level of punishment from its currently excessive and cruel (and thus, I assume, undeserved) levels.

But if one embraces the retributive value of never punishing in excess of desert, why not simply assert that value instead of talking, as Steiker does, about the need for more mercy? Her answer is that the philosophical language of retribution has been co-opted by the political forces of darkness. Because of this, it is positively pernicious to continue to use this language—whatever its theoretical merits—if one wants to make important changes in the actual world of crime and punishment as it operates, as she nicely puts it, "on the ground." This, of course, is the insight in the passage I quoted from Marx.

---

10. I am grateful to Michael White for forcing me to see the necessity of this qualification.

I think that Steiker has raised some legitimate concerns here. Indeed, these pragmatic concerns—supplemented by some insights from Nietzsche on the pathology that may underlie the urge to punish—had a great deal to do with the partial retreat from retributivism that Steiker herself has found in my American Philosophical Association presidential address.[11] Why, Steiker asks, use the language of what has, in the real world, become little more than a dangerous fiction? Why not try another language—the language of mercy—if there is good empirical evidence that this shift in language (and an accompanying change in thought) will indeed lessen the cruelty of our present system? Mercy language may still in some sense involve a fiction because it still essentially seems to aim at preventing people from being punished out of all reasonable proportion to their desert, and thus may deviate from what a strict philosophical analysis would call mercy. It is Steiker's hope, however, that any fiction here will likely have beneficent rather than evil results. Even if one has philosophical reasons for being reluctant to use the language of mercy, I think that Steiker's essential points could be captured just as well if one thought of her as advocating a larger role for empathy, compassion, or even love in our current system of criminal justice.

However, although I lack Steiker's knowledge of social science and most things empirical, I find it hard to share her confidence that a shift from the value of just deserts to the value of mercy (or empathy, or compassion, or love) will prove to be beneficent in the way that she hopes. The pragmatic or prudential payoff will depend largely on *institutional design*—on how we design social mechanisms that will indeed ratchet down the cruelty, lack of proper proportion, and downright stupidity that currently seem dominant. And Steiker is far more sanguine than I that a wider scope for official *discretion* will do the trick.

---

11. Jeffrie G. Murphy, "Legal Moralism and Retribution Revisited," *Proceedings and Addresses of the American Philosophical Association*, 80, no. 2 (November 2006).

To some degree we are all prisoners of the generation that framed our sensibilities, and most people from my generation who think of official discretion—from trial judges, prosecutors, or juries—probably have as the first example that springs to mind the phenomenon (made highly visible in the early days of the civil rights movement) of white officials and juries in the American South always finding a way to make sure that white people were never punished for violence against black people, even for murders. Abuse of discretion in the direction of harshness and cruelty is not a mere relic from the past, however. In my own county in Arizona, for example, we have a local prosecutor (our county attorney) who—in team with our cowboy county sheriff—uses the legal discretion at his disposal mainly to show how tough on crime he is. I do not know the degree to which his desire to appear tough is a matter of conviction or merely a strategy of appeal to the voters with an eye to reelection, but, given his and our sheriff's mania for self-glorifying self-advertisement, I strongly suspect that the latter plays a substantial role. Steiker recognizes dangers of this sort, but the recognition does not seem substantially to diminish her enthusiasm for expanded discretion and her faith that it is likely to be used in beneficent ways.

So I would not myself be too hopeful that increased exercise of discretion will move our criminal justice system in a more merciful direction. Ultimately, something must be done to change the general mood of the electorate so that out legislatures and public officials will be less inclined to exploit the fears of citizens (think of, for example, appeals to "remember 9/11!") as their best route to political power. I have no recipe for how we might do this, though I do have one relevant thought.

Liberals of my generation got into the very bad habit of expecting officials—particularly federal appellate courts—to bring about enlightened criminal justice (and other kinds of justice) by judicial fiat. This is a kind of judicial activism often welcomed, of course, if it is activism in pursuit of one's own values. I call this a bad habit because it encouraged many liberals (and I include myself) to disengage from the messiness of actual politics—of actually walking the streets for one's candidate for the state legislature, or contributing money to his or her campaign, or attending town meetings to express one's values in the hope of persuading others. In short, faith and hope in official behavior encouraged many of us to become bad because slothful citizens.

Those of us who want a more civilized system of criminal justice in America had better do a lot more than place our faith in the exercise of official discretion since officials—as Steiker herself notes—are political animals. That is, they are either required to seek election or are appointed by those who are required to seek election and are thus likely to reflect the mood currently dominant in the area where they live. With respect to crime and punishment, that mood remains dominantly fearful and cruel, and without a change in that mood there is little to hope for (and perhaps much to fear from) official discretion.

If that mood does change, then my guess is that our best hope for significant criminal law reform will lie not in official discretion, but in statutory reform, which is the job of the legislature. Statutory reform, in my view, should involve such things as significant decriminalization in a variety of areas, substantial reduction in the amount of punishment given for many offenses, rethinking of certain criminal law doctrines (felony murder, for example), expanded opportunities for rehabilitation, and significant reforms in the conditions of prison life. Furthermore, given the Supreme Court's general unwillingness to use its discretion to apply in a meaningful way the Eighth Amendment ban on cruel and unusual punishment to prison conditions, the only hope for reform in these areas must rest with state legislatures. The work to lessen the conditions of poverty and alienation that breed crime—conditions dramatically noted by Steiker—will also, I think, have to be directed mainly to legislative bodies. So perhaps it is time for philosophers of punishment to focus more on what Jeremy Waldron has called "the dignity of legislation."[12] Such is my guess. I am, however, very open to correction from Steiker, who knows much more about empirical and prudential matters than I do.

Let me close by drawing together themes from Zipursky's and Steiker's papers and by addressing the question of the sense in which I still—at least today—embrace retributivism as part of the justification of criminal punishment. To use Zipursky's phrase, I will try to "come clean"—or at least be a bit less dusty—on this issue.

(1) I embrace Kantian retributivism's grounding in the idea that our initial presumption should be that criminals have the dignity of free and responsible autonomous agents—agents who can legitimately be blamed, resented, and held accountable for what they do. I believe, however, that this presumption can sometimes be rebutted by evidence of a damaged character—a damaged character that, as Steiker notes, can be the result of terribly oppressive social situations. Sometimes these oppressive situations do not damage character per se but put temptations in the way of people who, even of very strong character, would find it extraordinarily difficult to resist. This too should guide our retributive responses.

(2) I embrace the classic retributive idea that punishment should be proportionate to the moral gravity of the crime and the culpability of the criminal. I believe that much, if not all, of the evil and irrationality of our present punitive practices is a result of a failure to respect this retributive norm. I also believe that empathy and compassion can play a significant role in allowing us to recognize the factors that

---

12. Jeremy Waldron, *The Dignity of Legislation* (Cambridge, UK: Cambridge University Press, 1999).

are relevant to the determination of criminal desert. Empathy and compassion, when conjoined with a proper humility, can also play a significant role in helping us to avoid the all-too-common mistake of confusing judgments of criminal desert with judgments that we are dealing with worthless monsters or mere scum who deserve whatever cruel indignity we choose to inflict on them. This will, I think, capture much of what Steiker wants to include under the heading of mercy. Also, and in line with something I said in response to Neu, I think that mercy is properly understood not merely as an act but as a disposition of character—a disposition of character that will make us better retributivists than we would be absent such a disposition. (By the way, my skepticism about placing weight on expressions of remorse and apology in criminal sentencing should not be read as skepticism about mercy in general.)

(3) Finally, I am currently charmed by what might be seen as a version of Hegel's annulment theory of punishment. Punishment cannot annul the crime in the sense of making it go away or making that it never happened. Such a claim would be nonsense. However, I think that punishment administered in the name of the community is a way in which the degrading message conveyed by the criminal about the victim's value or worth can be annulled—that is, not allowed to stand as even tacitly endorsed. Jean Hampton's view of punishment as vindicating the value of the victim—represented by what the victim could legitimately resent—seems to me to be a theory of this sort and also strikes me as having merit.[13] This view is retributive in the sense that it involves the righting of a wrong. Of course, this view is plausible only for some crimes. Also—and here is more of my "on the one

---

13. Hampton's first development of this idea was in "The Retributive Idea," in our co-authored book, Murphy and Hampton, *Forgiveness and Mercy* (Cambridge, UK: Cambridge University Press, 1988), chap. 4.

hand, but on the other hand" process of thought—there are ways other than punishment in which the value of victims might be vindicated. Truth commissions, for example, come to mind. However, whatever the mechanism of justice, I think that the victim—the victim's legitimate resentments and grievances—should never be forgotten as one pushes for compassion, empathy, love, mercy, or just deserts for the criminal.

In a letter to his nephew, Billy James, Henry James wrote: "Three things in life are important. The first is to be kind. The second is to be kind. The third is to be kind."[14] Although this is clearly an overstatement, it is an important corrective to the values that are currently dominant in contemporary life. I think that the criminal justice system—along with almost everything else in the world—would benefit from more kindness (or, if you like, more mercy) and I am not certain that it deeply matters—as a *practical* matter—if this is thought of as securing more accurate retributive justice, limiting retributive justice by a separate moral principle, or a prudential choice to use language (perhaps a philosophically inaccurate language) that will ratchet down the current cruelty of our system.[15]

---

14. Quoted in Leon Edel, *Henry James, Volume V: The Master, 1901–1916* (Philadelphia: Lippincott Williams & Wilkins, 1972), 124.
15. Although I have no basis for claiming certainty on any pragmatic or prudential matter, I do have at least a hunch that a *properly expressed* retributivism might actually be preferable to mercy language in bringing greater rationality and humanity into our present system. If those administering the current system are in fact using the language of retribution or just deserts, it might be very hard to bring them around by asking them to drop utterly their present conceptualization and get on board with a totally different value: mercy. I think it would be at least worth a try to approach them by saying initially that one is in agreement with them—that retribution (as just deserts) is indeed the right value around which to organize one's thinking about punishment—and then try to get them to see that their current understanding of this value is defective—that much of what some people call mercy is in reality just deserts properly understood. If one starts by expressing agreement with people, rather than expressing utter distaste for their preferred value, one might have a better chance of getting them to listen and then bringing them around. This is just a hunch, however.

I believe, however, that the choice between these competing conceptualizations—even if without much practical significance—does matter a great deal *philosophically*. I think that philosophers (and other academics) should be very cautious before framing their intellectual views around strategic concerns about the way in which misinformed and ill-motivated public actors might distort those views. Down that road lies, if not madness, then at least the dangers of intellectual dishonesty and the loss of the kinds of contributions their training qualifies them to make.

Steiker brings to the table the perspective of a gifted activist lawyer with a solid grounding in the social sciences. Valuable work done "on the ground" toward the goal of a more humane system of criminal justice depends greatly on people of her kind. In my view, however, the importance of this kind of work should not tempt philosophers to mold their work around it—to abandon theoretical views they believe to be correct because of a fear that those views might be misused by the forces of darkness. (They should be able to depend on people such as Steiker to point that out when it happens.) So I am glad, as a philosopher, to continue to embrace a version of retributivism, and I will hold up just deserts over mercy (as both are correctly analyzed) as the value that should, in my view, control our thinking about punishment.

J. L. Austin, when told that clarity was not enough, replied that there would be plenty of time to go into that when we finally achieved clarity on something. When told that I should shift the focus of my thinking on punishment from justice to mercy, I am inclined to reply that there will be plenty of time to consider that when we finally attain at least a reasonable degree of justice in this domain of law.

As a final word, let me once again express my gratitude to Neu, Zipursky, and Steiker for presenting me with a few things to lament, a few things to celebrate, and a great many things to think about.

Chapter 10

Jealousy, Shame, and the Rival[1]

ABSTRACT. This essay is a critique of the two chapters on jealousy in Jerome Neu's book *A Tear Is an Intellectual Thing*. The rival—as an object of both fear and hatred—is of central importance in romantic jealousy, but it is here argued that the role of the rival cannot be fully understood in Neu's account of jealousy and that *shame* (not noted by Neu) must be seen as central to the concept of jealousy if the role of the rival is to be fully understood.

When Jerome Neu's essay "Jealous Thoughts" was published in 1980, jealousy was widely regarded—at least in leftist intellectual and cultural circles—as an irrational and even evil "bourgeois" passion—one tied to a capitalistic market conception of human relations. The jealous person—according to this view—regards the loved person as a kind of object—as owned property over which the lover has rights. Jealousy is thus a kind of property fear—analogous to the fear of theft. The fear intrinsically involves the belief that one risks losing a possessed loved object to whose love one has a right.

---

1. This paper is a response to the essays "Jealous Thoughts" and "Jealous Afterthoughts" in Jerome Neu's essay collection *A Tear Is an Intellectual Thing* (Oxford: Oxford University Press, 2000). Since a part of this paper elaborates on some ideas contained in a student paper written by my wife, Ellen Canacakos, it would be appropriate (in spite of her wish to the contrary) to regard her as co-author.

Neu—rightly in my judgment—rejects this account of jealousy as psychologically shallow. He argues—in "Jealous Thoughts" and in the later "Jealous Afterthoughts"—that psychoanalytic theory teaches us that love gets its initial life and draws its basic character from the Oedipal situation. The child so needs and depends upon the mother that loss of the mother's love would appear both as biological and psychological annihilation—psychological because the very self of the child is identified with that of the mother. Any perceived rival for the mother's affections (initially the father) is seen as a threat to security and thus provokes in the child a fear of loss of love. It is here that love and jealousy begin, develop through what Winnicott calls "transitional objects," and assume forms that will persist in adult life. To love is, at least in part, to be so identified with another person that the loss of that person's love will be perceived as loss or annihilation of one's very self or personality. Jealousy, then, is simply the fear that one will lose the love of a person with whom one is psychologically identified—an instance of the fear of annihilation. "If others do not love us," Neu writes, "we will disintegrate."

This fear is not, according to Neu, grounded in a bourgeois or possessive model of human relations, for one can fear the loss of love without believing that one owns the loved person or that one has a right to that person's love. All that is required is that one has the love. Love, then, in part involves self-identification—when we lose it we lose ourselves, having our vulnerabilities open and unsupported. All human beings, regardless of social setting—bourgeois or communitarian—fear the exposure of vulnerabilities and the resulting loss of self. According to Neu, this fear is jealousy. Thus jealousy and love are necessarily connected—we cannot get rid of the former without losing the latter.

There are some questions that I immediately want to raise about this analysis. First, what about unrequited love? There are surely intense cases of jealousy where the jealous person knows full well that the love he feels is not returned. Not having it, he cannot fear its loss. Thus it cannot be literally true to say, as Neu does in the first essay, that "to be jealous over someone, you must believe that they love you or have loved you."

Unrequited love thus presents a problem for Neu's original analysis, but I think that the problem can be rather easily fixed. One might draw on some of the instructive things that Neu has to say in the later essay about the role of illusion and projection in erotic love, or one might suggest (think of the John Hinckley/Jodie Foster case) that what the jealous unrequited lover fears is not the loss of love (which he clearly does not have) but the loss of the *possibility* of love (which he may still hope for).

There is also, of course, the problem of jealousy over love that one believes is already hopelessly lost. Othello—often presented (as he is by Neu) as a paradigm of a jealous person—is frequently thought to be most jealous *after* he believes that he has lost Desdemona's love to Cassio. But surely this cannot be understood simply as the fear of loss of love, for how can one fear to lose what one has already lost?

In keeping with the spirit—if not the exact letter—of Neu's analysis, one might try to deal with the Othello case in this way: the fear that constitutes Othello's jealousy should not be seen as the fear of the loss of love (it is simply too late for *that* fear) but rather as the fear of the personal disintegration that may result from that loss.

Perhaps killing or other acts of revenge against the lost lover are strategies to defend against this possible consequence. Perhaps they are preventive strategies that seek not the prevention of the loss of love, but rather of the dire consequences that—according to Neu— may flow from that loss. Or perhaps they are *retributive* strategies— seeking to inflict punishment on the person who has caused such personal disruption and pain at the core of one's very self. Thus it is possible that the jealous person who inflicts pain over love lost is somewhat like the lover of a murder victim who believes (sometimes rightly, sometimes wrongly) that a kind of closure will result from the execution of the killer.

We are all, alas, familiar with newspaper reports that read, "He killed her in a jealous rage." Such a phrase might well describe Othello, but I am not sure. He was surely jealous when he suspected Desdemona of infidelity, but was he jealous at the time he murdered her? Perhaps he was simply vindictive. However, if such murderous rage is properly to be identified as "jealous," it surely cannot be motivated by the fear of losing love since the surest way permanently to lose love is to kill the lover. Dead people cannot love. So what goes on in these cases is either not jealousy at all but rather something else—vengeance perhaps—or it is jealousy motivated by something other than the fear of losing love. Perhaps it is motivated by a deep aversion to certain *consequences* of losing love. Neu would stress the consequence of annihilation or disintegration—since that is so integral to his analysis of love—but I shall later argue that one of these consequences may be *shame*.

Before moving to this issue, however, let me pause for a moment over this link that Neu claims exists between fear of lost love and fear of annihilation. Personal annihilation is certainly worth fearing, but is Neu correct in thinking that love—mature adult love—really involves the kind of identification that might lead to this? Is this love or rather what the psychiatrist Karen Horney called *neurotic* or *morbid dependency*—an excessive identification that she believed is particularly harmful to women?[2] If this really is love, then perhaps love is in greater competition with other values—autonomy, self-respect, even love of God—than we might have initially thought or hoped.

To lose the people whom I love would, of course, be a terrible blow because the presence of these people in my life plays a central

---

2. Karen Horney, *Neurosis and Human Growth* (New York: W. W. Norton, 1950).

role in my happiness and in the meaning that my life now has. So of course I fear to lose them—in the same way, although to a greater degree, that I fear a loss of hearing that would separate me from the deep joy and sense of meaning that I currently derive from music. But in neither case—unless I am deceiving myself—am I fearing annihilation. For I know that there are, if one is strong enough or resourceful enough or touched by grace, new sources of meaning and new sources of happiness that may be found in life—even after grave losses. But after annihilation there is nothing.

In Gluck's beautiful aria *Che faro*, Orfeo asks the questions, "What is life to me without thee? What is left if thou art dead?" These are questions that any lover would ask in the period of grief immediately after a loss, but a mentally healthy lover will surely not be haunted by these questions forever. (I suspect that there are evolutionary reasons why this has to be so, since the survival and reproductive potential of the permanently distraught would not be very high.) One reason, I think, that we are so saddened by the suicides of teenagers disappointed in love is that we realize that if they lived longer they would be more able to accept such disappointments simply as parts of the general fragility of human life. I fear that, in too closely linking love with a fear of annihilation, Neu may mistakenly be taking a model of love appropriate for some stages—e.g., adolescence, immediate grief over lost love, the first few weeks of a love affair—as a model for all stages. Freud wrote this about the death of a child: "Our hopes, our pride, our happiness, lie in the grave with him, we will not be consoled, we will not fill the loved one's place."[3] But even as one says such things and means them—thoughts particularly appropriate at the grave—one at some level knows that they are probably not literally true. One probably will go on with at least some hope, some pride, and some happiness intact.

---

3. Sigmund Freud, "Thoughts on War and Death," *Collected Papers*, Volume 4, trans. Joan Riviere (New York: Basic Books, 1959).

The "I die in you, you die in me" sort of thing that one finds in the stories of Orpheus and Eurydice, Tristan and Isolde, and other great love stories can be deeply moving, but this is art—not life—or, if it is life, it is mainly adolescent life, not adult life. Not surprisingly, these stories often lead to the early deaths of the lovers—before reality raises its ugly head—because who wants to imagine Tristan with a prostate infection, Isolde with menstrual cramps, or Orpheus and Eurydice arguing over who will drive the kids to the doctor this time? But that is real life and—one would hope—a valuable kind of real love. I suspect, however, that whatever kind of identification exists between such mature real lovers, though in some ways risky, will not involve risks as grave as annihilation.

One moral I would draw from this is that it is not always wise for life to imitate art or for philosophy to be too influenced by it. Imaginative literature, for dramatic reasons, often focuses on the extreme—even pathological—cases; and this is certainly true of much of the famous literature devoted to romantic love. For the picture of romantic love we often get in art is one where love, though thrillingly intense while it lasts, cannot last very long and is indeed ultimately infantile. Freud and other psychoanalysts talk brilliantly about the infantile origins of our loves, but surely one of our missions—as autonomous and rational human beings—is to attempt to transcend the limitations imposed by those origins, not to surrender to them.

I now want to move to the main worry that I have about Neu's analysis of jealousy. The worry is this: can he give an adequate account of the role that the *rival* plays in jealousy? Jealousy, after all, is not just *any* feared loss of love—if it were I would be jealous upon learning that my lover has terminal cancer—but specifically the fear of *loss to a rival*. Neu's analysis of jealousy acknowledges the role of the rival, but this acknowledgement is often in passing or in parentheses; and his only extensive treatment of the rival occurs in his discussion of envy. But can his analysis illuminate, and not merely acknowledge, the role of the rival in jealousy? This is the question to which I shall now pass.

When leftist radicals of the sixties and seventies deplored jealousy as a bourgeois passion, they surely had in mind a critique of any marketplace theory of human relations. But market thinking may be found not merely in the concepts of rights, property, and possession, but also in the concept of *competition*; and I think that the role of the rival in jealousy must be understood as, at least in part, based on a competitive account of human intimacy and love—competition that, at its most extreme, produces the pathological and dangerous "if I can't have her nobody can" response. Neu has many insightful things to say about competition in his discussion of envy, which he generally distinguishes from jealousy. Since I think that such a discussion must be put at center stage in order to understand the role of the rival in jealousy, the distinction between jealousy and envy will perhaps emerge as less sharp than Neu sometimes suggests.

If we think of the development of love and jealousy in evolutionary terms as well as psychoanalytic terms, we will surely see how the rival must loom large in our account. Mammalian biological life involves intense competition for viable mates, and jealousy—as an emotional strategy for dealing with such competition—would likely be a part of the psychological programming of successful competitors. It prompts one, for example, to take preventive measures. These measures might be such things as threatening or even killing a rival or more gentle things—e.g., being a particularly good provider and thus making one's mate less tempted to stray.

It is, of course, very tiresome to hear messianic sociobiologists and evolutionary psychologists talk as though they have the whole or even the most important story to tell about the nature and origin of human emotions. But surely they do have one important part of the story—one that we may miss if we look only to a psychoanalytic perspective. Biology may help to explain, for example, certain reported gender differences with respect to jealousy—e.g., the fact that jealousy in heterosexual men primarily involves a fear of sexual infidelity, whereas jealousy in heterosexual women primarily involves a fear of lost love and abandonment.[4]

Moving to a more phenomenological perspective, we can see the importance of the rival in terms of the *shame* that generally results in being beaten out in a competition over a loved person. Such shame is not present when that person dies, although the loss of love is the same.

Why is it painful to lose or fear to lose one's lover to a rival? Surely Neu has an important part of this story: the pain of lost love itself. But this is not, I think, the whole story. Neu focuses on the fear that one will lose the attention and availability of another. Important also, I would argue, is the fear that one will lose the *validation* that the other provides. In the second essay—where Neu speaks of the idealization of the lover and the need to be selected by that lover as a special object—Neu begins to see this and thus adds a perspective that enriches his earlier analysis. I would like to elaborate a bit on that perspective.

It is a perhaps sad but surely true claim that, to a substantial degree, people derive their sense of self-worth from the judgments of others. If we love a person, we tend to take that person's judgments in these matters quite seriously—i.e., we take them in some sense to be accurate judges of our own worth. (The mentally healthy among us—if there are any—would not follow Groucho Marx in contemptuously refusing to join any club that would have us for members; nor would we deeply mistrust the judgment of any person who could love us.) If we add to this the fact that nonmoral judgments of worth are generally comparative, then the fact that a judge whom we trust prefers

---

4. See David Buss, *The Dangerous Passion: Why Jealousy Is as Necessary as Love and Sex* (New York: Free Press, 2000). Buss is an evolutionary psychologist, and it would be interesting to learn Neu's views on the degree to which the evolutionary perspective is consistent with the psychoanalytic perspective adopted by Neu.

someone over us may make us doubt our own worth or value. So jealousy may stand as testimony not merely to our need for love and attention, but also to our need for validation by another. We are thus shamed by rejection.

It is, of course, not merely the judgment of the loved person who matters. The judgment of a wider circle of people matters as well, for even the strongest of us needs validation from some relevant reference group. Consider Achilles. His rage over the loss of Briseis to Agamemnon is to a substantial degree based on his loss of honor—face and standing—in the eyes of his fellow warriors. He has been shamed by having the girl taken from him.

I think that similar shame may be found in many contemporary cases of jealousy and loss. The jilted love is often ashamed to report this to others—thinking that it casts some bad reflection on his or her worth or standing. (Sometimes—for similar reasons I suspect—people are reluctant even to admit that they are divorced.) Being a victim of infidelity is, among other unpleasant things, shameful and embarrassing. Perhaps this in part explains the rage that is often found in those who have been jilted—a rage that may provoke expensive and vicious lawsuits, small or even major acts of retribution, and sometimes even murder. Why do people do these things? These acts will not get the love back, but they may go a long way—at least in the eyes of the perpetrator—toward saving face, restoring lost status and honor, and thus overcoming the shame of it all. If one believes that he has been brought down by another, he may find it therapeutic—or think he will find it therapeutic—to bring that person down as well. I am not, of course, saying that such a response is justified, only that it is—unfortunately—not unusual (particularly among men). As Norman Mailer (who ought to know) has asked: "Isn't human nature depressing?"

To summarize and conclude: I think that Neu has provided us with many profound insights on jealousy and its relation to love.

Indeed, if I were asked to recommend just one philosophical essay on jealousy, it would be Neu's. It is, I think, the best place to start—for its insights, the framework it provides, and the provocative questions it forces us to raise.

In raising these questions, however, I have come to think that Neu's account of jealousy needs to be supplemented in certain ways. In particular, I have suggested that *shame* needs to be stressed in order fully to account for the role of the rival in jealousy.[5]

---

5. I have elaborated my own views on shame in my "Shame Creeps through Guilt and Feels Like Retribution." *Law and Philosophy* 18 (4) (July 1999), 327–344.

Chapter 11

Moral Reasons and the Limitations of Liberty

I find myself in substantial agreement with Professor Dworkin, and I find this deeply disturbing—not merely because it will make my role as his commentator more difficult, but also for reasons of a more personal nature. I have long held the belief that developing a sympathy for conservative positions is simply a sign of growing old, and thus I view with considerable alarm my increasing sympathy for Lord Devlin's attack on John Stuart Mill's Harm Principle—a principle long considered central to the liberal theory of law, particularly criminal law.

Indeed, I am in much worse shape in this regard than Professor Dworkin because, a couple of years ago, I published an essay in which I expressed even greater support for Devlin's views than that expressed by Professor Dworkin and was even harsher in my criticisms of Joel Feinberg's liberal attempt to defeat those views.[1] In that essay, I argued not merely that most Mill-inspired arguments against Devlin were less successful than I had once thought, but also that Devlin had made some important points of his own against his opponent's liberal views.[2] I argued that Devlin had made a start

---

This commentary on Gerald Dworkin's essay *Devlin Was Right: Law and the Enforcement of Morality* was prepared for presentation at the conference "Reconstructing Liberalism" at The College of William and Mary School of Law, April 3–4, 1998. It is a response to the draft of the essay that Professor Dworkin presented at the conference.

1. *See* Jeffrie G. Murphy, *Legal Moralism and Liberalism*, 37 Ariz. L. Rev. 73, 73–88 (1995).
2. *See id.*

toward showing that some positions strongly favored by many liberals are not consistent with simply ruling out, as legally irrelevant, nonneutral judgments about personal goodness or the good life.[3] In particular, I argued that regarding certain constitutional rights as *fundamental* (e.g., free exercise of religion) presupposes a conception of the human good, as does a substantial amount of the *retributive* component in criminal sentencing.[4] I do not propose to rehearse here all that I wrote in that essay, but I do strongly recommend that you read it. At the very least, it will alert you to what you might expect of yourself as you grow old.

What, then, shall I do in my role as commentator on Professor Dworkin's essay? Rather than further explore the pros and cons of Lord Devlin's views, I shall instead—after a brief scholarly quibble—focus on the final section of Professor Dworkin's essay and on his suggestions, with which I generally agree, that the liberal position is sometimes best defended not with some abstract general principle claiming that private immorality is simply not the law's business, but rather with reflection on the particular judgments of immorality themselves—what they mean and whether they can be rationally defended. In pursuing this thought, I will focus on the criminalization of private homosexual sodomy between consenting adults—Lord Devlin's issue[5]—and will explore the concept of morality that was at work in the Supreme Court's decision in the 1986 case *Bowers v. Hardwick*.[6] In *Bowers*, the Court held that the supposed moral objection that a majority of Georgia citizens had to homosexual sodomy was a rational basis for criminalizing the practice.[7]

---

3. *See id* at 80–81.
4. *See id* at 81–84, 86.
5 *See* PATRICK DEVLIN, THE ENFORCEMENT OF MORALS 1–2 (1965).
6. 478 U.S. 186 (1986).
7. *See id.* at 196.

First, though, the scholarly quibble. In the cases in which Professor Dworkin does wish to defend certain liberal positions on principle, the principle he favors he characterizes as the "Kantian" principle of "the protection of autonomy and equal respect for persons."[8] Although it has been years since I have done serious Kant scholarship—and my memory may be defective here—it strikes me that Professor Dworkin's own understanding of the concepts of autonomy and respect for persons is not obviously Kantian in nature. Professor Dworkin is inclined to defend in principle, for example, a doctrine of free speech that includes the right to hurl "racial insults" as a part of a legitimate "sphere of autonomy for individuals to engage in."[9]

I am not at all sure, however, that Kant would protect the hurling of racial insults as an exercise of autonomy in his sense. In Kant's sense, autonomy is—I think—best understood not simply as doing whatever comes into one's mind for whatever motive, but rather as the exercise of one's capacity for practical reason—the use, in John Rawls' language, of one's "moral powers."[10] It is not obvious that a racial insult is an expression of autonomy in this sense; it is, indeed, far more likely to be expressive of heteronomy. One might still be able to make a case for the protection of racial insults by appealing to other aspects of Kant's philosophy—e.g., his notion in the *Rechtslehre* that coercion is justified only to prevent one citizen from using "external freedom" in such a way as to interfere with the external freedom of another citizen.[11] I think, however, that one distorts this notion of external freedom if one tries to interpret it in light of Kant's much more restrictive concept of autonomy—a concept that seeks to capture our status as rational

---

8. Gerald Dworkin, *Devlin Was Right: Law and the Enforcement of Morality*, 40 WM. & MARY L. REV. 927, 931.
9. *Id.* at 945.
10. John Rawls, *The Domain of the Political and Overlapping Consensus*, 64 N.Y.U. L. REV. 233, 236 (1989).
11. *See* IMMANUEL KANT, THE METAPHYSICAL ELEMENTS OF JUSTICE 35–37 (John Ladd trans., Bobbs-Merrill 1965) (1797).

and moral beings. This status is typically revealed when we seek to reason together, not when we let ourselves get carried away by base emotions and shout insults at each other.

With this scholarly quibble out of the way, let me now move to a discussion of *Bowers v. Hardwick*. I will discuss this case not as an expert in constitutional law—I am not one—but rather as a philosopher interested in finding out whether the Court's reasoning in this and other cases can inform and enrich our moral and political thinking about democratic government, a form of government that should be understood, as Ronald Dworkin has argued, not simply as winner-take-all majoritarianism but rather as incorporating the value of equal concern and respect for all citizens.[12] One way in which such concern and respect are shown is by placing limits on the kinds of reasons that may legitimately be used to justify the curtailment of liberty, and here I shall be asking this question: Should our philosophical theories about the reasons that we owe our fellow citizens when we propose to limit their liberty be guided by what the Court says about those reasons? Is there wisdom in the Court from which we all can learn? If *Bowers* is representative of the Court's general thinking about reasons, I am inclined to answer this question in the negative, and my discussion of *Bowers* will reveal the basis for my negative answer.

Most of you will recall that (for our present purposes) there were two important parts to Justice White's majority opinion in *Bowers*. In the first part, White considered the question of whether strict scrutiny should be applied in the case.[13] Obviously reluctant to expand the scope of the previous privacy cases, White refused to apply strict scrutiny on the grounds that private homosexual sodomy is not properly conceptualized as a fundamental right (one of the triggers for strict scrutiny).[14]

---

12. See RONALD DWORKIN, FREEDOM'S LAW: THE MORAL READING OF THE AMERICAN CONSTITUTION 1–38 (1996).
13. See Bowers v. Hardwick, 478 U.S. 186, 190–91 (1986).
14. See id. at 191.

He interpreted the previous privacy cases as concerned essentially with marriage, family life, and reproductive autonomy and argued that, because homosexual sodomy engages none of these values, it should not be conceptualized as a fundamental privacy right and thus that strict scrutiny was not required.[15]

Some dissenting Justices (Justice Blackmun in particular) challenged this view—arguing that White had selected the wrong level of generality to describe the issue before him.[16] The issue, Blackmun argued, was not about sodomy as a fundamental right but about personal intimacy as a fundamental right, and that even if the Framers and the previous privacy cases were not concerned with the former as such, they were concerned with the latter, which may plausibly be conceptualized as including the former.[17] Because I explored these issues in the essay I have already mentioned,[18] I will now move on to the second important part of the *Bowers* opinion.

In the second part of the opinion, Justice White, having rejected strict scrutiny, moved to the framework imposed by minimal scrutiny: the so-called "rational basis test."[19] Unlike strict scrutiny, which requires a showing by the government that it is pursuing a compelling state interest by means that are necessary for the attainment of that interest, minimal scrutiny imposes a much weaker burden on the government: the burden of showing that the liberty restriction it imposes serves, if not a compelling state interest, at least a state interest that is reasonable or rational.[20] (The actual language typically used is that the state interest must be legitimate and the liberty restriction employed must be rationally related to that

---

15. *See id.*
16. *See id.* at 199–200 (Blackmun, J., dissenting).
17. *See id.* at 206 (Blackmun, J., dissenting).
18. *See* Murphy, *supra* note 1, at 85–87.
19. *See Bowers*, 478 U.S. at 196.
20. *See id.*

interest.[21]) Let me turn now to how Justice White interpreted and applied this test in *Bowers*. He wrote as follows:

> Even if the conduct at issue here is not a fundamental right, respondent asserts that there must be a rational basis for the law and that there is none in this case other than the presumed belief of a majority of the electorate in Georgia that homosexual sodomy is immoral and unacceptable. This is said to be an inadequate rationale to support the law. The law, however, is constantly based on notions of morality, and if all laws representing essentially moral choices are to be invalidated under the Due Process Clause, the courts will be very busy indeed. Even respondent makes no such claim, but insists that majority sentiment about the morality of homosexuality should be declared inadequate. We do not agree, and are unpersuaded that the sodomy laws of some 25 states should be invalidated on this basis.[22]

The reasoning revealed here does not, in my judgment, show Justice White at his best. Even if we grant that, in a democratic society, the majority has a legitimate interest in building some of its moral beliefs into criminal law, we surely cannot interpret this to mean that the majority should be allowed to build just *any* of its beliefs and desires into the criminal law. This would deprive the rational basis test of any meaning at all, interpreting the mere fact that the majority wants to do something as equivalent to their having a rational basis for doing it. The Due Process Clause and its rational basis test may not place very onerous burdens on the government; on this interpretation, however, they place no burdens at all. The majority simply gets to do whatever it

---

21. *See, e.g.,* Pennel v. City of San Jose, 485 U.S. 1, 14 (1988) (holding that a rent control ordinance was "rationally related to a legitimate state interest" [quoting New Orleans v. Dukes, 427 U.S. 297, 303 (1976)]).
22. *Id.* at 196.

jolly well feels like—so long, at any rate, as it remembers to use the word "morality" somewhere in its supposed justification.

Justice White's basic mistake, I think, was his failure to see that any serious consideration of the role that moral conviction might legitimately play in justifying criminal law must regard as separate and discuss separately the following three questions:

(1) Is it in fact true that a majority of citizens have strong disapproval of the practice in question?
(2) If it is true that they do have strong disapproval, is there good reason to think that this disapproval is *moral* in nature—that the attitudes, beliefs, and judgments involved are *moral* attitudes, beliefs, and judgments?
(3) If the relevant attitudes, beliefs, and judgments are moral in nature, are these attitudes, beliefs, and judgments *reasonable* or *rational*? (The contrast here is with beliefs that may simply be silly superstitions or with beliefs that, to use Justice Kennedy's language from the 1996 case *Romer v. Evans*, reflect mere prejudice or animus.[23])

The fact that we can distinguish these three questions at the very least shows that the slogan "citizens in a democratic society have a legitimate interest in enforcing morality"[24] is open to a variety of interpretations, and that on some interpretations the slogan will be more plausible than on others. I will now briefly explore each of these three questions.

(1) THE FACT OF DEEP DISAPPROVAL. This is not itself a moral issue, but an examination of the factual assumptions being made by those claiming to enforce moral judgments will sometimes assist us

---

23. *See* Romer v. Evans, 517 U.S. 620, 632 (1996).
24. *See, e.g.,* Barnes v. Glen Theater, Inc., 501 U.S. 560, 569 (1991).

in determining if those judgments are genuinely moral and reasonable. As Justice Stevens pointed out in his dissent in *Bowers*, the actual facts about the beliefs of a majority of citizens are a bit harder to determine than Justice White thought.[25] Justice White was convinced that a majority of Georgia's citizens had strong moral disapproval of homosexual sodomy. What, though, was his evidence for this? Apparently the mere fact that the Georgia legislature (in company with the legislatures in many other states) voted for the statute criminalizing homosexual sodomy and the fact that the Georgia attorney general claimed that this vote was expressive of strong moral conviction on the part of Georgia's citizens were enough.[26] Of course, we do not really know why the Georgia legislature voted for this statute. Perhaps it was indeed because they believed that there was a deep level of moral repugnance against homosexuals among the citizens of Georgia. Perhaps, though, it was simply because they were under great pressure from the Christian Coalition and feared getting recalled if they did not toe the line on this issue. I really do not know; and neither, I suspect, did Justice White. Also, as Justice Stevens pointed out, the actual language of the statute is gender neutral, covering heterosexual sodomy as well as the practices of homosexuals.[27] Indeed, the statute replaced an earlier statute that explicitly targeted only homosexuals.[28] Thus, if the statute itself provides any evidence of what truly disturbs the citizens of Georgia, it would seem to provide evidence that they do not much like sodomy in any form, whether heterosexual or homosexual. One might ask, then, how could Justice White, if he wished to defer to majority sentiment, so easily support—as he did—the limitation of the enforcement of this statute to homosexuals?

---

25. See *Bowers*, 478 U.S. at 219 (Stevens, J., dissenting).
26. See id. at 196.
27. See id. at 215–16 (Stevens, J., dissenting).
28. See id. at 200–01, 200 n. l (Blackmun, J., dissenting).

There is, of course, one possible answer to this question, namely, that Justice White believed that the privacy cases would force him (logically) to apply strict scrutiny in the area of heterosexual activity and that such scrutiny would demand an interest more compelling than the mere enforcement of morality. Although he might have preferred enforcing the moral judgment across the board, he perhaps had to content himself with allowing its enforcement in the one area where (he had already argued) strict scrutiny was not available: homosexual relations. This position, of course, had considerable logic. If the citizens of Georgia morally deplore it all, they must surely deplore the part of it that the privacy cases permits the government to target. So let us at least, White may have been thinking, allow them to enforce their moral convictions in the one area where the privacy cases permit them to do so.

(2) Moral and Nonmoral Disapproval. Let us grant then, at least for the moment, the truth of the empirical claim that the majority of Georgia's citizens have strong disapproval of—perhaps even disgust and repugnance at—homosexual sodomy. It does not follow from this alone, however, that their disapproval is moral disapproval; for some disapproval, even strong disapproval that rises to the level of disgust and revulsion, is not plausibly regarded as moral in nature. It could, for example, be religious or aesthetic. I am confident that I find revolting the idea of someone eating "road kill" (the barbecued corpses of animals killed on the highway), but is my revulsion moral? I do not think so—any more than my revulsion at the so-called "art" of Jeff Koons is moral revulsion. Why not? Because of the nature of the *reasons* that are, in my view, intrinsic to morality. If I am actually disapproving of something on moral grounds, it seems that I ought to be prepared to make a case that the object of my disapproval involves at least one of the following: harm, injustice, or certain failures of human flourishing. If I am not prepared to make such a

case but can only say something like "This is ugly" or "Yuck! This makes me sick to my stomach!" or "God forbids this" (a constitutional nonstarter), there is no reason to regard my judgment as moral in nature. In short: the status of my judgment as a moral judgment is a function not of its intensity, but of the reasons I am prepared to give in support of that judgment.

In summary: Suppose we grant the principle that the majority has a right to enforce its moral convictions. Further suppose that we grant that the majority finds homosexual practices revolting. If I am correct in my claim that not all revulsion is moral revulsion, it does not follow from these two claims alone that the majority has the right to use the criminal law to target homosexual sodomy.

(3) MORALITY AND REASONS. If I am correct that a judgment is typically identified as moral through the kinds of reasons given in support of that judgment, it would seem that it would be important to distinguish good (rational) reasons from bad (irrational) reasons. In *Bowers*, however, this distinction was lost on Justice White; for in *Bowers*, once he had decided that citizen disapproval of homosexual sodomy was moral disapproval, he concluded that the rational basis test had been satisfied, with no inquiry at all into the question of whether the moral judgment involved is a rational or reasonable moral judgment or perhaps simply a judgment of unexampled stupidity, ignorance, prejudice, and animus.

The indifference that White showed to this question in *Bowers* was in marked contrast, as it happens, to his use of the rational basis test in his concurring opinion in the 1965 case *Griswold v. Connecticut*.[29]

---

29. 381 U.S. 479, 502–507 (1965) (White, J., concurring in judgment).

In that case, he actually ridiculed the claim made by the state of Connecticut that a ban on contraceptives for married couples is a rational means to the legitimate government objective of discouraging extramarital sex.[30]

It is possible, I suppose, that Justice White embraced noncognitivist metaethical views, that he viewed the reasons given by Connecticut as open to rational evaluation because they concerned matters of fact but viewed moral reasons as irretrievably subjective or relative and thus beyond the scope of rational evaluation. If this was his metaethical view, it is worth noting that it is a view rejected—at least in this simple form—by most contemporary moral philosophers. These philosophers generally see the place of reason in ethics to be an issue of central importance.[31]

What would it be like to give reasons of a moral nature to support the criminalization of homosexual sodomy? Consider the argument developed by Michael Levin in his essay "Why Homosexuality Is Abnormal."[32] According to Levin, scientific studies reveal that male homosexuals tend to be much more unhappy than heterosexual males, and he attributes this unhappiness both to their promiscuous lifestyles and to their use of their sexual organs in an exclusively unnatural way.[33] He then suggests that society has a moral duty to discourage lifestyle choices that have a tendency to produce great unhappiness and advocates using the law as one instrument in a comprehensive strategy for the social discouragement of homosexuality.[34]

---

30. *See id.* at 506 (White, J., concurring in judgment).
31. *See, e.g.,* STEPHEN EDELSTON TOULMIN, AN EXAMINATION OF THE PLACE OF REASON IN ETHICS (1950).
32. *See* Michael Levin, *Why Homosexuality Is Abnormal, in* ETHICS IN PRACTICE 233 (Hugh LaFollette ed., 1997). This essay originally appeared in 1984, but the 1997 printing is preferable because of the postscript added in 1995.
33. *See id.* at 236–39.
34. *See id.* at 240.

Now suppose some legislature develops a set of laws targeting homosexual conduct—some criminal, some not—and cites Levin's account in defense of those laws. This defense would, on my view, count as moral because it involves reasons based on both harm and human flourishing. Is the defense reasonable, though? Should it pass a rational basis test? I suspect that Justice White, if he remained on the Court, would give it a pass because in *Bowers* he gave a pass to a morals statute supported by no reasons at all. Is such a posture defensible, though? Should it be adopted by anyone wishing the rational basis test to have some bite, some meaning? Before simply signing off on the acceptability of the statute, one should first at least ask questions like the following (questions expressing the spirit of skepticism that Justice White himself displayed in *Griswold*): Is there any reason to believe that any of Levin's claims are true? Are homosexuals generally far more unhappy than heterosexuals? If they are, is this because of their homosexuality or because of society's treatment of them? Is homosexuality an elective lifestyle choice or is it genetically determined—something we discover about ourselves rather than choose? (If it is largely genetically determined, of course, we clearly will not have to worry much about people being lured into making harmful lifestyle choices here.[35]) My own belief is that Levin is largely wrong. As the one advocating interference with liberty, he bears the burden of proof and has failed rather dramatically to bear that burden. Any legislation based on his writings on homosexuality, in my view, therefore, would not be rationally based. If, in spite of this, the Court would still uphold the legislation as satisfying the rational basis test, all this shows is that the Court is probably confusing rationality with majoritarianism. It is thus operating with a concept of rationality that, whatever its constitutional merits, is uninstructive to those of

---

35. Levin considers the possible genetic basis for homosexuality and generally concedes this point in his 1995 postscript. *See id.* at 240–41.

us interested in the question about democratic theory that I posed at the outset: What sorts of reasons do we owe our fellow citizens when we propose to encumber their liberty?

This brings to a close my commentary on Professor Dworkin's essay. I have in my remarks attempted to build on the few brief suggestions made by Professor Dworkin in the closing section of his paper. By arguing that disapproval of homosexuality may not be moral disapproval and that moral disapproval of homosexuality may not be rational, I have tried to fill out in some detail my reading of two of Professor Dworkin's claims—the claim that our thinking about issues such as homosexuality requires a plausible account of what is involved in the making of moral judgments, and the claim (made in the final sentence of his essay) that the reason that homosexual conduct ought not to be criminalized is that there is nothing immoral in such activity. I hope that I have construed him correctly here and that he sees my efforts as involving the "honest toil" he advocates on issues of this nature.

Chapter 12

The Elusive Nature of Human Dignity

A mad animal
Man's a mad animal
I'm a thousand years old and in my time
I've helped to commit a million murders
The earth is spread
The earth is spread thick
with squashed human guts
We few survivors
We few survivors
walk over a quaking bog of corpses
always under our feet
every step we take
rotted bones ashes matted hair
under our feet
broken teeth skulls split open
A mad animal
I'm a mad animal

—*Peter Weiss, Marat/Sade*[1]

There seem to be two basic choices about how best to conceptualize morality and its claims on us. One possibility is to think of it as essentially a matter of *consequences*—the promotion of the best possible balance of

---

1. Peter Weiss, *Marat/Sade*, trans Geoffrey Skelton and Adrian Mitchell (Prospect Heights: Waveland, 2002) 32–3.

good over bad consequences—and the other is to think of it in terms of certain fundamental and perhaps even absolute *principles*. Utilitarianism is the best-known version of the consequential approach—a moral theory that sets "the greatest good for the greatest number" as the basic principle of morality and characterizes good as pleasure or happiness.

There are many problems with this vision of morality, of course. For one, it builds the idea of moral good around pleasure or happiness, and many of us think that there are more important things in life than these hedonic states—perhaps even sympathizing a bit with Friedrich Nietzsche's claim that utilitarianism is a shallow philosophy that would appeal only to pigs and English shopkeepers.

Even if one does not have these elitist and aesthetic objections to utilitarianism, however, it may strike some as leaving out the central values of *rights* and *justice*—an omission that would, so the classic objection goes, allow utilitarianism to justify making slaves of a minority or punishing the innocent if the greatest good for the greatest number would be served thereby. Utilitarianism actually can make a place for rights and justice, but the place will not be central or basic. Rights and justice will be *derivative* values—established only if called for by rules that themselves promote utility. Rights established by such rules might—indeed probably would—rule out slavery and punishing the innocent in most real-world cases. However, those who see this as the right result might understandably think that the result is reached for the wrong reason. The wrongness of treating individuals in this way, they would argue, does not depend on a determination that *others*—the majority—would be rendered insecure if social rules that allowed slavery or punishing the innocent were adopted. Is not avoiding such treatment simply wrong in principle, wrong in itself—something we *owe* to every particular individual regardless of the projected social consequence of making such treatment a general practice?

Finally, utilitarianism simply does not seem very inspiring—not the sort of value that could easily motivate a call to arms. As the philosopher Margaret MacDonald once observed, who would endure blood, toil, tears, and sweat for the sake of a little extra comfort?

If utilitarianism does not appeal—or does not appeal deeply enough to be the basic value—what might be tried as an alternative? What might capture the idea that some ways of treating human beings are intrinsically wrong and not merely instrumentally wrong? The most well-known alternative is a theory of justice grounded in the idea of *basic human rights*, rights that it is wrong in principle to violate. And how does this grounding work? According to Immanuel Kant, the most prominent philosophical defender of such a view, rights and justice must be based on the value of human *dignity*—the moral specialness of persons that makes them precious and perhaps even sacred, earning for them a kind of respect that is not available to any other sentient creature. On this view slavery, for example, will be rejected as a direct affront to the human dignity of each individual who is a slave—rejected as absolutely unacceptable from the moral point of view before any consideration of its impact on the general welfare has been taken.

This appeal certainly does not lack inspirational value, since the call to defend human dignity and rights can get the blood stirring in a way that appeals to a net gain in social utility cannot. Unfortunately, however, inspirational value alone is not sufficient; for inspiration will last only so long as the values on which it is based cannot be defeated by a variety of skeptical doubts—and doubts aplenty can be directed at the very idea of human dignity.

There are, of course, doubts of a deeply philosophical nature that can be raised against any attempt to establish human dignity on the basis of highly controversial metaphysical claims. Kant, for example, seemed to think that such dignity is grounded in human *autonomy*—an attribute of persons that he sometimes conceptualized as a radical freedom of the will, as "noumenal freedom," whereby rationality exercises a kind of contra-causal influence on human actions. Of course, anyone who knows even a little bit about metaphysical determinism will realize that demonstrating the existence of this kind of freedom—or even finding a satisfactory way to analyze coherently the concept of such freedom—may be impossible.

Kant's conception of autonomy was not always this metaphysically ambitious, however. Sometimes he conceptualized autonomy simply as a capacity to understand moral reasons and to be motivated by them—a capacity that renders persons morally responsible for what they do. Even this more modest view faces some problems, however, since some members of the human species do not possess this trait—small children, the mentally disabled, and those suffering from dementia, just to give three examples—and yet many would want to regard them as persons with dignity and rights.

Kant has often been characterized, with some justice, as attempting to find a secular translation for what is essentially a Protestant view of morality. Kant's theological critics will condemn this attempt as a failure—one of the great "nice tries" in the history of philosophy perhaps, but one that cannot produce a result that many regard as essential: including *all* human beings in the circle of dignity and not just those that possess Kantian autonomy. Christians, for example, claim to have a basis for regarding the Nazi execution of the mentally retarded and mentally ill—hardly candidates for Kantian autonomy—as assaults on human dignity just as grave as those found in the execution of normal and mature adults.

So what would the Christian put in the place of Kantian autonomy as a foundation for human dignity? Simply this: each human being—every single member of the human species—has dignity (is sacred and precious) because each has been created in the image of God and is one of God's beloved children.[2]

---

2. I am, of course, aware that Christianity is not the only religion that embraces this conception of human dignity. I use it as my example because it is the religion with which I am most familiar and the religion that informed the thinking of Immanuel Kant—the philosopher who has influenced much of my work in moral philosophy.

But surely at least as many skeptical doubts can be raised against the belief in God—and all of the surrounding claims about loving creation—as can be raised against the belief in Kantian autonomy as a foundation for human dignity. And, indeed, it is my hunch that it is people who are already committed to the value of human dignity who may be drawn to Christianity because it claims to enshrine that value. I seriously doubt that many people acquire that value solely through Christian teaching. (Kant's "moral proof" for the existence of God, for example, starts with a moral claim about the implications of human dignity and then uses that moral claim as a reason for embracing religious belief.)

Also, there is the problem of reconciling Christian teaching with Christian practice. The history of Christianity in power is filled with events—pogroms, crusades, and inquisitions, for example—that indicate that people who mouth the language of love and human dignity do not always avoid treating their fellow human beings in unspeakably evil ways. As Lutheran theologian Reinhold Niebuhr put it, "practically nothing can purify the symbol of Christ as the image of God in the imagination of the Jew from the taint with which ages of Christian oppression in the name of Christ have tainted it."[3] There have been, of course, many inspiring examples of Christians fighting oppression and defending human dignity—revealing themselves as models of the goodness of which human beings are capable—but it would be hard to establish that such Christians represent a majority within that group.

It would seem, given the above, that metaphysically inclined philosophers and metaphysically inclined theologians have not yet exhibited resources to save the idea of human dignity from the skeptical doubts that can be raised against it.

---

3. Quoted in Howard Lesnick, *Listening for God; Religion and Moral Discernment* (New York: Fordham University Press, 1998) 103.

As interesting and important as metaphysical attempts to ground or attack the idea of human dignity may be, Christianity's history of coziness with evil leads to another, and more empirical reason that might cause one to doubt human dignity. Indeed, I am inclined to think that the greatest obstacle to believing in human dignity—an attribute of persons that makes them morally unique within the universe—is to be found in the *actual history* of human behavior from earliest times to the present. This behavior provides strong evidence, as a character in the play *Marat/Sade* suggests, that man may indeed be a "mad animal." Human history is, to a substantial degree, a history of murder, rape, torture, exploitation, and callous indifference to the poverty and misery of those fellow humans who do not remind us closely of ourselves. How, one might ask, can we speak of the dignity of a species containing so many members who are murderers, rapists, torturers, or—if not themselves active agents of atrocity—at least quite willing to ignore or deceive themselves about the murders, rapes, and tortures committed by others in their name?[4] Reflecting on the Holocaust—just one dramatic example of the depths of evil human beings can reach—philosopher Robert Nozick draws some very disturbing conclusions. I will quote him at some length:

---

4. It is tempting to adopt the view that most of the great evils in human history have been the work of just a few people of particular nastiness. Books such as Daniel Jonah Goldhagen's *Hitler's Willing Executioners: Ordinary Germans and the Holocaust* (New York: Knopf, 1996), though not without their critics, provide at least some reason to resist that comforting temptation. In this regard, it is also instructive to think about the phenomenon of psychic distance and the way in which it encourages self-deception. A person who might be utterly unable to put a pistol to a baby's face and blow its brains out might easily be able to drop bombs from thirty thousand feet that will blow the brains out of many babies. (During the Vietnam War the *Doonesbury* cartoon strip would sometimes portray bomber pilots dropping napalm and being struck by the beauty of the little puffs of light and color they saw below them.) Finally, too much weight on the act-omission distinction can tempt one to minimize one's role in evil by saying, "But I did not do anything." Surely there are circumstances in which letting evil happen when one could have prevented it is just as culpable as doing evil. I am grateful to Chrystin Ondersma for reminding me of this point.

I believe the Holocaust is an event like the Fall in the way traditional Christianity conceived it, something that radically and drastically alters the situation and status of humanity.... Mankind has fallen.

I do not claim to understand the full significance of this, but here is one piece, I think: It now would not be a special tragedy if humankind ended, if the human species were destroyed in atomic warfare or the earth passed through some cloud that made it impossible for the species to continue reproducing itself.... Such an event would involve a multitude of individual tragedies and suffering...so it would be wrong and monstrous for anyone to bring this about. What I mean is that earlier [prior to the Holocaust], it would have constituted an *additional* tragedy, one beyond that to the individual people involved, if human history and the human species had ended, but now that history and that species have become stained, its loss would be no *special* loss above and beyond the losses to the individuals involved. Humanity has lost its claim to continue.

... [Of course there have been other earlier and later large-scale atrocities, but] the Holocaust alone would have been enough, all by itself. Like a relative shaming a family, the Germans, our human relatives, have shamed us all. They have ruined all our reputations, not as individuals—they have ruined the reputation of the human family... we are all stained.

... Humanity has desanctified itself.[5]

This is powerful language, and the thought behind it is deeply disturbing. But to what extent does it, along with Weiss's mad animal diagnosis, undermine the idea of human dignity, the moral specialness of each member of our species? This is a complex question that requires a complex answer.

---

5. Robert Nozick, *The Examined Life: Philosophical Meditations* (New York: Simon and Schuster, 1989) 237–39.

Let me make a start toward an answer by noting that the most that the passages from Weiss and Nozick could possibly show (and I am not at all confident that they show even this) is that it would not be a tragedy if certain human groups or even the whole human race ceased to exist—by a collective decision no longer to reproduce, for example. On this view, "Save the Human Race" might be a less defensible slogan than "Save the Whales." While such a view might, to some degree, undermine the idea that there is something particularly wrong about *genocide* to the degree that this is conceptualized as the loss of an entire human group, it would in no sense undermine the claim that the production of this result by *murder* would be a great evil, a grave wrong to each individual person who was murdered. As the passage shows, Nozick clearly agrees with this. So even a person who could contemplate with tranquility the loss of the entire human species might well also maintain that bringing this about through the murder of individual human beings would not only be perpetrating a great evil but would also be perpetrating an evil much *worse* than slaughtering, say, an equal number of mice or cattle. A person who holds such a view would seem to be acknowledging the value of human dignity even if that term is never mentioned.[6] But is it reasonable to subscribe to such a value? Can it be defended? I think that to some degree it can be, though perhaps not with the finality that many would desire.

Consider first Weiss's example of man's mad animal behavior and Nozick's description of the "desanctifying" evil of the Holocaust. What is so bad about these acts, so "desanctifying," *unless they are understood as assaults on the dignity of human beings*? Without such a view, one could not distinguish these acts from the killing of large

---

6. I do not mean to suggest that nonhuman animals, because they lack human dignity, necessarily lack all dignity. David Lurie, the central character in J. M. Coetzee's novel *Disgrace* (New York: Viking, 1999), begins to find some meaning in his life again when he takes a job that allows him, as he puts it, to make sure that the dogs euthanized in an animal shelter are killed and disposed of in a way that preserves their dignity. The view he takes on this matter strikes me as moving and not at all absurd.

numbers of cattle, chickens, or pigs in order to provide food for human beings. I would not for a moment want to suggest that it is unreasonable to feel significant moral qualms about such killings, but—not yet persuaded by some of the more radical animal rights advocates—I still regard the killing of human beings as much worse than the killing of the other animals. Some evidence that this view is widely (even if wrongly) shared is revealed in the linguistic fact that we call only the former acts *murder*. So I—and Weiss and Nozick—seem to be, at least tacitly, committed to some notion of human dignity.

Does this then establish that it is rational to subscribe to a doctrine of human dignity? Alas, not fully. The most it shows is that, if one wishes to undermine the concept of human dignity, one will have to do better than trot out multiple examples of atrocities perpetrated by human beings, since the very concept of atrocity seems impossible to understand except as an assault on human dignity. So unless one is willing to abandon such notions as "atrocity," "moral horror," "unspeakable evil," or "acts that cry out to heaven," it seems that one must grant the concept of human dignity, since the concept is presupposed by these terms of condemnation. This kind of "transcendental" argument (to use a Kantian term) reveals that the idea of human dignity may be a presupposition for the very intelligibility of the moral language that many of us want to use. And this is perhaps the best we can do by way of arguing for the value of human dignity. Those with no desire to retain the noted moral language—some utilitarians, some radical animal rights advocates perhaps—however, will, of course, not be impressed or persuaded by such an argument—after all, why should one care about the presuppositions of views that one does not hold? Those of us who would cling to some notion of human dignity can only hope that people of this sort are in the minority.

Even if one comes to grant that murder, rape, and other atrocities are assaults on human dignity, another important question remains: do *all* members of the human species merit being treated as creatures of human dignity—even those who themselves commit atrocities and thereby themselves assault human dignity? Consider this passage from Dostoevsky's *The Brothers Karamazov* (Ivan is speaking to his brother Alyosha):

> "One day a house-serf, a little boy, only eight years old, threw a stone while he was playing and hurt the paw of the general's favorite hound. 'Why is my favorite dog limping?' It was reported to him that this boy had thrown a stone at her and hurt her paw. 'So it was you,' the general looked the boy up and down. 'Take him!' They took him, took him from his mother, and locked him up for the night. In the morning, at dawn, the general rode out in full dress for the hunt, mounted on his horse, surrounded by the spongers, dogs, handlers, huntsmen, all on horseback. The house-serfs are gathered for their edification, the guilty boy's mother in front of them all. The boy is led out of the lockup. A gloomy, cold, misty autumn day, a great day for hunting. The general orders them to undress the boy; the child is stripped naked, he shivers, he's crazy with fear, he doesn't dare make a peep… 'Drive him!' the general commands. The huntsmen shout, 'Run, run!' The boy runs… 'Sic him!' screams the general and looses the whole pack of wolfhounds on him. He hunted him down before his mother's eyes, and the dogs tore the child to pieces…! Well… what to do with him?… Speak, Alyoshka!"
>
> "Shoot him!" Alyosha said softly.[7]

The case of the general is (and was intended by Ivan to be) a test of Alyosha's commitment to Christianity as a gospel of love. When confronted with evil of such extreme cruelty, Alyosha finds it

---

7. Fyoder Dostoevsky, *The Brothers Karamazov*, trans. Richard Pevear and Larissa Volokhonsky (San Francisco: North Point, 1990) 242–43.

impossible—at least as his first reaction—to feel any love in his heart for the general as the perpetrator of this atrocity. Is he then denying the general's human dignity? It is hard to say. If his desire to have the general shot is a desire for just punishment, then he must regard the general as a morally responsible agent and thus at least in that sense as possessed of a capacity that many would see as an important aspect of human dignity. But if he, to use Weiss's language, sees the general merely as a "mad animal" or as a kind of monster, then he must be seeking to have him killed in the same spirit in which we might seek to have a mad dog put down. This is to see the general, as many would see the psychopath or sociopath, as not fully human from the moral point of view and thus as not possessed of human dignity and lacking the rights that dignity generates.[8]

But is it ever permissible to regard any member of the biological human species in this way? Christians, I suppose, would have to say *no*, since they are committed to the view that all members of the species—even the general and those like him—are precious because they are created in God's image. But can one really see preciousness in creatures such as the general? Perhaps only if we view them with the eye of *love* as Simone Weil and, more recently, Raimond Gaita have said—a thought captured in Weil's observation that "love sees what is invisible."[9] Perhaps the invisible that one thinks one sees through love is a capacity for redemption, no matter how vile the wrongdoer's past. Or perhaps it is to believe that one sees some decent core of the person through all the layers of corruption. "Lost

---

8. For an argument that psychopaths may lack certain basic rights normally accorded to human beings, see Jeffrie G. Murphy, "Moral Death: A Kantian Essay on Psychopathy," *Ethics* 82.4 (July 1972) 284–98. I no longer subscribe to all the views I developed in that essay, but it strikes me as still retaining some insights.
9. See Raimond Gaita, *A Common Humanity—Thinking About Love and Truth and Justice* (London: Routledge, 2000) and his *Good and Evil: An Absolute Conception*, 2nd ed. (London: Routledge, 1999). What knowledge I have of Simone Weil is drawn from Gaita's presentation of her views.

within a man who murdered, there was a soul like any other soul, purity itself it surely once had been," as the novelist William Trevor says of the serial killer who is the central character of his novel *Felicia's Journey*—a moving sentence by a writer of great moral and spiritual sensitivity.[10]

However, even those who feel the emotional pull of this sentence, or appreciate the spiritual idea of seeing through the eye of love, will surely have to admit that such a point of view has no clear rational foundation. Perhaps it can be adopted only within a framework of radical religious *faith*—a faith that would allow a believer to see the neighbor even in the general and thus be able to extend the command to love one's neighbor as oneself even to him.

But what is the nonbeliever to do? Should the person incapable of radical faith feel free to regard the general and his kind as less than human, as devoid of dignity, and thus as mad animals or monsters that merit no respect and can thus be treated in any way that one might desire?

Even for complete secularists, who are unlikely to recognize any absolute reasons of principle, there are at least powerful *historical* and *pragmatic* reasons that should give them pause before utterly abandoning the idea of human dignity. The twentieth century, for example, gave us many demonstrations of the terrible dangers that can arise when individual human beings or their governments presume to discard as not really human—and thus treat as monsters, animals, or vermin—members of their own species. These dangers are not merely the terrible things that acting on such a view can bring about to those deemed nonhuman, but also the terrible things that acting on such a view can bring about in the souls of those who would presume to treat others as nonhuman. To guard against these dangers, it is always a good idea to keep vividly in mind Nietzsche's wise counsel that

---

10. William Trevor, *Felicia's Journey* (New York: Viking, 1995) 212.

"whoever fights monsters should see to it that in the process he does not become a monster. And when you look long into an abyss, the abyss also looks into you."[11]

Nietzsche's counsel is in part consequential in nature since it warns of what could happen to the world and to us if we felt free to apply the human/nonhuman distinction to members of our own species and then act upon it. His counsel is not strictly utilitarian, however, because it is concerned not merely with social consequences to the general welfare but also with negative influences on our own virtue of character.

The case against acting on a human/nonhuman distinction applied to members of our own species is not limited to these consequential considerations, important as these are. I would also raise what I will call considerations of *moral humility*. If we can overcome our comforting self-deceptions about our own wisdom and goodness, we will surely realize how limited our cognitive powers to read the heart of another are and how great our own potential for evil is—realize that perhaps we do not know enough and are not good enough to presume to dismiss any other human being from the dignity club. A Christian will think here of Jesus' remark, "Let him who is without sin among you be the first to cast a stone," but the insight in that remark as a check to human pride as unjustified self-confidence in one's own virtue can surely be embraced by even the most secular of readers—an insight that might even incline such a reader to accept W. H. Auden's counsel to "love your crooked neighbour/With your crooked heart."[12]

"But wait a minute," the secular skeptic might say, "I have never had my dogs rip a child apart or committed any other atrocity—have never raped, tortured, or murdered. Surely I am without sin in the

---

11. Friedrich Nietzsche, *Beyond Good and Evil: Prelude to a Philosophy of the Future*, trans. Walter Kaufmann (New York: Vintage, 1989) 89.
12. W. H. Auden, from "As I Walked Out One Evening," *Collected Poems*, ed. Edward Mendelson (New York: Vintage, 1991) 135.

relevant sense and can feel free to cast as many stones as I like at the general and his kind—even the stone of refusing to regard him as possessing human dignity. My heart may be a little bit crooked—I was rude to my secretary yesterday, for example—but not so crooked that I must consider loving the general or even according him the kind of respect as a human that he, being a monster and not really a human, does not merit. He is moral excrement, and excrement pretty clearly lacks dignity."[13]

This response strikes me as too hasty and shallow a response to the insight expressed in Jesus' remark, which invites those of us who have been virtuous and law-abiding to ask ourselves *why* this has been the case. Is it, as we would like to think, because our characters are splendid all the way down? Or is it perhaps because our circumstances—of upbringing, need, temptation, and all the other things that John Rawls called "our luck on the natural and social lottery"—have been favored?[14] And might it not even be possible that we are virtuous and law-abiding simply because we are *afraid* of the consequence of disobedience? Imagine yourself possessed of Gyges' ring—a ring that, in the stories told by Herodotus and Plato, makes its wearer invisible—and then try to answer honestly what you might do under such circumstances. I suspect that for most of us an honest answer will be an important lesson in moral humility. This lesson might incline us not to condone what the general has done nor to

---

13. One of the most powerful moments in Stanley Kramer's film *Judgment at Nuremberg* (1961) is when the former Nazi judge finally brings to full consciousness the magnitude of the evil of which he was an agent and says this of himself: "I have turned my life into excrement." My interest here is in whether one can ever legitimately make such a judgment of another, but it would also be worth considering if one might ever legitimately make such a judgment about oneself.
14. John Rawls, *A Theory of Justice* (Cambridge, MA: Belknap, 1971). In Sections 12, 13, and 14, Rawls uses the idea of a lottery in the distribution of natural and social advantages to reject what he calls "liberal equality" in favor of "democratic equality" (65–90). Liberal equality is rejected because (in Rawls' view) it unjustly allows natural and social advantages, which are morally arbitrary because they are simply a matter of luck, to influence the formation of a principle of distribution as part of the basic structure of a society.

free him from punishment, but to resist the temptation to distance ourselves from him too far—so far that we would presume to dismiss him from the human race and attribute to him no human dignity at all and thus make him a target of whatever cruelty we might desire to inflict on him.[15] The question, "Who am I to presume to make such a judgment?" combined with the worry that "there but for the grace of God go I," should make us at least travel part way down the road sketched for us by Walt Whitman in his poem, "You Felons on Trial in Courts":

> Beneath this face that appears so impassive hell's tides continually run,
> Lusts and wickedness are acceptable to me,
> I walk with delinquents with passionate love,
> I feel I am of them—I belong to those convicts and prostitutes myself,
> And henceforth I will not deny them—for how can I deny myself?[16]

---

15. The Eighth Amendment of the United States Constitution bans "cruel and unusual punishments." In theory, if not always in practice, this shields even the worst criminals from treatment such as torture or mutilation—treatment that would assault their dignity as human beings and would compromise the dignity of those who would inflict such punishments.

16. Walt Whitman, *Leaves of Grass* (New York: Vintage/Library of America, 1992) 511. Perhaps I cannot imagine myself joining Dostoevsky's general and sending my dogs to kill a small boy, but I can—alas—imagine myself a different general who, in time of war, might order a cannon bombardment of a village while knowing that many small boys and other innocent people will be torn to bits. How big, then, is the moral gap between the two generals? My brief exposition of the idea of moral humility and its relevance to judgments of what I call the "deep character" of wrongdoers and of their worth as human beings is a summary of thoughts I pursue at length in two of my published essays: "Moral Epistemology, the Retributive Emotions, and the 'Clumsy Moral Philosophy' of Jesus Christ," *The Passions of Law*, ed. Susan A. Bandes (New York: New York University Press, 1999) 149–67, and "Legal Moralism and Retribution Revisited," *Criminal Law and Philosphy* 1.1 (January 2007): 5–20. This essay was my 2006 presidential address to the American Philosophical Association, Pacific Division, and may also be found in *Proceedings and Addresses of the American Philosophical Association* 8.2 (November 2006): 45–62.

Aided by the insights of Jesus, Nietzsche, Auden, Rawls, and Whitman, I have tried to develop a case for the relevance of the virtue of moral humility in thinking about excluding wrongdoers, even ones as terrible as the general, from the range of those regarded as having human dignity. The arguments presented in no sense establish the objective correctness of the claim that each human being has dignity. I think that they do, however, provide some reasons why abandoning this claim might be a very bad idea.

Nozick—very gifted at making a point through humor—once gave this characterization of some philosophers' dream of a perfect philosophical argument: it sets up a chemical reaction in your opponent's brain so that, if he accepts your premise but denies your conclusion, he explodes and dies. No philosophers actually have this standard of perfection, of course, but many do aim for a level of precision and proof to which the subject matter under investigation may not be susceptible. Much of ethics tends to be like this, and I agree with Aristotle that it is a mistake in this rather messy area to aim for a level of precision that one might legitimately expect in other fields of philosophy. Those with such an aim often manage to produce not illumination, but only what H. L. A. Hart once called "uniformity at the price of distortion."

This does not mean that anything goes, of course, but it does make one justifiably suspicious of aspirations for grand theory in ethics. Indeed, I sometimes think that the next great book in ethics—one that would do justice to the complex and conflicted nature of our actual moral lives—might not have as its title "A Theory of..." but rather something more like "Stumbling Along" or "Muddling Through."

On the subject of human dignity and its place in morality, I certainly have no final theory to offer in the hope that it will settle once and for all the significant disputes over what role, if any, this concept should play in our moral lives. I have simply tried, using Richard

Rorty's fine phrase, to "advance the conversation" a bit—trying to highlight and clarify some of the issues at stake, to alert my readers to some of the problems and difficulties that confront any attempted philosophical account of those issues, and in particular to note some issues that merit additional thought. Perhaps the discussion will allow at least some of my readers to muddle through and stumble along with a somewhat steadier gait than they might previously have been able to manage. That, at any rate, is my hope.

Chapter 13

Kant on the "Right of Necessity" and other Defenses in the Law of Homicide

There are a number of cases where Kant seems to be admitting that, although in some sense a defendant ought to be punished (even with the death penalty), special circumstances undermine even the legal right and duty to punish (or to apply the death penalty), e.g., shipwreck "necessity" cases, and, in defense of "honor," a soldier killing in a duel and a mother killing her illegitimate newborn infant. Apparently, these are not bizarre cases of a legal duty of officials to punish despite a moral prohibition against doing so, but rather cases of moral grounds for limiting the legal right to punish in special circumstances.

Thomas E. Hill, Jr.[1]

INTRODUCTION

This essay was originally written for a projected essay collection to honor the work of Thomas Hill, Jr. This collection is to be edited by Robert Johnson and Mark Timmons and should appear at some time in the future. Tom Hill is a man whose friendship I value and whose work always stimulates my own thinking, and thus I dedicate this essay to him with affection and esteem. I have decided to use the

---

1. Hill 2000: 177–178.

above passage from his essay on Kant on punishment as a springboard for my own essay for three reasons. First, the fact that I have devoted so much of my own philosophical career to the topic of criminal punishment will, I hope, give me some chance that I might have something both informed and useful to say about the three criminal defenses in the law of homicide that Kant notes in his *Doctrine of Right* (*Rechtslehre*) with some approval: killing as a life-saving necessity, killing in a military duel, and bastard infanticide. The final two are conceptualized by Kant as shame-avoiding honor killings.[2] Second, although I some years ago published an essay of my own on Kant and punishment, it has been a very long time since I—generally moving away from Kant studies—could claim anything like Hill's scholarly expertise on the Kantian texts.[3] I will here try to hide my scholarly inadequacies, however, by focusing on a quite specific issue: three defenses in the law of homicide, topics on which Kant provides a highly compressed but also highly puzzling and sometimes even disturbing discussion. I select this issue both because of its intrinsic and continuing interest in criminal law theory and because much of what Kant says about it strikes me as quite unhelpful for a variety of reasons. Third, I have always admired Hill's ability to make sense of and render plausible many Kantian claims that, on first

---

2. Kant generally does not offer the defenses in these honor killings as complete defenses—ones that should result in complete aquittal—but rather as mitigating defenses that should qualify the convicted defendant for a sentence less severe than the sentence (death) normally and properly given for murder. In the necessity cases Kant seems to favor total acquittal.
3. For my early essay on Kant on punishment, see Murphy (1987). What I said in the essay about Kant on honor killings now strikes me as quite superficial and even wrong, and I hope that my expanded discussion of such killings in the present essay is a significant improvement. What I say in the present essay about Kant on the necessity defense overlaps some of what I said in my earlier essay, but involves some nontrivial modifications—indeed a complete change of mind on my part with respect to some central claims. I am not sure that I was ever in a position to claim expertise on Kant comparable to Hill's. My teacher, Lewis White Beck, once told me—after reading one of my early Rawls-inspired essays on Kant's moral and legal philosophy—that he thought I was destined to become America's leading authority on what Kant *should* have said. This was definitely *not* a compliment.

inspection, seem confused or otherwise unacceptable, and it is my hope that I can provoke him into engaging that ability by addressing the issue of Kant on these selected criminal defenses. What Hill says about them in the essay is found in the quoted passage—a passage that offers little commentary, pro or con, about Kant's discussion of the three defenses noted. Does Hill find what Kant says about these defenses intrinsically acceptable and consistent with the larger theoretical claims in Kant's moral and legal philosophy, or does he agree with me that they have significant—and perhaps fatal—shortcomings? I am anxious to hear what he might have to say about this and expect that, as usual, I will find what he says illuminating.

HONOR, SHAME, BASTARDS, AND DUELS

Before exploring the complex issues involved in claiming a "right of necessity" as a legal defense to a charge of murder, I would like briefly to discuss the two other Kantian examples mentioned by Hill: a soldier killing a fellow soldier in a duel, and a woman killing her illegitimate newborn infant. Some of Kant's arguments on these two issues strike me as instances of unexampled feebleness and in no sense worthy of perhaps the greatest philosopher of the eighteenth century.

I believe that Hill is quite correct in interpreting Kant to be saying that these are not cases where there is a legal duty to punish despite a moral prohibition against doing so, but rather cases of moral grounds for limiting the legal right to punish in certain circumstances—in short, morally justified legal defenses. But are Kant's arguments persuasive? For the most part—absent some creative rational reconstruction—I think that they are not. Let me consider primarily the bastard infanticide case, since I think that what I will say about that will hold, *mutatis mutandis*, for the case of a soldier killing in a duel.

If there is a moral reason for limiting the legal right to punish in this case, what is it? One possible reason, of course, would be to claim that the child, being illegitimate, is not a human person at all in any morally relevant sense and thus totally lacks the rights and dignity generally attributed to human persons and protected by just systems of law. But this is surely a vile view and one cannot imagine Kant, of all people, holding such a view. But, alas, consider the following passage:

> A child that comes into the world apart from marriage is born outside the law (for the law is marriage) and therefore outside the protection of the law. It has, as it were, stolen into the commonwealth (like contraband merchandise), so that the commonwealth can ignore its existence (since it was not 'right' that it should have come into existence in this way), and can therefore also ignore its annihilation.[4]

As a first and rather obvious objection to this line of reasoning, consider this: Since the infant presumably loses is status as a relevant object of legal protection because it was not legally right that it come into existence in this way, how would a bastard *ever* earn a right to legal protection since the *origin* of its existence will remain the same throughout its entire life? And why is the right to kill limited to the mother? Should we not *all* have a legal right to kill this individual, because of its illegal origin, whether it is three days old or thirty years old? And what should our attitude to adult illegal immigrants be, given they that have *intentionally* stolen illegally into our society? This would seem to support an even stronger case that killing them should not be regarded as murder—or at least not as the most severe degree of murder, murder to be punished by death. Finally, if it is really the case that, with respect to an illegitimate child, we may ignore its

---

4. Kant 1996: 477.

annihilation, then why punish such infanticide at all instead of merely reducing the sentence to a degree of homicide that does not require the death penalty? We do not punish people at all simply for throwing out their garbage, and Kant's discussion—whatever its actual intention—invites us to think of the illegitimate infant in an analogous way.

How could Kant have been drawn to such a vile view? Although he at least has the decency to add the phrase "as it were," he tries out the following analogical argument in defense of his view: The illegitimate child is, as it were, like a smuggler who sneaks contraband (in this case himself) into society—who has, in Kant's words, "stolen into the commonwealth." But this of course will not work since the use of the word "stolen"—suggesting intention or what the law calls *mens rea*—seems to attribute responsibility to an infant, and that is absurd. Kant quickly abandons this absurdity by adopting a view that is, at least morally, even worse: namely, he conceptualizes the infant *as itself contraband*, as a *thing* or *object* rather than a person who is an end in itself. This would seem to be exactly what the second formulation of the categorical imperative in the *Groundwork* (*Grundlegung*) commands us not to do.[5]

I am reluctant, of course, to convict Kant of the kind of moral imbecility I have so far described. So, to interpret him more sympathetically, we might see in these tortured passages Kant groping toward a distinction not clearly analyzed until much later in the development of criminal law: the distinction between *excuse* defenses and *justification* defenses. To justify is to argue that what the defendant has done was *right*. To excuse is to argue not that what the defendant has done was right, but rather that the defendant was *not responsible*—at least not fully—for the wrong that he has done.[6] All

---
5. Kant 1996: 78–85.
6. Some defenses—for example, provocation—seem to straddle the distinction since the provocation that reduces a homicide from first- to second-degree murder or manslaughter must be a provocation that would have aroused a reasonable person.

just legal systems will regard some conduct normally wrong (intentionally killing, for example) as in some circumstances justified (intentionally killing in self-defense, for example) and will sometimes not punish even for wrong conduct if the individual who engaged in the conduct was not a free and responsible agent (as in the insanity defense, for example).

How might this distinction bear on Kant's discussion? Consider his introduction of the concept of *shame* with respect to the woman who kills her illegitimate infant: "No decree can remove the mother's shame when it becomes known that she gave birth without being married."[7]

The fact that a woman, given prevailing social conventions, will feel deeply ashamed in giving birth to an illegitimate child certainly cannot justify the intentional killing of that child—particularly if the conventions are themselves, to use Kant's language, "barbarous and undeveloped."[8] But perhaps the psychological pressure of such shame might at least mitigate to some degree the appropriate legal punishment for such killing—making the killing of a less serious grade, perhaps, than killing done out of cruel malice. Kant speaks of "being constrained by public opinion" in the case of the soldier who kills in a duel, and surely a similar kind of constraint could apply in the case of bastard infanticide as well. If one acts from allegiance to conventions that are irrational and immoral, one surely cannot claim that one's conduct was (all things considered) justified; but the oppressive nature of social conventions just might be regarded by some as mitigating—arguably reducing the crime from capital murder to a lesser degree of homicide carrying a lesser punishment—life imprisonment, perhaps. I have no idea if Kant was trying to grope toward some idea of excuse, but I can see no other reason why he would

---

7. Kant 1996: 477.
8. Kant 1996: 477.

introduce the concept of shame at all.[9] Also, Kant's claim that legal punishment is justified in such cases, but that the death penalty may not be, is best explained in terms of a mitigation excuse.[10]

There are, of course, grounds for being skeptical that the kind of shame endured from acting against a powerful social convention is adequate to trigger a legitimate excuse, even a mitigating excuse.[11] Down that road perhaps lies excusing the gang banger who murders because of a fear that if he does not, he will—given the social conventions operating in certain gangs—be shamed in

---

9. My colleague Mary Sigler has suggested that fear of social ostracism may be just one motivating factor. Another might be the realization that one has done a shameful thing and killing as a desire to distance oneself from that by obliterating its object.
10. Fearing shame and social ostracism are typically not such powerful emotions as to render a person delusional or powerless. They are not a kind of insanity. They might, however, make it more difficult to comply with the relevant criminal law than would be the case for persons who lack these fears, and thus fairness might point to a lesser punishment for killings motivated by these fears than for killings motivated in other ways—particularly if the motives in question are thought to be less evil than, say, malicious cruelty. Also, it might be argued that a person who kills in compliance with powerful social conventions can to some degree blame those conventions and argue that society to some degree shares responsibility for what has been done. I would not, however, be too hasty in going down this excusing road—particularly if the excuse is regarded as a total defense and not merely a mitigating defense. It is, of course, to ask a lot of a person when one asks that person to go against common social conventions or practices. But it is also true, it should be remembered, that criminal law must target people at the point when they are most strongly tempted to act contrary to what the law requires. Because of this, one must be cautious about recognizing difficulty of compliance as a criminal defense. The American Model Penal Code 2013(1)(b) provides for a defense of "extreme emotional disturbance." The defense reduces murder to manslaughter if the emotional distress in question has "a reasonable explanation"—that is, is a kind and level of distress that we think would have a tendency to deeply upset a reasonable person. Though similar to provocation in some ways (see note 6), this defense does not require a provoking act.
11. I am interested in whether Kant's discussion can cast any light on controversies in contemporary criminal law theory. In fairness to Kant, however, I must admit that I have no knowledge of the degree of shame occasioned *in his day and culture* by the violation of the two social conventions he discusses. Dueling has the interesting feature that both parties willingly participate in the duel, but in contemporary criminal law consent is generally not a defense to homicide. When I later discuss the issue of the right of necessity, however, I will discuss the possibility (only to be rejected) that certain kinds of consent—hypothetical rational consent or what is sometimes called actual tacit consent—might render some intentional killings justified.

the eyes of his fellow gang members and perhaps dropped from the gang. Or is it only the shame occasioned by violation of the social conventions of "respectable" middle-class people that is to count in the realm of excuses for homicide? That does not seem very decent.

Consider a recent case in Phoenix, Arizona. Faleh Hassan Almeleki, a forty-eight-year-old conservative Muslim immigrant from Iraq, was convicted of second-degree murder and sentenced to thirty-four years in prison for running down his daughter with his car and killing her. Why did he do this? Because, according to most reports, his honor demanded it—demanded it because his daughter had become so Westernized that she was exhibiting a level of sin that, in his view, shamed the entire family. (The United Nations Population Fund estimates that more than 5,000 women a year die in honor killings for such so-called crimes as speaking to unrelated men or being raped.) It is sad that there are still places in the world that condone such mindless barbarism, and surely no civilized society would regard such actions as anything but culpable criminal homicides.[12] But are they murders of the very worst sort—murders that require the death penalty? Kant thought not, and if he was thinking of mitigating excuses (leading to conviction of a lesser degree of homicide) rather than justifications (leading to total acquittal) the essence of his view may not be so feeble after all.

---

12. For a brief summary of this case see www.cbsnews.com/8301-504083_162-20054930-504083.html (last accessed September 28, 2011). For initial local newspaper coverage of the case, see the *Arizona Republic*, November 8, 2009, page B14—Leonard Pitts's "Viewpoint" essay "Father, daughter, caught in class of cultures in Ariz." A month later (December 18, 2009, A2) the *Republic* reported a case in which a London judge sentenced to life imprisonment a Kurdish father for murdering his fifteen-year-old daughter because she fell in love with a follower of a different branch of Islam. Although the killing in the Arizona case was almost certainly premeditated, the prosecuting attorneys decided not to seek the death penalty—perhaps because they thought a jury might contain some aggrieved parents inclined to be somewhat sympathetic to a strict father driven to despair by the disobedient behavior of a near-teenage child.

With this background, let me now return to the case of bastard infanticide. There are, even in contemporary America, instances of killing an illegitimate child that might reasonably be regarded as open to a mitigating excuse—classification, perhaps, as a degree of homicide that does not demand the most severe penalties set down for first-degree murder. However, this generally will not be regarded as appropriate simply because the defendant faces shame. Rather, it will be because the defendant is, for example, very young (in high school, perhaps), is poor, is very unsophisticated, and faces not just shame, but perhaps brutal punishment at home or even being thrown out of the house and made homeless on the streets. These worries impose pressures far more grave than the mere fear that one will endure the shame that comes from violating certain social conventions. Imagine, however, a woman who does not labor under the other fears that I have noted but who simply fears shame before, let us suppose, her country club circle of white friends who would shun her if she revealed herself as the parent of an illegitimate black baby. I see no place for a mitigating excuse of any kind in this case. Indeed, I am rather inclined to see killing an infant for this reason to be an aggravating factor.

One final point worth noting in Kant's highly compressed discussion is his introduction of the concept of the *state of nature*:

> Legislation cannot remove the disgrace of an illegitimate birth any more than it can wipe away the stain of suspicion of cowardice from a subordinate officer who fails to respond to a humiliating affront with a force of his own rising above the fear of death. So it seems that in these two cases people find themselves in the state of nature, and that these acts of *killing* (*homocidium*), which would then not have to be called murder (*homocidium dolosum*) are certainly punishable but cannot be punished with death by the supreme power.[13]

13. Kant 1996: 476.

This strikes me as astoundingly weak as an argument that acts of bastard infanticide and killing in (some) duels are "crimes deserving of death, with regard to which it still remains doubtful whether *legislation* is also authorized to impose the death penalty."[14]

First, it is by no means obvious that "legislation cannot remove the disgrace of an illegitimate birth any more than it can wipe away the suspicion of cowardice." Legislation alone cannot perhaps totally and immediately *remove* such disgrace, but it can surely reduce it— and perhaps in the long run assist in its total removal. Strictly enforced laws against dueling would surely have some effect in undermining cowardice as the only reason why a law-abiding and law-respecting person would refuse a duel, and strictly enforced laws against bastard infanticide might ultimately lead to social conventions that make killing an illegitimate infant more shameful than giving birth to it. We now generally punish as murder killing in duels and bastard infanticide, and we would no longer take shame over such matters as either an excuse or justification for such killing.[15] Our community norms have changed, and the law has probably played some role in this normative shift—just as United States Supreme Court decisions declaring unconstitutional laws criminalizing homosexual sodomy and laws mandating racially segregated schools have probably played some nontrivial role in increasing social tolerance in areas of sexual orientation and race. In short, the law does not always have to follow. It can sometimes lead.[16]

---

14. Normally one argues that a mitigating excuse should reduce the penalty because of a belief that, morally, the individual having that excuse does not deserve the death penalty. So what could it possibly mean to say—as Kant does—that the individual deserves to be executed but that legally the penalty should not be imposed?
15. As I have discussed earlier, if we add some complexities to the case and find ourselves dealing not merely with shame but with such things as youth or mental instability (diminished capacity), then we may have grounds for a mitigating case.
16. For a stimulating discussion of how the law and the punishments provided by law can play a role in the formation of beliefs in wrongfulness, see Kahan 2000. Kahan argues that when the goal is to change a deeply entrenched norm (for example, to replace the norm that tends to

Second, even if legislation happens to be powerless to remove certain social conventions that stigmatize when violated, it hardly follows—as Kant seems to suggest—that with respect to actions in accord with those conventions, individuals "find themselves in a state of nature." If there are powerful social conventions that are motivationally operative, then this is certainly not a state of nature of the kind Hobbes described—a condition in which people are motivated to act solely to avoid pain and violent death. But then what kind of state of nature is it? Kant seems to be claiming that legal punishment for the killings in question would be legitimate, but not the death penalty. But what kind of state of nature is it that provides for any *legal* punishments at all? If there is legitimate punishment, then there is a legitimate civil society and thus no state of nature in any sense that I can understand. If one of the primary purposes that would prompt rational beings to form civil society in the first place is not being realized for certain groups of people (minorities not getting police protection to prevent their being murdered or criminals being put in prisons in effect run by the Aryan Brotherhood, for example) then I can understand why one might say that those people have been in effect thrown back into the state of nature. I am not, however, tempted to say this for people whose only complaint is that one of their familiar social conventions points one way and, if the law points in another way, they will be put in an uncomfortable bind: face criminal punishment or face the shame of social stigma. This is a tough situation for one to face, no doubt, but to call it the state of nature strikes me as nothing more than grandiose and misleading rhetoric.

But perhaps the above is a bit too quick. Even if it cannot be literally true that those who kill from honor find themselves in a state of

---

trivialize date rape with a norm that condemns it as "real" rape), the best strategy is to employ a relatively mild sanction expressing condemnation of the old norm since juries will often not convict if they think the punishment is too severe. This would be a non-Kantian reason for thinking that Kant may be right when he suggests that the criminal punishment for honor crimes should not be the most severe in our punitive arsenal.

nature, perhaps talk about the state of nature could be a way—a metaphorical way—of highlighting a worrisome problem that could have legitimate impact on determinations concerning severity of punishment, or at least condemnation. If one believes that a legal system gets its legitimacy in part by enforcing shared social or community norms—by encouraging compliance with those norms rather than punishing for loyalty to them—then might one not be at least tempted to feel outside the scope of a legitimate rule of law if one is punished for doing what most people in the community think is the right thing to do, even if some, being more enlightened perhaps, would not agree?[17] Southern white segregationists in the early days of the civil rights movement often expressed opposition to integration as "a challenge to our very way of life." Justice required, of course, that force be used to bring them into line on this matter, but one can still—I think—have a certain limited sympathy for their view that their expectations concerning the rule of law were being undermined by the federal government. And this sympathy could to some degree mitigate the unambiguous harshness with which we might otherwise condemn them for peacefully expressing the view (which they had a constitutional right to express) that integration was wrong and should not be forced on them. This might at least make us see such people as something more than simply evil and ignorant racist thugs. They certainly deserve some condemnation (many white Southerners did, after all, see the evil of racial segregation) but surely not the same level of condemnation appropriate to apply to Sheriff "Bull" Connor (and those who applauded him) when he unleashed attack dogs on peaceful civil rights demonstrators or those jeering whites who shouted abuse and spit on the children being escorted by the National Guard to recently integrated schools. If one is inclined to mitigate at

---

17. Lord Patrick Devlin's belief that one of the law's primary purposes is to uphold the shared moral norms of society came to be called "legal moralism." For elaboration and discussion of this view, see Devlin 1965 and Murphy 2006.

least to some small degree the condemnation that one addresses to those who opposed segregation because they saw it as an attack on their way of life, then perhaps one is—at least in a metaphorical sense—seeing them as in some sense in a state of nature. That, at any rate, is the best that I can do in trying to make at least a little bit of sense of Kant's claims on the matter.[18]

So much for honor, shame, bastards, and duels. Let me now move to a more complex issue: Kant on the right of necessity.

SHIPWRECKS AND KILLING TO PRESERVE ONE'S OWN LIFE

In a passage that matches very closely what Kant says in his other writings about the so-called right of necessity, he says this in the *Doctrine of Right (Rechtslehre)*:

18. That this is the best I can do does not, of course, mean that it is the best that can be done. Tom Hill called my attention to a splendid essay by David Sussman (Sussman 2008). Mustering far more Kant scholarship than I currently possess, Sussman argues that "Kant takes agents to have a moral right to defend their honor. Unlike other rights, however, this right of honor can only be defended personally, so that individuals remain in a 'state of nature' with regard to any such rights, regardless of their political situation. According to Kant we should be lenient in these cases because the malefactors are caught between two kinds of authentic normative demand, at a point when the moral authority of the state collides with a certain authority which individuals must claim for themselves" (p. 299). Also, Justin Tosi, responding to a version of this essay that I presented at a conference, suggested the following in an email to me: "The state of nature ... is a relational concept. Persons are in the state of nature relative to each other, concerning certain disputes, if there is no sovereign power in place to resolve those disputes. So, before civil society, Smith and Jones are in the state of nature relative to each other about every dispute they might have. After they join a sovereign commonwealth, they are in the state of nature with each other only with respect to disputes that [the commonwealth] does not regulate ... Kant might mean that two officers, Smith and Jones, are in the state of nature relative to one another concerning some shameful incident—[Smith insulting Jones in certain ways, for example] ... The law does enjoin citizens from dueling. But it does not forbid all actions that bestow shame. So in response Jones may rightly insult Smith's honor in some way. But in killing him, he takes more than is owed. And killing is an action that the law is concerned with, so it may of course sanction Jones. But it may also take into account Jones's right to reclaim some of his honor from Smith. So if

This imagined right is supposed to give me permission to take the life of another person when my own life is in danger, even if he has done me no harm. It is quite obvious that this conception implies a self-contradiction within jurisprudence, since the point in question here has nothing to do with an unjust assailant on my own life, which I defend by taking his life.... The question under discussion is whether I am permitted to use violence against someone who himself has not used it against me.

It is clear that this allegation [of a right based on necessity] is not to be understood objectively, according to what a law might prescribe, but merely subjectively, as the sentence that might be pronounced in a court of law. There could be no penal law assigning the death penalty to a man who has been shipwrecked and finds himself struggling with another man—both in equal danger of losing their lives—and who, in order to save his own life, pushes the other man off the plank on which he had saved himself. For the first man, no punishment threatened by the law could be greater than losing his life. A penal law applying to such a situation could never have the effect intended, for the threat of an evil that is still uncertain (being condemned to death by a judge) cannot outweigh the fear of an evil that is certain (being drowned). Hence, we must judge that, although an act of

---

Smith's (private) offense was serious enough, the state could have reason to withhold imposing the death penalty [the most severe penalty for homicide] on Jones." Finally, Guyora Binder emailed me the following comment after reading a draft of my essay on a flight back to Detroit after presenting a very stimulating paper at Arizona State University: "I think I understand what Kant means by characterizing the two honor killings as taking place within a state of nature. A society according status on the basis of honor (rather than viewing all moral agents as equals) is not governed by the moral law, and—insofar as status must be maintained through violence—rejects the rule of law. Just as punishment is impossible in the international arena (Binder 2009) it is impossible in a society where security of life depends on a willingness to defend one's honor. Think of Jack Abbott's portrayal of life in a maximum security prison, of Maxine Hong Kingston's portrayal of Chinese village life in *The Woman Warrior*—which opens with a description of a young woman giving birth out of wedlock forced not only to kill the baby but also to commit suicide."

self-preservation through violence is not inculpable...it still is unpunishable, and this subjective immunity from punishment, through a strange confusion among jurists, is identified with an objective (legal) immunity from punishment.[19]

I do not know enough about German legal history to know if what Kant says here captures the law of his day. My interest here, however, is not historical. Rather, I want to see if what Kant says can provide illumination for contemporary criminal law theory—particularly illumination of defenses to homicide. I found very little illumination in exploring his mitigating defenses for bastard infanticide and killing in duels, and I now want to see if his discussion of the right of necessity fares any better.

The example that Kant uses to frame his discussion of the right of necessity—Cicero's (originally Hecaton's) famous example of two men in danger of drowning contending for a floating plank after a shipwreck—is not an ideal case around which to build a discussion of a right of necessity with respect to homicide. The fact that Kant describes the man who pushes the other off the plank as taking the life of that other man suggests, along with the rest of Kant's discussion, that this is to be understood as a case of murder. But murder is typically understood as the *intentional* and *wrongful* killing of another human being, and it is by no means obvious that this is the proper way to understand Cicero's case.

First, it should be noted that this case involves two men contending (each "struggling with another man" in Kant's words) for a plank in the hope that this plank will serve as a life preserver. This is a plank to which neither man has a right (unless the fact that one man at the moment has it in his control constitutes a kind of squatter's right), and thus the fact that one man ultimately wins out in this competitive

---

19. Kant 1996: 391–392.

struggle does not obviously constitute wrongdoing on the part of that man. It would be extremely nice—perhaps even heroic—for one of these men to withdraw from the competition so that the other might live, but surely there is no wrongdoing in a refusal to withdraw and criminal law does not punish people for failing to be extremely nice. If this is going to be understood as wrongdoing, then an argument for this is surely needed.[20]

Second, and more important, murder typically is understood as requiring a *mens rea* of intention or purpose—that is, the actor, to be guilty of murder, must have as his purpose (what the American Model Penal Code calls his "conscious object") the death of the person whose life is lost. It seems to me, however, highly unlikely that the man in this particular shipwreck case has as his purpose the death of the person who loses the struggle. The victor, surely, would be perfectly happy if the man over whom he has been victorious found another plank and saved his life as well.[21] The law will sometimes treat knowledge that one will bring about death as equivalent to intention if the knowledge is certain or of extremely high probability, but we have no evidence that that kind of knowledge was present in the case before us. Perhaps there were other planks in swimming distance and the victor over the one plank (perhaps viewed as a particularly splendid plank) hoped that his rival would find another plank that was at least adequate and

---

20. In a rich essay (Finkelstein 2001), Claire Finkelstein outlines the history of the plank example from its origins in Hecaton through Cicero, Grotius, Pufendor, Bacon, Blackstone, and, finally, Kant. In her own discussion of the example, she argues that each of the contending men has an equal right to the plank. It does not follow, of course, that because each man has an equal right to the plank that each man may do whatever is in his power to secure the plank. The idea of two men contending for the plank tacitly assumes, I think, that the competition between them is approximately equal—or at least not grotesquely unequal. Suppose one of the men has a pistol and shoots the other between the eyes in order to keep him from having a chance at the plank. Here I think we would have wrongdoing unless one wants to subscribe to the (to me) utterly implausible principle "if X has a right to Y, then X may do anything at all to secure Y."
21. The absence of relevant *mens rea* in this case is noted by Suzanne Uniacke in a valuable article (Uniacke 1996).

would survive. At any rate, no civilized legal system would (absent more information) regard the death of the sailor who lost the struggle for the plank as a case of murder—reckless or negligent homicide perhaps (although I suspect not even this) but nothing that would engage even a discussion of the death penalty.

Suppose, however, we consider for a moment the case as Kant considers it: namely, as a case of murder that, as a matter of law, should be punished with death but for which the defendant should receive a sentence less than death or even no sentence at all.[22] Here, in his contrast between the *objective* and the *subjective* view of the matter, Kant seems to be noting an important distinction between what might be relevant at a trial to establish guilt and what might be relevant at a later stage at which a judge sets the sentence after conviction—a stage at which certain subjective features of the defendant, perhaps not thought possible to specify in advance and build into the statutory definition of the crime, can play a role.[23]

What might these be? Somewhat surprisingly, at least for those who want to hold on to the view that Kant is primarily a retributivist, Kant offers only one argument that the sentence for this case of murder should be less than death—namely, that such a sentence can have no deterrence value. There are possible retributivist arguments

---

22. There seems to be a lack of parallel here with the shame/honor cases. With respect to those, I have suggested that Kant may have been groping toward the articulation of a mitigating excuse rather than a justification—an excuse that reduces the crime from one requiring the death penalty to one that carries a lesser punishment. (However, when Kant says that the law may "*ignore* the annihilation" of the illegitimate infant, that one isolated remark could be taken as a justification for recommending no punishment at all.) A mitigation excuse, as Austin once said, gets the defendant out of the fire and into the frying pan—but a frying pan that is still in a fire. With respect to the shipwreck case, however, Kant does not say that the punishment should be less than death but rather says that the conduct in question is "unpunishable" and enjoys "immunity from punishment." So total acquittal and no punishment at all seems to be what Kant is suggesting.
23. For this and other reasons, it might be better to consider such matters at the pardon or clemency stage. For a defense of this view, see Murphy 2007. Also, for a brief discussion of the dangers of pardon and clemency, see Kant 1996: 477–478.

that could be given—for example, the argument that one who kills under the extreme psychological pressure of fear of death does not *deserve* the same punishment as one who kills out of malice—but Kant seems to have no interest in arguments of this nature.

Even his deterrence argument leaves much to be desired. Kant claims, as though it is an obvious fact, that one facing certain immediate death cannot be affected by a criminal statute that threatens as punishment only a possible future death. I believe, however, that this is by no means obvious—at least not when one sees the full nature of the way in which the law can control behavior. As I noted in my earlier discussion of the shame cases, the law can sometimes be understood as an expression of community norms and can even have some effect in molding those norms. So one might respect and obey such a law not merely because one fears the threatened punishment, but because one sees the law as a particularly emphatic reminder (by imposing the death penalty) of an important community norm that one should obey out of duty and not just fear. I believe that philosopher C. D Broad, in speaking of a situation of lifeboat survival, once said that he hoped that if he were ever faced with such a situation, he would not engage in some unseemly fight over the small bit of remaining food but would rather, like a gentleman, go to his death in good order.

Even if we consider only the simple motive of fear of death, however, is it possible that Kant might have been tempted by the fairly common view that the fear of immediate death is so strong that it will trump all other motivational considerations? This view is clearly mistaken, of course, as we know from the many cases in which sailors will, at great risk to themselves, save passengers before themselves on a sinking ship and ship captains, at least in the old days, felt a duty to go down with their ship or at least not to leave the ship—again at great risk to themselves—until they were certain that all passengers and crew had been evacuated. These people, like those who sacrifice for comrades in battle, we regard as heroes, although they probably think of themselves as simply doing their duty or what is honorable. At any rate, the cases, although perhaps not the norm, certainly show that it is not beyond human possibility for a person to regard some non-self-interested considerations as of sufficient importance to justify his facing immediate death. These heroic sailors and captains surely feared death, but they feared something else even more: a shameful death, one in which they failed to do their duty and thereby failed to live up to what Freud called their ego-ideal. And their sense of duty may have been formed at least in part by the fact that the law provides severe penalties for a failure to suppress what Kant called "the dear self" (which would include the fear of immediate death) and, in some circumstances, requires the willing sacrifice of one's own life.[24]

Of course, if one accepts Kant's fear-based version of a deterrence rationale, his claim that there should be no punishment at all in the shipwreck case he discusses makes perfect sense. Since he rules out the death penalty because of his belief that it will not deter (the fear of immediate certain death always being stronger than the fear of a possible future death), then *a fortiori* any punishment less than death must be ruled out as well. However, if one adopts (as I have suggested here) a richer interpretation of the deterrence rationale—or employs a different (perhaps retributivist) rationale—one might find a basis for a mitigating excuse that would reject the death penalty but still allow some other punishment.

In spite of these noted shortcomings, Kant's discussion does show some appreciation of two important matters: (1) the distinction between what is relevant in defining a crime (of primary relevance

---

24. Recall that Kant, in discussing a soldier fighting a duel with another soldier, accepts that motivational considerations of honor can represent "a force...rising above the fear of death." And sometimes, as noted by Suzanne Uniacke (1996: 120), "people can refrain from wrongful conduct because they believe it to be wrongful."

at trial and conviction) and what may be relevant at the sentencing stage, and (2) the related distinction between regarding conduct as objectively justified as a matter of right and seeing that, given certain subjective features present in the defendant, the conduct of that defendant might be at least partially excused for doing something he has no objective right to do. As noted in my earlier discussion of shame defenses to homicide, Kant sometimes seems to be groping toward a distinction in law and morality that is now quite familiar: the distinction, not always sharp of course, between justification (the defendant had a right to do it) and excuse (the defendant cannot be fully blamed for doing something he had no right to do).

But is Kant correct in thinking that other than in cases of legitimate defense against an unlawful aggressor, intentionally killing to save one's own life or the lives of others, though perhaps sometimes excusable, is never a matter of objective right—that there is no legitimate doctrine of a right of necessity? Is the very concept of such a right, as Kant says, "a self-contradiction within jurisprudence"? This is the issue to which I shall now pass.

ANOTHER SHIPWRECK: THE CASE OF REGINA V. DUDLEY AND STEPHENS

Like many other teachers of criminal law, I often start my class with this famous case of murder and cannibalism on the high seas—a much better illustration of a shipwreck necessity case than Cicero's.[25] In 1884 the yacht *Migonette* went down very far away from land. The

---

25. [1884] 14 QBD 273 DC. This is a better illustration because it is a clear case of intentionally killing another human being—seeking the death of another human being as one's conscious object. This claim will not be defeated by someone saying that their conscious object was to save their lives. For full details of the situation faced by Dudley and Stephens and of the case itself, see Simpson 1984 and Hanson 2000.

four crewman Dudley (the captain), Stephens, Brooks, and Parker (a young boy at sea for the first time) managed to get into a small lifeboat—a boat with very little food or water packed on board—in the hope that they might find land or be rescued. They drifted for twenty days, and two cans of turnips in the lifeboat and one small turtle, which they managed to catch, was their only food. They ran out of water and began what they reasonably believed was their rapid progress to certain death from starvation and dehydration. Parker, with no experience at sea, made the mistake of drinking sea water and became so ill and delirious that it was reasonably believed by the others that he was fading fast—that his death, given the poison nature of sea water and his illness and delirium, was inevitable.

On the nineteenth day Dudley, Stephens, and Brooks discussed killing Parker in order that they might eat his flesh and drink his blood and thereby increase their chances that they would survive long enough to be rescued. Dudley proposed the drawing of lots to determine who would be sacrificed—often thought of as the custom of the sea in such cases. Brooks wanted no part in any of this, saying that he would rather die than murder or be murdered, and lots were not drawn.[26] Dudley and Stephens then agreed to kill Parker, selecting him both because they believed he had no chance of survival anyway and because, unlike Dudley and Stephens, he had no family responsibilities. Dudley then approached Parker, said a prayer asking forgiveness "in case they should perform a rash act," told Parker his time had come, and then killed him by slitting his throat. Dudley, Stephens,

---

26. One might, of course, be tempted by the cynical view that Brooks was simply taking advantage of the fact that he believed that Parker would be killed (and provide Brooks with life-sustaining sustenance) because Dudley and Stephens would cast two votes for the killing and Brooks would cast only one against, thereby giving Brooks the best of both worlds: retaining his moral (and legal) purity while still getting something to eat. Even if this was true of Brooks (and we have no way of knowing) it would in my view be overly cynical to assume that any person who expressed the view expressed by Brooks would simply be engaged in strategic behavior.

and Brooks (willing to eat the flesh but not to kill in order to do so) all fed on the body of Parker and drank his blood. They regained some of their strength, certainly enough to live a few more days, and four days later they were rescued.[27]

When they arrived at their home port, they were warmly welcomed—most of those in this community of mariners apparently believing that they had, of course, done the right thing in killing one so that they could survive—particularly since it was believed that Parker could not have survived no matter what.[28]

Their warm welcome did not last very long, however, since those administering the English criminal law system—a group not dominated by individuals socialized as mariners—took a dim view of intentionally killing "a weak and unoffending boy" not in self-defense against unlawful aggression, but simply to prolong one's own life. They saw this as the intentional killing of an innocent and thus a noncontroversial case of murder—the kind of premeditated killing that would require the punishment of death.

Dudley and Stephens, however, thought they had a defense that ought to earn them a total acquittal: *necessity* (what is now sometimes called a choice of evils or a lesser evil defense). The intuitive idea was this: It is better that one person die rather than that all die—what they reasonably believed would happen if they did not kill and eat one of the crew members. In short, it was reasonably believed that such killing (clearly an evil) was *necessary* in order to avoid the greater

---

27. Why did Dudley say a prayer asking forgiveness if he thought his action justified? He actually was said to offer a prayer "asking forgiveness of them all if either of them should be tempted to commit a rash act, and that their souls might be saved." Did the reference to the possibility of a rash act perhaps involve a recognition of human fallibility—a realization that even reasonable beliefs are sometimes not true beliefs?
28. I think that this is a much less controversial justification for selecting Parker than the argument that Dudley and Stephens had families and Parker did not. Having family responsibilities is a morally relevant factor, of course, but so is the loss of any opportunity to have a family or participate in other aspects of adult life.

evil of all dying. Also, it was reasonable to believe that Parker should be selected primarily because of his already terminal condition.

But was such a defense to be recognized in English law? The trial court was unwilling to rule on this matter. They simply agreed on the facts (as sketched above) and then sent the case to the House of Lords (the institution in England that is closest in function to the United States Supreme Court in that it has the last word as a matter of existing law) for a special verdict. The special verdict would function to answer this one question: If the facts were indeed as presented (mainly facts about what was reasonable for Dudley and Stephens to believe), did this constitute capital murder or was there rather a defense, often called the right of necessity, that would merit acquittal or at least a reduced sentence?

The Law Lords refused to recognize such a defense. They noted that the available legal authorities (with the possible exception of Lord Bacon) recognized as a defense only the necessity of self-defense involved in repelling an unlawful aggression—certainly not the issue in the present case. Given this absence of legal precedents, and no statutory authority either, the Lords were unwilling to preempt the legislative function and carve out, on their own, a new defense to murder. So, given existing law, Dudley and Stephens were found guilty of murder and sentenced to death.

The Lords did not merely state existing law, however, but they also spoke with some eloquence in defense of their view that the existing law was absolutely right and that it would be unjust, unwise, unflattering to human nature, and even un-Christian, for anyone to introduce such a defense of necessity into English law. It would be unjust because this was a case of intentionally killing the innocent (a crime that surely deserves the death penalty), unwise because such a defense could so easily be abused (letting a man judge necessity when he is likely to profit from such a judgment), unflattering to human nature since it failed to take note of the recorded heroic deeds of sailors sacrificing themselves so that others might live (thereby proving that human nature is not as cowardly as those favoring a necessity defense seem to think), and un-Christian because the example set by "the Great Example whom we profess to follow" set for Christians the standard of sacrificing ourselves for others, not a standard of sacrificing others for ourselves.[29]

In short, the Law Lords reached exactly the same conclusion as Kant on the supposed right or defense of necessity: *there is no such legal right*.[30] Interestingly, they also hinted that they, like Kant, held the view that no punishment or at least a reduced sentence would be appropriate in a case like this. The Lords suggested that *mercy* should probably be shown to individuals such as Dudley and Stephens, suggesting that this might be a good case for the sovereign to exercise the power of pardon or at least reduce the sentence.[31] Although they agreed with Kant on conclusion, however, Kant used none of the Lords' rationales to get to that conclusion and the Lords did not use the only one that Kant offered: the argument that no deterrence purpose would be served by a criminal law threatening the possibility of a future death to someone believing that he now in fact faces the certainty of immediate death.

---

29. It is not strictly correct, of course, that those standing to profit would make a legally binding decision since a *jury* would typically have to agree that the killing was indeed necessary (or at least reasonably believed to be so) before an acquittal on grounds of necessity.
30. I am not, of course, suggesting that the Law Lords had any knowledge of Kant's views on the matter.
31. As reported in Simpson 1984 and Hanson 2000, there was a behind-the-scenes deal struck between the Law Lords and the crown—perhaps explaining why the possibility of a manslaughter conviction was not considered. Dudley and Stephens were to be convicted of murder and sentenced to death, and the crown was to pardon them—a way of being sympathetic to the great stress under which Dudley and Stephens operated that would not involve recognizing a new defense and thereby changing the definition of murder. Sovereign pardon does not recognize a new defense or change the definition of murder since it sets no precedent. In spite of what may have been agreed to behind the scenes, Dudley and Stephens were not pardoned. Their conviction stood but their sentence was reduced to six months.

When I first wrote on the necessity defense, I thought that both Kant and the Law Lords were mistaken about this matter and that, at least as a matter of principle, a defense of necessity should be recognized in cases such as Dudley and Stephens.[32] The argument I gave I took to be Kantian in spirit since it drew on some of the hypothetical contractual or bargaining models that one occasionally finds in Kant and that are present (apologies to the ghost of Lewis White Beck) in the greatest Kantian in twentieth century moral philosophy: John Rawls.[33]

Simply put, I suggested the following: Imagine a group of rational sailors coming together to agree on rules to govern lifeboat survival situations of the kind faced by Dudley, Stephens, Brooks, and Parker. It seemed to me that they would surely select a rule of the form "kill one to save the many," since each sailor would stand a better chance of survival given this rule than if they adopted the rule "never kill one even if that means that all will die." If Sailor Bill found himself in a grim situation comparable to that faced by Dudley, Stephens, Brooks, and Parker, he would, of course, not be at all pleased if he became the one selected to be executed and served as food and drink to his shipmates. But neither would he be pleased to die along with the rest of his shipmates if nobody is sacrificed. So, as a rational being seeking to maximize his chances of survival in lifeboat situations, Sailor Bill would surely agree (as would all other rational sailors) to a rule allowing sacrifice of one to save many in circumstances of the kind here described.[34]

---

32. Murphy 1987.
33. See note 3, in which I talk about Beck's less-than-enthusiastic response to my Rawlsian interpretations of Kant. As an example of the use by Kant of agreement models to illustrate rational and moral choice, see his "On the Common Saying: That May be Correct in Theory but is of No Use in Practice" (Kant 1996: 277–306) and, for an analysis of that essay, Murphy 1998. The Rawlsian use of hypothetical consent models is to be found in Rawls 1971.
34. In a famous essay (Posner 1985), Richard Posner discusses the Dudley and Stephens case and argues, in defense of recognizing a right of necessity in the case, that "at some point the sacrifice of one person so that others will live must increase social welfare." He then

I have now, under pressure from some very astute critics, come to the conclusion that my earlier view simply will not work and only seems to by begging some very important questions.[35] Some sailor (take Brooks as an example) might believe that it is always wrong to kill the innocent, no matter the circumstances, and I now see no good reason for thinking that someone who subscribes to such an absolute principle (a version of the venerable principle "do no evil even if good will come of it") is in any sense irrational—even if he subscribes to this principle out of religious conviction that does not rest on what Rawls calls "public reason."[36] Of course, the sailor who feels this way could always volunteer to be the one sacrificed—unless, of course, he regards that as suicide and regards suicide as absolutely wrong, another view that does not clearly establish him as irrational. These problems show some of the limitations of hypothetical consent models—particularly the danger of getting the result one wants (and tacitly begging the question at issue) by placing arbitrary constraints on what can count as rationality.

---

discusses the principle of drawing lots and the principle of sacrificing the weakest and finds advantages and disadvantages in both. Finally, he briefly notes in passing that hypothetical antecedent agreements might be relevant if they are indeed ways of establishing economic efficiency since he believes that we should "always [assume] that economic efficiency is to be the guidepost for criminal law doctrine." Posner offers what are in effect utilitarian arguments (arguments of wealth maximization or economic efficiency) as the foundation for his conclusion, and it is thus not surprising that a defense of necessity emerges as justified on such a theory. Posner, like all utilitarians, would no doubt brush aside Kantian or religious scruples here as a kind of sentimental irrationality. For a critique of the employment of Posner's economic analysis to issues in moral, legal, and political philosophy, see Murphy 1986.

35. I am grateful to Guyora Binder, Richard Dagger, Antony Duff, Carissa Hessick, Sandra Marshall, Herbert Morris, Jerome Neu, Mary Sigler, Justin Tosi, and Michael White for very helpful comments on this and other issues discussed in the present essay. My thoughts on necessity have been greatly influenced by Marshall 2005—a critical response to Ripstein 2005. Ripstein's rich and stimulating essay provides me with another embarrassing reminder of how out of touch I now am with Kant scholarship. His nonmoralistic approach to criminal law doctrine is quite different from my moralistic approach. Unlike Ripstein's, my approach—perhaps overly influenced by Kant's sole reference to targeting "inner viciousness" (*inneren Bösartigeit*) in his doctrine of criminal liability—seeks to retain some elements of moral retributivism in Kant's account of punishment.

36. Rawls 1993.

Of course, a rational sailor will not agree to a principle that one may be sacrificed for all unless there is a *procedure of selection* to determine who that one will be—a procedure that will guarantee that he is no more likely than others to be the one selected for sacrifice. Thus the principle of selection must guarantee to each sailor that the person sacrificed does not, for reasons that are unreasonable or unfair, make him more likely to be selected than relevantly similar others. So I believe that rational sailors would select as the principle of selection the drawing of lots—the standard custom of the sea. This gives each sailor an equal chance of avoiding his own sacrifice. (An exception to the principle of drawing lots might be made in a case where the one to be sacrificed is, like Parker, reasonably believed to already be on the verge of certain death.) In short: *If one is to be sacrificed that the rest might live, then drawing lots is generally the rational and fair principle of selection.* This is a big if, however, and does nothing whatever to establish that it is ever proper to sacrifice anyone.

If hypothetical consent will not work, how about actual consent? What I have in mind is a kind of actual *tacit* consent. Suppose (as was probably true for nineteenth-century sailors) that there is a socially evolved principle, known to all sailors as part of the established custom of the sea, that in extreme situations of the kind here discussed lots will be drawn to determine a person to be sacrificed so that others might live. If this is the case, it might be plausible to argue that any sailor, *simply by agreeing to ship on*, tacitly agrees to this custom.

Even if there is tacit consent in such cases, however, this will not necessarily make any resulting murders justified (and thus, though homicides, not really murders). Why not? Because in criminal law, at least in the Anglo-American legal tradition, we do not generally accept victim consent as a defense to homicide, and several plausible rationales have been given for this:

1. The right to life is generally regarded as an *inalienable* right, and this simply means a right that cannot be waived or forfeited.
2. Because the right to life is inalienable, *suicide* and assisting suicide has long been regarded as criminal. If one does not have a legal right to kill oneself, then *a fortiori* one does not have a legal right to allow someone else to do the job.
3. Crimes are generally and properly regarded as offenses, not just against individuals, but against the entire community—something revealed in the fact that criminal cases, unlike cases in private or civil law, carry the name "*State* v. X" or "*Regina* v. X" and not "X v. Y." Thus victim consent cannot eliminate the state's legitimate interest in prosecution and punishment—unless, of course, we are dealing with a crime such as rape where absence of consent is part of the very definition of the crime itself.
4. A context in which one might be called upon to consent to his own death is likely to be one in which the individual will feel great psychological pressure from others to consent. Thus we might have reasonable doubts that any consent given in such a context will be free enough to count as valid consent. The problem of Ulysses and the sirens might also arise here. What should be counted as the *real* consent—consent given when the matter is being conceived in the abstract with no strong emotional involvement or consent given when actually faced with the terrifying prospect of being killed?

Of course, not everyone will accept the above four reasons as sufficient to undercut the kind of tacit consent that might be assumed when a sailor embraces the custom of the sea. Some will see the arguments above—particularly 1 and 2—as depending on controversial religious or philosophical beliefs, such as Kant's strange argument in the

Groundwork against the moral impermissibility of suicide or Peter Geach's argument that it is not rational to accept any absolute moral principles unless they are grounded in a belief in God and the doctrine of divine providence.[37] And others might point out that the practical worries raised in number 4 might not apply in the context of signing on to go to sea as a sailor—a context that may not involve the kind of psychological pressure likely to be present in an actual lifeboat situation where others might pressure you into thinking that your going to your death in order that they might live is your duty. The Ulysses and the sirens problem still remains, however.

Even though these arguments against consent as a defense to homicide may not be conclusive, I think that they do have some power—at least enough to give us rational grounds to proceed with caution before using the custom of the sea as a basis for assuming a kind of valid tacit consent that keeps a so-called a right of necessity from remaining highly problematic and dangerous—both morally and legally.

I think the best argument that one might give for a right of necessity in the Dudley and Stephens situation would be an argument that they are in a lawless state of nature—an argument that I previously argued would be hard (if not impossible) to defend with respect to honor killings but perhaps has some plausibility in a case of starving men killing to save their lives in survival situations on the high seas. Kant, however, does not use the state of nature argument in necessity cases—only in the less persuasive cases of honor killings. Of course, this argument would at most address the legality (as a kind of jurisdictional matter) of what Dudley and Stephens did and not the morality of what they did.

Even as a legal matter, however, the state of nature argument would face an uphill fight. The Law Lords did consider and reject an

---

37. Kant 1996: 73–74 and 80, and Geach 1969.

absence of jurisdiction claim—rejected because the *Migonette* was a registered British vessel and all crew members were British subjects. You may be inclined to dismiss the Law Lords' argument as little more than a case of rigid legal formalism, but before doing this consider this case: Suppose that Dudley and Stephens were malicious sociopaths who killed Parker simply for the fun of it or suppose they decided to repeatedly rape him through acts of forced sodomy. Would you want to say that since they were in a state of nature that no law applied to them, and thus they could not legitimately be punished by an English court?

CONCLUSION

My purpose in this essay has been to evaluate three claims made by Kant with respect to criminal defenses to homicide: the claim that we should not punish as a capital murderer the soldier who kills in a duel, the claim that we should not punish as a capital murderer the woman who kills her illegitimate baby, and the claim that there is no just and rational right of necessity in shipwreck survival situations (but that it would, for deterrence reasons, be pointless to punish such injustice as murder). I think that he is generally quite wrong with respect to the first two—at least to the degree that he is thinking in terms of justification—but that in his discussion of shame he may have partially laid the foundations for at least considering a mitigating excuse in some cases of this nature. On the third issue, necessity as a justification, I am now inclined to think that he (and the Law Lords in Dudley and Stephens) may have reached the right conclusion: namely, that the law should not recognize a justifying right of necessity in cases that involve the murder of a person innocent of any wrongdoing. In reaching this conclusion, however, the Law Lords and Kant part company. Kant relies on a very unpersuasive deterrence argument (an argument of a kind never even considered by the Law Lords) and he, unlike the Law Lords, does not recommend sovereign mercy on compassionate grounds for those in situations of the kind faced by Dudley and Stephens—a recommendation that strikes me as showing a proper understanding of the pressures under which Dudley and Stephens made their decision without setting a precedent and thus changing the law so that an improper justification would be legally recognized. If Kant and the Law Lords had been able to think more clearly about the justification/excuse distinction—a distinction Kant sometimes seems to flirt with in his discussion of the two honor/shame cases—they might even have been able to build an appropriate excuse into the prevailing doctrines of criminal law. Absent that, sovereign mercy strikes me as better than nothing.

I do not, however, want to end on such a negative note about the great Kant, whose moral vision has been an inspiration to me throughout much of my philosophical career.[38] When I find myself tempted to reject a right of necessity in cases such as Dudley and Stephens, I find that my temptation has a Kantian foundation—not a foundation in what he actually says about necessity cases, but a foundation in the very essence of his moral theory. As I see this theory it makes respect for the inherent dignity of each person foundational—a value commitment that forbids that any person be used merely as a means rather than as an end in himself, as a mere resource to be exploited for the benefit of others. Killing an innocent person that others might live strikes me as a possible example of the very thing that Kant's moral theory requires us to reject (far more powerful than a bogus deterrence argument) or a least to make us engage in a great deal more serious moral reflection before we endorse the recognition of a justifying right of necessity for homicide. We will

---

38. Often as that vision has been articulated by Tom Hill. My work on forgiveness, for example, was greatly influenced by his two essays on servility and self-respect (Hill 1991: 4–24).

thereby take seriously, as I think we should, the question that Sonja puts to Raskolnikov (who seeks her approval for killing the pawnbroker) in Dostoevsky's *Crime and Punishment*: "Who put me here to judge who is to live and who is not to live?"

LIST OF WORKS CITED

Binder, Guyora (2009), "States of War: Defensive Force Among Nations," *Ohio State Journal of Criminal Law* 7: 439–461.

Devlin, Lord Patrick (1965), *The Enforcement of Morals*, Oxford: Oxford University Press.

Finkelstein, Claire (2001), "Two Men on a Plank," *Legal Theory* 7: 279–306.

Geach, Peter (1969), "The Moral Law and the Law of God," in *God and the Soul*, London: Routledge and Kegan Paul.

Hanson, Neil (2000), *The Custom of the Sea*, New York: Wiley.

Hill, Thomas E. Jr. (1991), *Autonomy and Self-Respect*, Cambridge: Cambridge University Press.

——, (2000) *Respect, Pluralism, and Justice—Kantian Perspectives*, Oxford: Oxford University Press.

Kahan, Dan M.. (2000), "Gentle Nudges vs. Hard Shoves: Solving the Sticky Norms Problem," *University of Chicago Law Review* 67: 607–645.

Kant, Immanuel (1996), *Practical Philosophy*, translated and edited by Mary J. Gregor, Cambridge: Cambridge University Press.

Marshall, Sandra (2005), "Life and Death on a Plank–Ripstein and Kant," *Ohio State Journal of Criminal Law* 2: 435.

Murphy, Jeffrie (1986), "The Justice of Economics," *Philosophical Topics* 14 (2): 195–210.

——, (1987) "Does Kant Have a Theory of Punishment?" *Columbia Law Review* 87 (3): 509–532.

——, (1998) "Kant on Theory and Practice," *Character, Liberty and Law—Kantian Essays in Theory and Practice*, Dordrecht: Kluwer.

——, (2006) "Legal Moralism and Retribution Revisited," *Proceedings and Addresses of the American Philosophical Association* 80 (2): 45–62. Also published in *Criminal Law and Philosophy* 1 (1) (2007): 5–20.

——, (2007) "Remorse, Apology and Mercy," *Ohio State Journal of Criminal Law* 4: 423.

Posner, Richard (1985), "An Economic Theory of Criminal Law," *Columbia Law Review* 85: 1229–1230.

Rawls, John (1971), *A Theory of Justice*, Cambridge, MA: Harvard University Press.

———, (1993) *Political Liberalism*, New York: Columbia University Press.
Ripstein, Arthur (2005), "In Extremis," *Ohio State Journal of Criminal Law* 2: 415.
Simpson, Brian A. W. (1984), *Cannibalism and the Common Law*, Chicago: University of Chicago Press.
Sussman, David (2008), "Shame and Punishment in Kant's Doctrine of Right," *Philosophical Quarterly* 58 (231), 299–317.
Uniacke, Suzanne (1996), "The Limits of Criminality: Kant on the Plank," in *Punishment, Excuses, and Moral Development*, edited by Henry Tam, Aldershot: Avebury, 113–126.

INDEX

Abbott, Jack, 287n18
absolution, 213n50
Achilles (fictional character), 242
acquittal, 275n2, 295, 297n29
Adam and Eve, 95n3, 102–3
Adams, Marilyn, 22n5, 141n15
Adams, Robert Merrihew, 141n15
"Advent Preparation" (*The Living Church*), 146–47
Aeschylus, 13
agape (love of neighbor), 43, 49–51, 60
   capital punishment and, 60–61, 63
   as compassion, 47
   indifference and, 58
agapic forgiveness, 49, 57–58
agenbite of inwit (remorse), 140, 194
Ainsworth, Janet, xiv, 177
Allen, Woody, 221
"All Kinds of Guilt" (Deigh), 95
Almeleki, Faleh Hassan, 281
American Model Penal Code, 189, 280n10, 289
American Philosophical Association, 66
   presidential address to, xii, 125, 227
   "The Work of Herbert Morris," 94n1
   "The Work of Jeffrie G. Murphy," xi–xii, 215
Amnesty International, 213

animus, xvi
annulment theory of punishment, 126, 231
Anti-Defamation League, 169
apartheid, 4, 9, 148
apology
   Austin on, 165–68, 165n45, 170
   culture of, 144–48, 177
   mercy and, 164–72
   promises and, 166–67, 167n46
   public, 148, 170–72
   remorse, mercy and, 129–80
   remorse and, in criminal sentencing, 138–39, 138n13, 174–76, 231
   remorse and repentance compared to, 165
   retribution from, 170–71, 173, 175
   in tort law, 148, 148n24
Arendt, Hannah, 135, 209
Aristotle
   on doctrine of mean, 12
   ethics and, 5
   on friendship, 49
   on habituation, 51, 217
assembly line justice, 172
atheism, 44, 81, 152
atonement, 141, 152
   mandated *versus* chosen, 200n29
   penance and, 198, 198n26, 200
atrocities, 265–66

INDEX

Auden, W. H., 18, 205, 269
Augustine (saint)
 on capital punishment, 61–63
 The City of God, 61
 "hate the sin but not the sinner," 15, 29
Austin, J. L., 5
 on apology, 165–68, 165n45, 170
 on clarity, 184n5, 233
 A Plea for Excuses, 167–68, 184, 184n5
authoritative commands, guilt and, 95–105
autonomy
 Kant on, 246, 259–61
 racial insult as expression of, 246
 right of, 50

backsliding, 153, 194
bad conscience, 96, 105–9, 111–13
Bandes, Susan A.
 on death penalty, 176–78
 "The Heart Has Its Reasons," xiv, 178
bankruptcy, 173, 177
Barthelme, Donald, 108–9
base and irrational passions, 22
bastard infanticide, 275, 276–79, 282–83, 288
Beck, Lewis White, 275n3, 298, 298n33
Belfi, Donald E., 124n20, 131n3
Benedict, Pope, 182n2, 199–200
Bennett, Jonathan, 128
Beowulf, 130, 190n16
Between Vengeance and Forgiveness: Facing History After Genocide and Mass Violence (Minow), 4, 5
Beyond Good and Evil (Nietzsche), 42n37
Bibas, Stephen, xiv, 149, 175
Bierschbach, Richard A., 149
Biggar, Nigel, 213n50
Binder, Guyora, 287n18
Blackmun, Justice, 248
Blake, William, 79–80
Bowers v. Hardwick, xv, 74, 245, 247–55
Broad, C. D., 87, 291
The Brothers Karamazov (Dostoevsky), 181–214. See also Dostoevsky's general
Browning, Christopher R., 208
Burgh, Richard, 80

Bush, George W., 137, 137n11
Butler, Joseph
 on resentment and forgiveness, x, xi, 10–12, 53n9, 185, 185n8
 "Upon Forgiveness of Injuries," 6, 6n6, 52
 "Upon Resentment," 10–12, 52

cannibalism and murder, 293–304, 293n25, 294n26, 295nn27–28, 297n31, 298n34
capital punishment, 89. *See also* death penalty
 agape and, 60–61, 63
 Augustine on, 61–63
 personal rebirth and, 61–62
Cartesian dualism, 36n28
categorical imperative, 102, 198n26, 209
causal determination, 36n28
character. *See also* evil character
 deep, 89–90, 150–51, 208n41, 271n16
 forgiving, 217
 mens rea and, 35–36, 35n26, 151
 reform, prisons and, 51–52
 remorse, repentance, punishment and, 150–51, 155, 160, 161n39
character retributivism, 28–31, 28n13, 120–21
 choice retributivism compared to, 121n12
 cognitive obstacles to, 35–39, 35n25, 36n28
 in criminal sentencing, 73, 75–76
 cruelty and, 31–33
 definition of, 29
 grievance retributivism compared to, 28n13, 120, 159–61, 159n37, 161n39
 Moore on, 28n13, 29
 moral obstacles to, 35n25, 39–41
charity, 69
cheap grace, 145
Che farò (Gluck), 238
Cheney, Dick, 169
children
 bastard infanticide, 275, 276–79, 282–83, 288
 death of, 238
 guilt and, 97, 107–10
 illegitimate, 274, 276–79, 282–83, 290n22, 303
 love, jealousy and, 235
choice retributivism, 121n12
Christian Coalition, 251

308

INDEX

Christianity. *See also* Jesus
   death penalty and, 60–63, 137–38, 137n11
   evangelical, 143, 158
   forgiveness and, x–xii, 17–20, 45–46
   human dignity and, 260–63, 260n2, 267–70
   moral emotions and, xii
   necessity defense and, 296–97
Christian love, x, xi, xiii
   commandment, x, 46–52, 182, 203
   criminal punishment and, 43–65
   politics and, 45
   soul and, 47
Cicero, 288, 293
Cioran, E. M., 36n27
The City of God (Augustine), 61
civil rights movement, 285
clarity, 184n5, 233
clemency
   pardon or, 290n23
   rehabilitation and, 159
   remorse and, xiv, 124, 137–39, 162–64, 168, 174, 175–76
Clinton, Bill, 108, 173
coerced repentance, 163n42
coercion
   Kant on, 246
   legal moralism and, 67–69, 71–72
Coetzee, J. M., 16, 115, 115n3, 149–50, 152, 156, 171, 264n6
cognitive obstacles to character retributivism, 35–39, 35n25, 36n28
cognitive restructuring, 219
Colb, Sherry F., xiv, 175
commandment, Christian love, x, 46–52, 182, 203
A Common Humanity (Gaita), 59
common good, 59, 60, 61–62
communicative punishment, 114–28, 120n11
compassion
   agape as, 47
   empathy and, 230–31
   forgiveness as, 213n50
   liberal, 47, 49
   sympathy and, 219, 219n4
competition, 240
condemnation, ix
Connor, Sheriff "Bull," 285

conscience
   bad, 96, 105–9, 111–13
   guilt, shame and, 105–13
   moral guilt and, 96
conscious object, 289, 293n25
consent, tacit, 280n11, 300–302
consequential approach to morality, 257–58
consequentialism, 68–69, 77
contempt for victim, 116, 118–19, 127
contractarian retributivism, 221, 221n6
contrition, 182n1
cosmic justice, 213n50
Coward, Noel, 185n8, 224
crimes
   hatred and, xv–xvi
   mens rea as requirement for conviction of, 43, 121n12, 278, 289
   ranking of, 80–81
   symbolic message of, 76, 119, 119n9, 154, 159–60, 195
Crime and Punishment (Dostoevsky), 305
crime control
   goal of, 90
   justice and, 8, 14, 55
   retribution and, 77–78, 221n6
criminal justice, 174
Criminal Law Conversations, xiv
criminal punishment
   Christian love and, 43–65
   deterrence and, 157, 291–92, 297, 303–4
   justification of, 7–8, 37–38, 38n32, 55, 59, 61–62, 157, 230
   rehabilitation and, 157–59
criminal sentencing, xiii–xiv. *See also* reduced sentences
   character retributivism in, 73, 75–76
   Federal Sentencing Guidelines, U.S., 15, 156n34
   increased sentences, 117
   inner wickedness and, 35n26
   mercy and forgiveness in, 7–8, 55
   remorse and apology in, 138–39, 138n13, 174–76, 231
   repentance and, xiv, 75–76, 116–17, 116nn4–5, 120n11, 127, 158
   victim desires in, 8, 8n7, 55

INDEX

critical morality, 97
Critique of Pure Reason (Kant), 33–34
cruelty
    character retributivism and, 31–33
    hatred and, 58
    self-deceptive, xiii, 31–32, 85
cultural shame, 192, 192n18
culture of apology, 144–48, 177
The Cure at Troy (Heaney), 20

dark sayings, 95n3, 183
dead, forgiveness of, 6, 7, 53, 55
Dead Man Walking (film), 40n33, 164
dear self
    Kant on, xxii, 119, 198, 198n26, 200n29, 219n4, 292
    repression of, 182n1, 199–200, 200n29
death
    of children, 238
    love and, 236–39
Death in Summer (Trevor), 94, 99
The Death of Ivan Ilych (Tolstoy), 164n43
death penalty. *See also* clemency
    Bandes on, 176–78
    Christianity and, 60–63, 137–38, 137n11
    homicide law and, 274, 278, 280–81, 281n12, 283–84, 283n14, 287, 287n18, 290–92, 290n22, 296
    views on, 163–64, 176–79
"The Decline of Guilt" (Morris), 144–45
deep character, 89–90, 150–51, 208n41, 271n16
Deigh, John
    "All Kinds of Guilt," 95
    on guilt, 95–96, 99n11, 105
deliberative repentance, 163n42
democratic equality, 205n38, 270n14
Derrida, Jacques, 184
desert (deserved reward or punishment). *See also* just deserts; moral desert
    analysis of, 37–38
    as debt owed for free riding, 28, 78–81
    five senses of, 28
    as guilt, 28, 77–78
    justice and, xii, 22

mens rea and, 28
Nietzsche on, 27n11
noumenal self and, 36, 36n28
punishment in proportion to, 226–27, 230–31
responsibility and, 28, 36n28, 86
retributivist concept of, 68
six accounts of retributive, 120–27
despair, sin of, 142n18, 143–44
determinism, 35, 259–60
deterrence, 157, 291–92, 297, 303–4
The Devils (Dostoevsky), 141, 141n16, 144
Devlin, Lord Patrick, 67–68, 244. *See also* Hart-Devlin debate
disapproval
    fact of deep, 250–52
    moral and nonmoral, 252–53
Disgrace (Coetzee), 16, 115, 115n3, 149–50, 152, 156, 171, 264n6
divine justice, 81–82
divine providence, 302
Doctrine of Right (Kant), 275, 286–88
Doctrine of Virtue (Kant), 11, 218–19
Dolinko, David, 80
Donne, John, 192
Doonesbury cartoon strip, on Vietnam War, 208, 262n4
Dostoevsky, Fyodor, 151
    Crime and Punishment, 305
    Stavrogin's suicide in *The Devils*, 141, 141n16, 144
Dostoevsky's general (*The Brothers Karamazov*), 181–214
    human dignity and, 187n13, 193, 202–9, 266–68, 270–72, 271n16
    loathing and shunning of, 191, 193, 201, 201n31, 210, 213
    mental illness of, 189–90, 190n16
    morality and, 187–89, 193, 197
    as paradigm, 181–83
    remorse and repentance of, 194, 197–98, 197n25, 200–201
    as responsible agent, 190, 190n16
double effect, doctrine of, 209n43
drawing lots, 294, 299n34, 300
Dressler, Joshua, 80

INDEX

duel, killing in, 275, 276, 279, 280n11, 283, 286n18, 288, 292n24, 303
Due Process Clause, 249
Duff, Antony
   influence of, 80, 114n1
   on rehabilitation, 157
   on repentance, 114–17, 120n11, 127–28
Durrenmatt, Friedrich, 95n3
duty, 291–92
Dworkin, Ronald
   on governmental neutrality, 72
   on moral reasons and limitations of liberty, 244–46
   on political liberalism, 50

Eating Crow (Rayner), 145, 173
ego-ideal, 292
Eichmann, Adolf, 135, 136, 136n10, 209
Eighth Amendment, 207n40, 229, 271n15
Eliot, T. S., 224
Elizabeth I, Queen, 151
emotions. *See also* moral emotions
   control of, 216–18
   moral epistemology and, 23, 24–27, 27n11
   testing philosophical account of, 107
empathy, 230–31
empirical self, 36n28
"The Enforcement of Morals" (Devlin), 67
Enright, Robert, 223
envy, 240
Ernaux, Annie, 106
eros (erotic love), 43
ethics, 5. *See also* virtue ethics
evangelical Christianity, 143, 158
"Every night and every Morn" (Blake), 79–80
evil
   choice of evils or lesser evil defense, 295
   horrendous, 141n15
   in human history, 262–65, 262n4
   potential for, 41, 204, 269
   punishment for, 9, 57, 77–78
   struggle against, 19
   suffering for, 27, 41
evil character, 37n29, 41

excuse
   forgiveness and, 7, 54, 189–90, 206n39
   justification compared to, 278, 290n22, 293, 303–4
   mitigating, 280–82, 280n10, 283nn14–15, 290n22, 292
eye for an eye, 78, 141
eye of love, 90, 202–3, 267–68

Facing Evil (Kekes), 37n29
fact of deep disapproval, 250–52
fairness, principle of, 38n32, 78–79
fake remorse and repentance, 154–56, 158, 161–63, 169–70
"Father Sergius" (Tolstoy), 141, 144, 198, 200
fear, 234–39, 241
Federal Sentencing Guidelines, U.S., 15, 156n34
Feinberg, Joel, 69, 75–76, 244
Felicia's Journey (Trevor), 18, 40n33, 94n2, 202, 268
Ferguson, Colin, 124n20, 131n3
Fingarette, Herbert, 96, 122n14, 125–26, 198–99
Finkelstein, Claire, 289n20
First Amendment, Establishment Clause of, 158
Flanigan, Beverly, 184
forgiveness
   as absolution and compassion, 213n50
   agapic, 49, 57–58
   Christianity and, x–xii, 17–20, 45–46
   of dead, 6, 7, 53, 55
   definition of, 6, 9
   excuse and, 7, 54, 189–90, 206n39
   hasty, dangers of, 10–13, 53
   justification and, 6–7, 54
   Kolnai on, 12
   mercy and, 7–8, 54–55
   movement, 13n16
   nature of, 6–10
   punishment and, 45–46, 52–60
   reconciliation and, 3–20, 53, 56–57
   repentance and, xi, 15–17, 53, 154, 216
   resentment and, x–xi, 10–13, 53n9, 185–87, 185n8, 186n9, 223

INDEX

forgiveness (*continued*)
    responsible agency and, 6, 7, 54
    self-forgiveness, 186, 186n12
    third-party, 185–86, 189
    of unforgivable, 181–214
    from victim, 183, 185–86, 185n7
    victimization and, 4, 53
    vindictive passions and, 8, 10, 12–14, 52–53, 56, 58
    as virtue, 4, 9–10, 13–17, 52, 217
    as waiving of right, 9
Forgiveness and Mercy (Murphy and Hampton), x, 4, 29, 81, 126
"Forgiveness in the Law" conference, xii
forgiving character, 217
Forgiving the Unforgivable (Flanigan), 184
Forgiving the Unforgivable (Stoop), 184
"Forgiving the Unforgivable" (Thomas), 182n1
Foxman, Abraham H., 169
free riding
    desert as debt owed for, 28, 78–81
    Morris on, 28, 37–38, 122–23, 123n16
free speech, 72
free will, 35
Freud, Sigmund
    on ego-ideal, 292
    influence of, xii, 96
    on love, 238, 239
friendship, 49
fundamental rights constitutionalism, 73–74, 245, 247–48
Furtwängler, Wilhelm, 134–36, 135n8, 136n10

Gaita, Raimond, 59, 202, 267
gangs
    rape, 51–52, 87, 157, 225
    shame and, 280–81
Garvey, Stephen, 161n39
Geach, Peter, 302
Geddes, Jennifer, 213n50
gender, jealousy and, 241
general, Dostoevsky's. *See* Dostoevsky's general
genetic basis for homosexuality, 255
genetic fallacy, 24, 85
genocide, 4, 264

Georgia, homosexual sodomy in, xv–xvi, 245–54
Getting Even–Forgiveness and Its Limits (Murphy), xi
Gibson, Mel, 168–69
Gluck, Christoph, 238
Goebbels, Joseph, 188, 199
A Good Man Is Hard to Find (O'Connor), 164n43
good deeds, reduced sentences for, 117
good life, 51, 73, 245
Good Samaritan, parable of, 47
governmental neutrality, 72–74
grievance morality, 75–76
grievance retributivism, 121–22
    character retributivism compared to, 28n13, 120, 159–61, 159n37, 161n39
Griffin, Lisa, xiv, 176, 177
Griswold v. Connecticut, 253–54, 255
Groundwork of the Metaphysics of Morals (Kant), 216–17, 278, 301–2
group forgiveness and reconciliation, 4
guilt, 94–113. *See also* moral guilt; nonmoral guilt
    authoritative commands and, 95–105
    children and, 97, 107–10
    Deigh on, 95–96, 99n11, 105
    desert as, 28, 77–78
    Hampton on, 96
    Morris on, 95–99, 99n11, 101–5, 107, 110n24, 111–13, 112n28, 113n30
    punishment, innocence and, 68–69, 161
    remorse and, 101, 140, 152
    resentment and, 26–27, 26n10
    retribution and, 23, 26
    shame, conscience and, 105–13
Guilt and Innocence (Morris), 110n24, 112–13, 113n30
Gyges' ring, 41, 41n35, 83, 207, 270

habituation, 51, 217
Hampton, Jean
    Forgiveness and Mercy, x, 4, 29, 81, 126
    on guilt, 96
    legal moralism and, 75–76
    on punishment, 231
Häring, Bernard, 60–61

INDEX

harm principle
   Devlin on, 67–68, 244
   Holmes on, 67
   Mill and, 67–68, 71–72, 74, 244
Hart, Herbert
   Law, Liberty and Morality, 68
   on retribution, 77
   on uniformity at price of distortion, xi, 5, 207n39, 272
Hart-Devlin debate, 67–68, 69–76, 223, 285n17
hasty forgiveness, dangers of, 10–13, 53
"hate the sin but not the sinner" (Augustine), 15, 29
hatred. *See also* retributive hatred
   crimes and, xv–xvi
   cruelty and, 58
Heaney, Seamus, 20, 130
"The Heart Has Its Reasons" (Bandes), xiv, 178
Hegel, Georg, 126, 231
Herodotus, 83, 207, 270
Herrin, Richard, 28n13, 31n19
Hessick, Carissa, 117, 117n7
heuristic guides to moral truth, 25
Hijuelos, Oscar, 21
Hill, Thomas, E., Jr., xvii, 274–76
Hiroshima, 199–200, 200n30
Hoffman, Martin, 101
Holmes, Oliver Wendell, Jr., 67, 103, 118, 118n8
Holocaust, 192, 262–65
homicide law, 56n10, 81, 160, 274–306.
   See also killing; murder
   acquittal in, 275n2, 295, 297n29
   death penalty and, 274, 278, 280–81, 281n12, 283–84, 283n14, 287, 287n18, 290–92, 290n22, 296
   mercy and, 297, 304
   reduced sentences in, 278n6, 279, 280n10, 297, 297n31
   responsibility and, 278, 294, 295n28
homosexuality, 74, 254–56
   genetic basis for, 255
   sodomy, xv–xvi, 70, 245–54
honor killing, 275nn2–3, 281n12, 284n16, 292n24
   shame and, 275, 281, 284, 290n22
   state of nature and, 284–85, 286n18, 302

Horney, Karen, 237
horrendous evil, 141n15
human dignity, xvi–xvii, 202–9
   Christianity and, 260–63, 260n2, 267–70
   Dostoevsky's general and, 187n13, 193, 202–9, 266–68, 270–72, 271n16
   elusive nature of, 257–73
   human rights and, 187n13, 193, 210, 212–13, 259
   moral humility and, 204, 210, 212, 269–72, 271n16
   religion and, xvi, 202n34, 203–6
   retribution and, 85–86
human fallibility, 295n27
human relations
   bourgeois or possessive model of, 235
   marketplace theory of, 240
human rights, 187n13, 193, 210, 212–13, 259
humbling of the will, 122n14, 125–26, 198–99
Hussein, Saddam, 211–12

Ibsen, Henrik, 104
"The Idea of Perfection" (Murdoch), 219–20
illegitimate children, 274, 276–79, 282–83, 290n22, 303
immorality, private, 245
Incline Our Hearts (Wilson), 100–101, 101n12, 109
indifference, 58–59, 63
infanticide, bastard, 275, 276–79, 282–83, 288
inner viciousness, 56n10, 78, 81, 89, 120–21, 160, 299n35
inner wickedness. *See also* inner viciousness
   criminal sentencing and, 35n26
   punishment in proportion to, 29, 37n29
   responsibility and, 36–37, 36n28, 37n29
innocence, guilt and punishment, 68–69, 161
insanity defense, 189, 279
instrumental and moral justification, 9–10
intention, 119n9. *See also mens rea*
interpersonal forgiveness and reconciliation, 3

Jackson, George, 162–63, 163n41
James, Henry, 232
Japan, 199–200, 200n30

INDEX

"Jealous Afterthoughts" (Neu), 235, 236
"Jealous Thoughts" (Neu), xv, 234–36
jealousy
    children, love and, 235
    competition and, 240
    envy compared to, 240
    fear and, 234–39, 241
    gender and, 241
    love and, 234–43
    Neu on, xv, 234–43
    shame, rival and, 234–43
Jesus, xii. *See also* Christian love
    disciples' weakness of will, 153
    Moore on, 24, 24n8, 39–40, 82–83
    on prisons, 212
    on sin and casting stones, 24, 39–40, 82–83, 204, 269–70
Jewish law, 46, 150
Jews, 157. *See also* Nazis
Johnson, Samuel, 62, 177
Johnson v. Phelan, 84
Judaism, 48
Judgment at Nuremberg (film), 187, 193, 270n13
judicial activism, 228–29
Judy, Steven, 132n4
just deserts
    capital punishment as, 61–62
    hypocrisy regarding, 39
    Kant on, 30n18, 56n10
    retributive, 178–79
justice
    assembly line, 172
    cosmic, 213n50
    crime control and, 8, 14, 55
    criminal, 174
    desert and, xii, 22
    divine, 81–82
    love and, 44
    Rawls on, 43
    restorative, 170
    retributive, 88, 170, 232
    rights and, 258–59
justification
    of criminal punishment, 7–8, 37–38, 38n32, 55, 59, 61–62, 157, 230

excuse compared to, 278, 290n22, 293, 303–4
forgiveness and, 6–7, 54
instrumental and moral, 9–10
nonretributive, 21n1
retributive, 21n1

Kahan, Dan, 106
Kant, Immanuel
    on autonomy, 246, 259–61
    categorical imperative and, 198n26, 209
    on coercion, 246
    Critique of Pure Reason, 33–34
    on dear self, xxii, 119, 198, 198n26, 200n29, 219n4, 292
    Doctrine of Right, 275, 286–88
    Doctrine of Virtue, 11, 218–19
    Groundwork of the Metaphysics of Morals, 216–17, 278, 301–2
    homicide law and, 274–306
    influence of, 44, 260n2, 304
    on inner viciousness, 56n10, 78, 81, 89, 120–21, 160, 299n35
    on just deserts, 30n18, 56n10
    on love, 48
    The Metaphysical Elements of Justice, 83
    The Metaphysics of Morals, 28–30
    on moral proof of God, 30n18, 261
    necessity defense and, 275n3, 286–93, 297–98, 302, 304
    on punishment, 28–29, 81, 117
    Religion Within the Limits of Reason Alone, 33–34, 40, 83–84, 206, 206n39
    on retribution, 77, 78, 83–84, 226, 230, 290–91
Karajan, Herbert von, 135n8
Kekes, John, 37n29
Kennedy, Anthony
    Lawrence v. Texas and, 73–74
    Riggins v. Nevada and, 125n22, 132n5
    Romer v. Evans and, 250
Kierkegaard, Søren
    on love, 47–48, 203
    on remorse, 164, 194
    Works of Love, 48

INDEX

killing. *See also* honor killing
  bastard infanticide, 275, 276–79, 282–83, 288
  in duel, 275, 276, 279, 280n11, 283, 286n18, 288, 292n24, 303
  as life-saving necessity, 275, 291–304
  murder compared to, 277–78
  in self-defense, 279, 296
  shame and, 275, 279–82, 280nn9–11, 283n15, 284, 290n22, 293
  social conventions and, 279–84, 280nn 10–11
  state of nature and, 284–86, 286n18, 302
kindness, 232
King, Florence, 161–62
Kingston, Maxine Hong, 287n18
Klein, Melanie, 101
Kohut, Heinz, 111n27
Kolnai, Aurel, 12

Law, Liberty and Morality (Hart), 68
Lawrence v. Texas, xv–xvi, 73–74
legal moralism
  coercion and, 67–69, 71–72
  Hampton and, 75–76
  Hart-Devlin debate and, 67–68, 69–76, 223, 285n17
  Mill and, 69, 75
  Morris and, 69, 75–76
  retribution and, 66–93
  sexuality and, 70–71, 73–75
Lehrer, Tom, 145
Levin, Michael, 254–55
Lewinsky, Monica, 173
lex talionis, 78, 87
liberal compassion, 47, 49
liberal equality, 205n38, 270n14
liberty
  moral reasons and limitations of, 244–56
  religious, 73, 74
  Supreme Court and, xv–xvi, 71, 73–74
The Living Bible, 147
The Living Church, 146–47

loathing and shunning, of Dostoevsky's general, 191, 193, 201, 201n31, 210, 213
"Lost Innocence" (Morris), 95n3, 102–3
love. *See also* agape; Christian love; *eros*; *philia*
  death and, 236–39
  eye of love, 90, 202–3, 267–68
  Freud on, 238, 239
  jealousy, children and, 235
  jealousy and, 234–43
  justice and, 44
  Kant on, 48
  Kierkegaard on, 47–48, 203
  pathological, 48, 216–17, 218
  practical, 48, 216–17, 218
  shame and, 242
luck
  moral, 99–100
  on natural and social lottery, 40, 79, 83, 205, 205n38, 206n39, 270, 270n14
Lynd, H. K., 97

MacDonald, Margaret, 259
Maciel, Father Marcial, 199–200, 200n29
Mailer, Norman, 242
Maimonides, 163n42
malice, 12–13, 291
mandated *versus* chosen atonement, 200n29
Mandela, Nelson, 4
Marat/Sade (Weiss), 257, 262–65
Marx, Karl, 225
"Marxism and Retribution" (Murphy), 79–80
Massaro, Toni, 106
mass violence, 4
McCleskey, Warren G., 124, 124n19, 131, 131n2
mean, doctrine of, 12
mens rea (intention, knowledge)
  character and, 35–36, 35n26, 151
  desert and, 28
  as requirement for conviction of crime, 43, 121n12, 278, 289
mental health, 147
mental illness, 189–90, 190n16

315

INDEX

mercy
  apology, remorse and, 129–80
  apology and, 164–72
  forgiveness and, 7–8, 54–55
  homicide law and, 297, 304
  repentance, communicative punishment and, 114–28, 120n11
  retribution and, 226–27, 232n15
The Metaphysical Elements of Justice (Kant), 83
The Metaphysics of Morals (Kant), 28–30
Michael Kohlhass (von Kleist), 14n18
Midwest Studies in Philosophy, ix
Migonette (yacht), 293–94, 303
Mill, John Stuart
  on free speech, 72
  harm principle and, 67–68, 71–72, 74, 244
  legal moralism and, 69, 75
  On Liberty, 67, 71
minimalist versions of retributivism, 221n6, 223
minimal scrutiny, xv
Minow, Martha, 4, 5
mitigating excuse, 280–82, 280n10, 283nn14–15, 290n22, 292
monsters, Nietzsche on, 42, 42n37, 91, 204, 268–69
Montaigne, Michel de, 16, 154–55
Moore, Michael
  on character retributivism, 28n13, 29
  on emotions and moral epistemology, 25–27, 27n11
  on Jesus, 24, 24n8, 39–40, 82–83
  "The Moral Worth of Retribution," xii, 23–24, 24n8, 28n13
  on remorse, 132n4
  on retribution, 27n11, 31n19, 81–83, 123–24
moral and nonmoral disapproval, 252–53
moral and spiritual rebirth
  agape and, 50
  insincere claims of, xiv
moral balance theory, 38, 78–81
moral desert, 77–78, 81, 85
moral emotions
  Christianity and, xii
  definition of, ix

moral epistemology, emotions and, 23, 24–27, 27n11
moral guilt, 96–99, 99n11, 103
moral horror, 141, 141n15
moral humility
  deep character and, 208n41, 271n16
  human dignity and, 204, 210, 212, 269–72, 271n16
  Nietzsche on, 24, 24n7, 31–33, 41
  retribution and, 31–35, 41
morality. *See also* shame morality
  consequential approach to, 257–58
  critical, 97
  Dostoevsky's general and, 187–89, 193, 197
  grievance, 75–76
  and reasons, 253–56
moral luck, 99–100
morally culpable negligence, 196–97
moral obstacles to character retributivism, 35n25, 39–41
moral order, 11–14
moral proof of God, Kant's, 30n18, 261
moral reasons, limitations of liberty and, 244–56
moral shame, 106–7, 110–12, 110n24, 111n27
"The Moral Worth of Retribution" (Moore), xii, 23–24, 24n8, 28n13
moral truth, heuristic guides to, 25
moral universalism, 48
Morris, Herbert, 22n5, 186
  "The Decline of Guilt," 144–45
  on free riding, 28, 37–38, 122–23, 123n16
  on guilt, 95–99, 99n11, 101–5, 107, 110n24, 111–13, 112n28, 113n30
  Guilt and Innocence, 110n24, 112–13, 113n30
  influence of, 94–95, 94n1
  on justification of criminal punishment, 37–38, 38n32
  legal moralism and, 69, 75–76
  "Lost Innocence," 95n3, 102–3
  "Nonmoral Guilt," 95, 97–99, 101
  "Persons and Punishment," 78–79, 122n15
  on public apology, 148
  "Reflections on Feeling Guilty," 112, 113n30

316

INDEX

murder, 264–65
    cannibalism and, 293–304, 293n25, 294n26, 295nn27–28, 297n31, 298n34
    definition of, 288–89, 297n31
    killing compared to, 277–78
    right of necessity as defense for, 276, 286–305
Murdoch, Iris, 87, 190, 219–20
Murphy, Jeffrie G.
    Forgiveness and Mercy, x, 4, 29, 81, 126
    Getting Even–Forgiveness and Its Limits, xi
    "Marxism and Retribution," 79–80

Nagel, Thomas
    on philosophy, 190
    on retribution, 37
narcissism, 111, 111n27
Nathanson, Donald L., 101n12, 104n17
Nazis, 135n8, 136n10, 209. See also *Judgment at Nuremberg*; specific individuals
    remorseful repentance of SS soldier, 133–36, 134n7, 195–96, 197n25
    Wiesenthal on, 133, 134n7, 185n7, 195
necessity defense
    Christianity and, 296–97
    Kant and, 275n3, 286–93, 297–98, 302, 304
    killing as life-saving necessity, 275, 291–304
    right of necessity as defense for murder, 276, 286–305
    shipwrecks and, 287–304, 289n20, 290n22
negligence, morally culpable, 196–97
neighbor, love of, 18, 46–51, 203, 205, 269. See also *agape*
Neu, Jerome
    "Jealous Afterthoughts," 235, 236
    "Jealous Thoughts," xv, 234–36
    on jealousy, xv, 234–43
    response to, xi, 216–21, 231
    A Tear Is an Intellectual Thing, 234
neurotic or morbid dependency, 237
New Yorker cartoons, 146, 146, 173, 219n4
Niebuhr, Reinhold, 261
Nietzsche, Friedrich
    Beyond Good and Evil, 42n37
    on desert, 27n11

    on monsters, 42, 42n37, 91, 204, 268–69
    on moral humility, 24, 24n7, 31–33, 41
    on philosophy, 190
    on punishment, xii, xiii, 19, 21–22, 21n1, 27n11, 42, 42n37, 85, 227
    on *ressentiment*, xii, xiii, 22–23, 26, 26n10, 39, 42n37, 55–56, 60, 85, 179
    on retribution, 21–24, 21n1, 39, 41
    on soul that squints, 22, 88
    on utilitarianism, 258
    on vindictiveness, 14
non-consequentialist theory of punishment, 37–38
nonmoral guilt, 96–99
"Nonmoral Guilt" (Morris), 95, 97–99, 101
nonretributive justification, 21n1
noumenal freedom, 259–60
noumenal self, 36, 36n28
Nozick, Robert, 80
    on Holocaust, 192, 262–65
    on perfect philosophical argument, 272
    on principle of fairness, 38n32

O'Connor, Flannery, 164n43
On Liberty (Mill), 67, 71
Ordinary Men (Browning), 208
Oresteia (Aeschylus), 13
ostracism, 280nn9–10
Othello (fictional character), 236, 237
Ozick, Cynthia
    on remorse, 153
    on remorseful repentance of SS soldier, 133–36, 195–96, 197n25
    on repentance, 121n13

Paradise (Barthelme), 108–9
pardon, 290n23, 297, 297n31
Parker, Richard, 124n19
pathological love, 48, 216–17, 218
Paul (disciple), 212
penance, 198, 198n26, 200
Perelman, S. J., x, 11, 11n11, 53
perfectionist liberals, 74
personal rebirth, 61–62

INDEX

"Persons and Punishment" (Morris), 78–79, 122n15
Petrovich, Porfiry (fictional character), 151
philia (friendship love), 43, 49
philosophical argument, perfect, 272
philosophical retributivist, 178–80
philosophy
    Marx on, 225
    Nagel on, 190
    Nietzsche on, 190
    views on, 190–91, 222–24
Plato, 41, 83, 207, 270
A Plea for Excuses (Austin), 167–68, 184, 184n5
political liberalism, 50
politics
    Christian love and, 45
    punishment and, 228–29
pop self-help psychology, 223
pornography, 50
Posner, Richard, 32–33, 83, 84, 298n34
practical love, 48, 216–17, 218
Prager, Dennis, 61
Prejean, Sister Helen, 40n33, 137–38, 137n11, 164
primary, secondary and third-party victims, 192n19
prisons
    character reform and, 51–52
    conditions in, 58, 60, 84, 86–87, 89, 157, 157n36, 176, 225–26, 229
    Jesus and Paul on, 212
    sodomy in, 58
Prison Dog Project, 51
Prison Rape Elimination Act, 51–52
problem of other minds, 35
promises
    apology and, 166–67, 167n46
    breaking, 140–41
provocation, 278n6, 280n10
psychopaths, 132, 267, 267n8
public apology, 148, 170–72
punishment. *See also* capital punishment; consequentialism; criminal punishment; criminal sentencing; desert; retribution
    annulment theory of, 126, 231
    character, remorse and repentance, and, 150–51, 155, 160, 161n39
    for common good, 59, 60, 61–62
    communicative, 114–28, 120n11
    discretion in, 227–29
    for evil, 9, 57, 77–78
    forgiveness and, 45–46, 52–60
    guilt, innocence and, 68–69, 161
    Hampton on, 231
    Kant on, 28–29, 81, 117
    Nietzsche on, xii, xiii, 19, 21–22, 21n1, 27n11, 42, 42n37, 85, 227
    non-consequentialist theory of, 37–38
    politics and, 228–29
    in proportion to inner wickedness, 29, 37n29
    remorse, repentance and, 148–64
    ressentiment and, xii, xiii
    shaming, 106–7, 171
    state, retribution and, 29–30
    system of, xiii
    vindictive passions and, 58, 60

racial insult as expression of autonomy, 246
rape, gang, 51–52, 87, 157, 225
rational basis test, xv–xvi, 248–49, 253, 255
Rawls, John, 298
    on consequentialism, 68–69
    influence of, 224
    on justice, 43
    luck on natural and social lottery and, 40, 79, 83, 205, 205n38, 206n39, 270, 270n14
    on political liberalism, 50
    on reflective equilibrium, 27n11, 85, 123
    on retribution, 221n6
Rayner, Jay, 145, 173
reactive attitude, x
reasons
    limitations of liberty and moral, 244–56
    morality and, 253–56
reconciliation, 8
    forgiveness and, 3–20, 53, 56–57
    group forgiveness and, 4
    interpersonal forgiveness and, 3
    vindictive passions and, 8, 10, 56

INDEX

reduced sentences, xiv, 56, 76, 116–17, 127
   for good deeds, 117
   in homicide law, 278n6, 279, 280n10, 297, 297n31
   "Reflections on Feeling Guilty" (Morris), 112, 113n30
reflective equilibrium, 27n11, 85, 123–25, 125n22
rehabilitation
   clemency and, 159
   criminal punishment and, 157–59
   Duff on, 157
   religion and, 158
religion
   human dignity and, xvi, 202n34, 203–6
   rehabilitation and, 158
   religious conversion, 129, 137–38, 137n11, 142–44, 142n18, 158, 161–62
   religious liberty, 73, 74
   repentance, remorse and, 129, 137–38, 137n11, 142–44, 142n18, 150–52, 161–62
Religion Within the Limits of Reason Alone (Kant), 33–34, 40, 83–84, 206, 206n39
reluctant retributivist, 86, 87
remorse. *See also agenbite of inwit*
   absence of, 130–33
   apology, mercy and, 129–80
   and apology, in criminal sentencing, 138–39, 138n13, 174–76, 231
   clemency and, xiv, 124, 137–39, 162–64, 168, 174, 175–76
   culture of apology and, 144–48, 177
   guilt and, 101, 140, 152
   Kierkegaard on, 164, 194
   Moore on, 132n4
   Ozick on, 153
   two kinds of, 139–42
remorse and repentance
   acknowledgment of wrongdoing compared to, 156n34
   apology compared to, 165
   character, punishment and, 150–51, 155, 160, 161n39
   of Dostoevsky's general, 194, 197–98,
   197n25, 200–201
   fake, 154–56, 158, 161–63, 169–70
   insincere, xiv, 197
   punishment and, 148–64
   religion and, 129, 137–38, 137n11, 142–44, 142n18, 150–52, 161–62
   retribution and, 159–61
   social consequences of, 153–54
remorseful repentance, 126–27, 126n24
   of SS soldier, 133–36, 134n7, 195–96, 197n25
repentance. *See also* remorse and repentance; remorseful repentance
   coerced and deliberative, 163n42
   criminal sentencing and, xiv, 75–76, 116–17, 116nn4–5, 120n11, 127, 158
   Duff on, 114–17, 120n11, 127–28
   forgiveness and, xi, 15–17, 53, 154, 216
   mercy, communicative punishment and, 114–28, 120n11
   Ozick on, 121n13
repression of dear self, 182n1, 199–200, 200n29
resentment
   as assertion of self-respect, 26n10
   as fitting response, 224n8
   forgiveness and, x–xi, 10–13, 53n9, 185–87, 185n8, 186n9, 223
   guilt and, 26–27, 26n10
   overcoming, 217
responsibility
   desert and, 28, 36n28, 86
   homicide law and, 278, 294, 295n28
   inner wickedness and, 36–37, 36n28, 37n29
responsible agency
   Dostoevsky's general and, 190, 190n16
   forgiveness and, 6, 7, 54
   retribution and, 86, 230
ressentiment
   definition of, 26
   Nietzsche on, xii, xiii, 22–23, 26, 26n10, 39, 42n37, 55–56, 60, 85, 179
   punishment and, xii, xiii
restitution, paying of, 152
restorative justice, 170

319

INDEX

retribution, xii–xiii, 21–42, 67–91. *See also* character retributivism; choice retributivism; contractarian retributivism; desert; grievance retributivism
   from apology, 170–71, 173, 175
   condemnation and, ix
   consequentialism and, 68–69, 77
   crime control and, 77–78, 221n6
   digression on, 28–30
   five senses of, 28
   guilt and, 23, 26
   Hart on, 77
   human dignity and, 85–86
   Kant on, 77, 78, 83–84, 226, 230, 290–91
   legal moralism and, 66–93
   mercy and, 226–27, 232n15
   minimalist versions of retributivism, 221n6, 223
   Moore on, 27n11, 31n19, 81–83, 123–24
   moral humility and, 31–35, 41
   Nagel on, 37
   Nietzsche on, 21–24, 21n1, 39, 41
   Rawls on, 221n6
   remorse, repentance and, 159–61
   responsible agency and, 86, 230
   rethinking retributivism, 77–85
   state punishment and, 29–30
   Steiker response and, 225–33
   two faces of, 85–91
retributive hatred, x, xiii, 29, 81
retributive just deserts, 178–79
retributive justice, 88, 170, 232
retributive justification, 21n1
retributivist
   definition of, 77
   philosophical, 178–80
   reluctant, 86, 87
revenge, 13
Riggins v. Nevada, 125n22, 132n5
rights. *See also* human rights
   of autonomy, 50
   forgiveness as waiving of, 9
   justice and, 258–59
   to life, 301
   of necessity as defense for murder, 276, 286–305

Rilke, Rainer Maria, 19
Ripstein, Arthur, 299n35
rival, jealousy, shame and, 234–43
Romer v. Evans, 250
Rorty, Richard, xi, 222, 272–73
rule-utilitarianism, 69

sacrifice, 291–92, 294, 297–300, 298n34
Schwarzenegger, Arnold, 124n18, 162–63, 168, 174
segregation, 285–86
selection, principle of, 300
self. *See also* dear self; empirical self; noumenal self
   annihilation of, 235, 238
   moral shame and, 110–12, 110n24
self-deceptive cruelty, xiii, 31–32, 85
self-defense, killing in, 279, 296
self-forgiveness, 186, 186n12
self-respect
   moral order and, 11–14
   resentment as assertion of, 26n10
self-restraint
   law abiding people and, 122
   moral balance theory and, 38, 78–81
self-worth, 241–42
sexuality, 70–71, 73–75. *See also* homosexuality
Shaffer, Thomas, 45–46, 57, 60
shame
   cultural, 192, 192n18
   gangs and, 280–81
   guilt, conscience and, 105–13
   jealousy, rival and, 234–43
   killing and, 275, 279–82, 280nn9–11, 283n15, 284, 290n22, 293
   love and, 242
   moral, 106–7, 110–12, 110n24, 111n27
   narcissism and, 111, 111n27
Shame and Necessity (Williams, B.), 103–4
Shame and Pride (Nathanson), 101n12, 104n17
shame morality, 110n24, 201n30
shaming punishments, 106–7, 171

INDEX

shipwrecks
   drawing lots and, 294, 299n34, 300
   necessity defense and, 287–304, 289n20, 290n22
Sigler, Mary, 58, 280n9
sin
   and casting stones, Jesus on, 24, 39–40, 82–83, 204, 269–70
   of despair, 142n18, 143–44
   "hate the sin but not the sinner," 15, 29
slavery, 258, 259
social conventions, 279–84, 280nn10–11
social utility, 145, 147, 259
societies of radical inequality, 38n32, 79–80
sodomy
   homosexual, xv–xvi, 70, 245–54
   in prisons, 58
soul
   Christian love and, 47
   soul that squints, Nietzsche on, 22, 88
   stain on the soul, 136n10, 193
South African Truth and Reconciliation Commission (TRC), 9, 16, 57, 147–48, 155–56, 156n34, 170–71
stain on the soul, 136n10, 193
state
   power of, 50–51, 71–74
   punishment, retribution and, 29–30
   right to execute, 61
state of nature, 284–86, 286n18, 302
statutory reform, 229
Stavrogin's suicide (fictional character), 141, 141n16, 144
Steiker, Carol, xi, 225–33
Stevens, Justice, 251
Stewart, Jon, 169
Stoicism, 48
Stoop, David A., 184
Strawson, Peter, x
strict scrutiny, 247–48, 252
Stump, Eleonore
   on Goebbels, 188, 199
   on stain on the soul, 193
suicide, 301, 302
The Sunflower (Wiesenthal), 134n7, 185n7, 195

Supreme Court, U.S. *See also specific cases and justices*
   discretion of, 229
   liberty and, xv–xvi, 71, 73–74
Sussman, David, 286n18
The Swimming Pool (film), 66
sympathy, 219, 219n4
Szymborska, Wislawa, 130

tacit consent, 280n11, 300–302
A Tear Is an Intellectual Thing (Neu), 234
Temple, William, 44
terrorism, 143
third-party forgiveness, 185–86, 189
Thomas, Laurence, 182n1
"to err is human; to forgive supine" (Perelman), x, 11, 11n11, 53
Tolstoy, Leo
   The Death of Ivan Ilych, 164n43
   "Father Sergius," 141, 144, 198, 200
tort law
   apology in, 148, 148n24
   remedy, 141
torture, 207n40, 271n15
Tosi, Justin, 286n18
transitional objects, 235
Traps (Durrenmatt), 95n3
TRC. *See* South African Truth and Reconciliation Commission
treason, 70
Trevor, William
   Death in Summer, 94, 99
   Felicia's Journey, 18, 40n33, 94n2, 202, 268
truth commissions, 232
Tucker, Karla Faye, 129, 137–38, 137n11, 161–62
Tutu, Desmond, 9, 147–48, 155–56, 170, 223

Ulysses and the sirens, 301, 302
unforgivable
   as concept, 183–88
   forgiveness of, 181–214
unforgivable injuries, 188
unforgiving servant, parable of, 14, 59

321

INDEX

uniformity at price of distortion, xi, 5, 207n39, 272
universalism, 48
"Upon Forgiveness of Injuries" (Butler), 6, 6n6, 52
"Upon Resentment" (Butler), 10–12, 52
utilitarianism, 258–59, 299n34. *See also* rule-utilitarianism

validation, 241–42
van Camp, Julie, 215
vice, virtue and, 75
victims
    contempt for, 116, 118–19, 127
    desires, in criminal sentencing, 8, 8n7, 55
    forgiveness from, 183, 185–86, 185n7
    primary, secondary and third-party, 192n19
    victim impact statements, 154, 154n32
    victim vindication, 126–27, 176
victimization, 4, 53
vindictiveness, 14
vindictive passions, 185n8. *See also* malice; resentment
    forgiveness and, 8, 10, 12–14, 52–53, 56, 58
    punishment driven by, 58, 60
    reconciliation and, 8, 10, 56
virtue
    forgiveness as, 4, 9–10, 13–17, 52, 217
    vice and, 75
virtue ethics, 88, 98
von Kleist, Heinrich, 14n18

Waldron, Jeremy, 230
Walker, Margaret, 148
weakness of will, 153
Weil, Simone, 59, 90, 95n3, 202, 267
Weiss, Peter, 257, 262–65
White, Justice, xvi, 247–55
Whitman, Walt, 41n36, 207–8, 271
"Why Homosexuality is Abnormal" (Levin), 254–55
Wiesel, Elie, 182n2
Wiesenthal, Simon, 133, 134n7, 185n7, 195
Williams, Bernard, 103–4
Williams, Stanley, 124, 124n18, 131, 131n1, 162–63, 168, 174
Wilson, A. N., 100–101, 101n12, 109
Winch, Peter, 128
Winnicott, Donald, 235
Works of Love (Kierkegaard), 48
"The Work of Herbert Morris" (American Philosophical Association), 94n1
"The Work of Jeffrie G. Murphy" (American Philosophical Association), xi–xii, 215

"You Felons on Trial in Courts" (Whitman), 41n36, 207–8, 271

Zipursky, Benjamin, xi–xii, 221–25

Printed in Great Britain
by Amazon

79693318R00202